Summa Kitharologica, Volume 1
The Physiology of Guitar Playing: Functional Anatomy and Physiomechanics

by Ricardo Iznaola

Video Contents

Intro

1-1	Shoulder Girdle
1-2	Shoulder
1-3	Elbow, Forearm and Wrist
1-4	Fingers
1-5	Thumb

2-1	Hand-at-rest and Anatomical Frame
2-2	Technical Frames
2-3	Right-Arm Leverage
2-4	Mixed Stroke Frame Example

3-1	Left-Hand Alignment
3-2	Shifting
3-3	Upbeat Moment
3-4	Barrés
3-5	Slurs
3-6	Vibrato

1   2

Visit us on the Web at www.melbay.com — E-mail us at email@melbay.com

MEL BAY PUBLICATIONS, INC   #4 INDUSTRIAL DRIVE   PACIFIC, MO 63069-0066
SUMMA KITHAROLOGICA, VOL. 1
PHYSIOLOGY OF GUITAR PLAYING:
FUNCTIONAL ANATOMY AND PHYSIOMECHANICS

Anatomical Illustrations

Figures 1-5, 1-6, 1-11, 1-13, 1-14, 1-15, 1-16, 1-17, 1-18, 1-19, 1-20, 1-21, 1-22, 1-26, reproduced from *The Biology of Musical Performance and Performance-Related Injury* by Alan H. D. Watson, Ph. D. Copyright © 2009 by Alan H. D. Watson. The Scarecrow Press: Plymouth (UK). Used under license.

Figures 1-3, 1-7, 1-8, 1-9, 1-10, 1-23, 1-24, 1-25, reproduced from *Basic Human Anatomy – A Regional Study of Human Structure*, by Ronan O'Rahilly, Fabiola Müller, Stanley Carpenter, Rand Swenson. Copyright © 2008 By Ronan O'Rahilly. Revised online edition, (http://www.dartmouth.edu/~humananatomy/index.html) of the original print edition, published by W. B Saunders (Philadelphia, 1983). Reproduced with permission of the authors.

Figures 1-1, 1-2, 1-4, 1-12 by Mariana Ruiz Villareal (http://commons.wikimedia.org/wiki/User:LadyofHats), 2007. Public Domain.

Photography

Wayne Armstrong, Denver, CO, USA, 2013.

Videography

Justin Rounds and Wayne Armstrong, Switch10 Productions, Littleton, CO, USA, 2013.

ACKNOWLEDGEMENTS

...to my wife Victoria, stalwart and spine of my life, and my son Rick, who nurtures me with his wisdom, strength and humor, with my unending love for *their* love, unwavering support and encouragement, for leaving me alone when needed, and always there when asked for, especially during this *annus horribilis*...

...to my dad Alfonso, my first teacher, actor, poet, supreme auto-didact, who taught me the best lesson I ever received about performing: if you ever want to 'feel at home' on stage, stay at home...

...to my students, past, present and future, partners in the search...

...to my colleagues across the continents, an inexhaustible source of amazement and stimulus, who keep taking the art form to ever higher levels of mastery...in particular my 'brothers-in-arms', Gilbert Biberian, Jonathan Leathwood, Masakazu Ito, Jorge Morel, Richard Boukas, Simone Fontanelli...

...to Henry Adams, life-long friend, 'tío Enrique', for his help with proof-reading...and so many other things...

...to Jim and Irma, without whom life in Denver is inconceivable (the ranch!)...

...to Dave and Jane, without whom Thanksgivings in the last three decades are hard to imagine...(the pies!)...

...to the University of Denver and the Lamont School of Music, my academic home for thirty years, and the Faculty Research Fund, for much needed grant support for this project...

...to my brilliant colleagues and dear friends at Lamont, Richard Slavich and Joe Docksey, without whom life at the school will *never* be the same...

...to the eminent hand surgeon, Dr. Charles (Charlie) Hamlim, for invaluable advice on the scientific content of the book, and for providing important resources, most particularly the precious article by his mentor, J. William Littler...

...to the great pioneers who cleared the path toward a more scientific and, at the same time, humane musical pedagogy: Matthay, Steinheusen, Ortmann, Havas, Taubman, Shearer... I consider myself a humble disciple...

...to Mel Bay Publications, with whom I started what is now a long-standing, fruitful relationship when Bill was at the helm, and now bearing fruit again with Collin, Bryndon and their team...

...and to my hero, my greatest teacher and my model, my son Victor, gone but increasingly, achingly present as the lessons of his fortitude, kindness, generosity and calm passion bore ever more deeply into my soul...

Thank you...

CONTENTS

PREFACE

The most beautiful thing we can experience is the mysterious. It is the source of all true art and science. He to whom this emotion is a stranger, who can no longer pause to wonder and stand rapt in awe, is as good as dead: his eyes are closed.

Albert Einstein
(Einstein 1931)

This book is the first volume of *Summa Kitharologica,* a treatise that deals comprehensively with the art of guitar performance, from its pre-technical aspects to the act of doing music in public.

The author's previous publications, *Kitharologus: the Path to Virtuosity and On Practicing* (also published by Mel Bay) are, in fact, applied foot-notes to *Summa.*

The present text is an attempt to present a basic introduction to the scientific foundations of guitar technique, an area of growing importance in music pedagogy during the last hundred years. As Otto Ortman said in his pioneering study on the physiological mechanics of piano playing, "...the [piano] teacher, selling lessons in physiological mechanics hour after hour, day after day, should at least know the tools with which he works" (Ortmann 1929).

Chapters 1 and 3 substantially expand and revise previously published texts (Iznaola, Physio 2000, Iznaola, Left Hand 2001) while Chapter 2 includes a totally new exposition of biomechanical properties of right-hand technique and a positional framing theory for the right hand.

The information provided in Chapter 1, a survey of common knowledge in functional upper limb anatomy, physiology and kinesiology, has been drawn from the following sources (see full listings in Bibliography): Palastanga and Soames 2012; O'Rahilly, et al. 2008; Watson 2009; Tubiana 2000; Adrian and Cooper 1995; Sataloff, Brandfonbrenner and Lederman 1991; Hay and Reid 1982; Guyot 1981; Piscopo and Baley 1981; Thompson 1981.

An important consideration to keep in mind as the reader peruses this chapter is that anatomical information, for musical performers, is *not* a necessity, nor will it, by itself, help improve their technique or their artistry. In fact, it is not advisable to provide it to students until they reach quite advanced levels of maturity and mastery, both technical and artistic.

It is, however, important for teachers and method book authors, who are , after all, responsible for providing an objective foundation for good practices on the instrument, thus assuring the physical (and emotional) well-being of their pedagogical charges.

Much of the text in Chapters 2 and 3 is speculative. Indeed, even in the objective scientific realms of anatomy and physiology, there are areas of disagreement among prominent specialists, particularly regarding the awe-inspiring complexity of the neuromuscular interactions that control the joint movements of the hand and its digits.

It is not entirely surprising, then, that in the didactic literature for the guitar these varying viewpoints, as well as the pervasiveness of unquestioned traditions, have produced an array of interpretations that have tainted with ambiguity and confusion even some of the most forward-thinking and otherwise sound advice presented in a number of prestigious method books and pedagogical writings.

Thus, Chapters 2 and 3, dealing with the specifics of right- and left-hand technique, take the risk of providing the author's personal but hopefully cohesive theory of fingerwork on the guitar. Approached from a physiomechanical standpoint, it treads cautiously because, although based on thoroughly contrasted factual information and extensive personal experience, this type of 'forensic' investigation still needs conclusive scientific validation through well-developed myographic, kinetics and kinematics studies of the guitarist's hands in action. Current equipment and methods of observation and measurement in these fields are not yet developed enough to thoroughly assess the inner workings of the neuromuscular fine-motor control mechanisms, but, as in all areas of technology, progress is made constantly.

Numerous photographs, anatomical figures, musical charts and examples and an accompanying DVD, whose contents are well-referenced in the book, help illustrate important structures, functions and procedures described and discussed in this text. The DVD highlights a few of those elements but it is by no means comprehensive nor detailed enough to be a substitute for the book.

The author's desire to share these perspectives is perhaps justified by the fact that, both as player and teacher, he and his students have derived substantial benefits from such research. Not least the advantage of establishing a vocabulary whose terminology, borrowed from the sciences, allows for exact descriptors that leave no room for ambiguity, once the terms are well-assimilated (granted, not an easy task initially). Indeed, if nothing else, it is hoped that the book will help advance the gradual adoption of pedagogical language that, because of its clarity and precision, leaves no doubt about the intended meaning of a teacher's or a method book's instructions.

It is sincerely wished that readers will also find useful tools in this text to enrich their daily playing and pedagogical activities. It hopes to help awaken, or keep stimulating, a questioning stance in the face of inherited tradition through which a possible better understanding of the 'what' and 'how' at the technical core of guitar playing may arise. Paraphrasing the well-known Socratic aphorism, the unconsidered technique is not worth using.

The sense of wonder, however, will never dissipate, for, as Einstein points out, the more we observe and study, the more we will "stand rapt in awe" at the breath-taking beauty of these natural structures and processes. The more we feel the awe, the more we will feel the pinch of our curiosity, the itch of our desire, prodding us to keep on pondering, in the hope to eventually elucidate the deeper mystery of their 'whence' and 'why'.

Ricardo Iznaola
Denver, August 2013

To the beloved memory of my son

Victor S. Fernández (1979 – 2012)

Forever present

Chapter 1

Reason does not preach
Albert Camus
(Camus 1956, 221)

GENERAL OVERVIEW: Basic Limb Anatomy, Biomechanics and Pedagogical Considerations

Section 1. Musculoskeletal Framework

In the act of playing the guitar, we utilize our musculoskeletal system in two ways: a part of this system is involved in providing a base of stability and support, while other parts are involved in movements whose coordination is the goal of technical training. The support base (the relatively static part) is articulated skeletally through the linkage between the **axial skeleton** (Figure 1-1), made up of the head (the skull), the spinal or vertebral column, the sternum and the rib-cage (the thorax), with the lower extremities, which are part of the **appendicular skeleton** (Figure 1-2), made up of the shoulder and pelvic girdles, and the upper and lower limbs.

In the standard sitting position of the classical guitarist, these parts of our skeleton provide the necessary positional stability for the free-moving parts that actually play, the dynamic part: the upper limbs. Of course, it is evident that the stability provided by the more static structures is not a total constraint on mobility. On the contrary, in the course of playing, mobility in the head and spine, and to some extent in the legs, is a normal part of efficient execution.

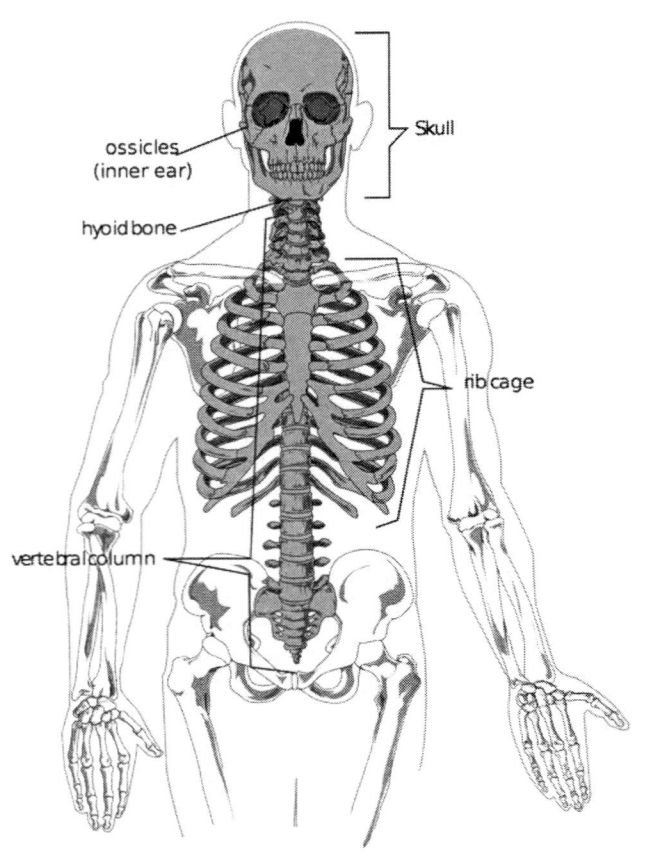

Figure 1-1. The axial skeleton

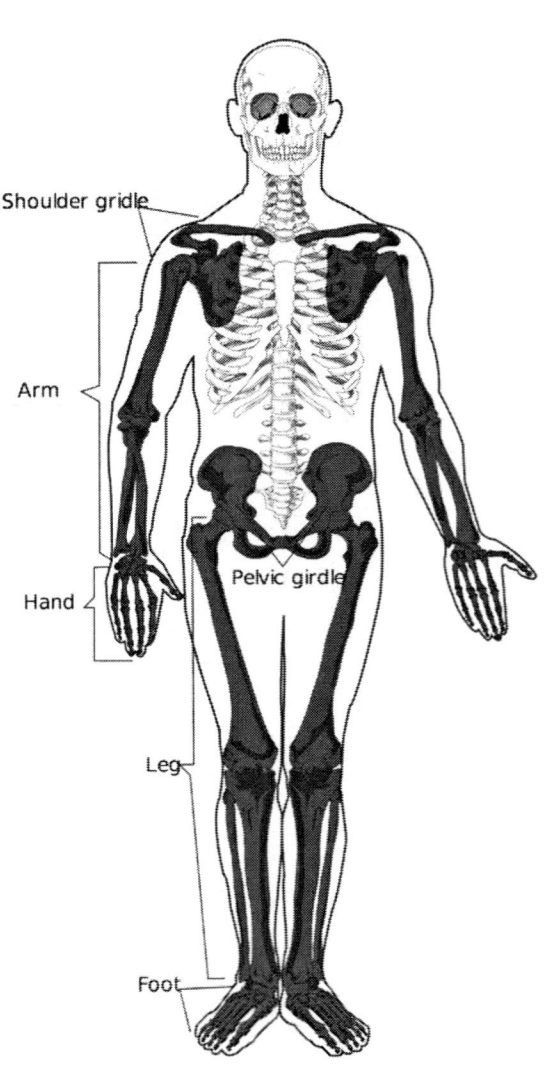

Figure 1-2. The appendicular skeleton

The axial skeleton (Fig. 1-1) consists of the bones in the head and trunk of the human body. It is composed of five parts: the human skull, the ossicles of the inner ear, the hyoid bone of the throat, the chest, and the vertebral column. The appendicular skeleton (Fig. 1-2) includes the pectoral girdle, the upper limbs, the pelvic girdle, and the lower limbs. The appendicular skeleton and the axial skeleton together form the complete skeleton. Mariana Ruiz Villareal, 2007.

The connections between the axial and the appendicular skeleton are made through the **shoulder or pectoral girdle** (Figure 1-12), a marvelously designed structure through which the upper arm articulates with the torso, and the **pelvic girdle**, which is to the lower extremities what the shoulder girdle is to the upper ones.

The skeletal structure of the arm and hand is similar to that of the leg and foot, although anatomically better designed for motion rather than positional stability. These differences, and similarities, point to an important characteristic of our body structure: a limited number of design features, used repeatedly in different parts of the anatomy, are made distinct by their specific functional roles.

The lower extremities have the responsibility of carrying our whole body-weight and, so, their design is a balanced compromise between sturdiness and mobility, while our upper limbs, having lost their primary support functions when humans adopted an erect posture, have specialized as tools for nimble and precise motion.

Bones, which provide the framework for position and movement, articulate with each other through **joints**. Depending on their degree of mobility, joints are classified as **synarthrodial** or fibrous (no mobility, as in the head bones), **amphiarthrodial** or cartilaginous (some limited mobility, as between vertebrae) and **diarthrodial** or synovial (fully movable, as in the limbs). We will be concerned, primarily, with **diarthrodial joints**. If no external force is present, joints can only move through the **pull** of **muscles**.

Usually, the point of origin of a muscle is on a bone closer (**proximal**) to the trunk, and the point of insertion is on a bone farther away (**distal**) from the trunk. Muscles may act on one or more joints. Joint movement is normally the result of a fairly complex coordination of activity in various muscles acting in a complementary way.

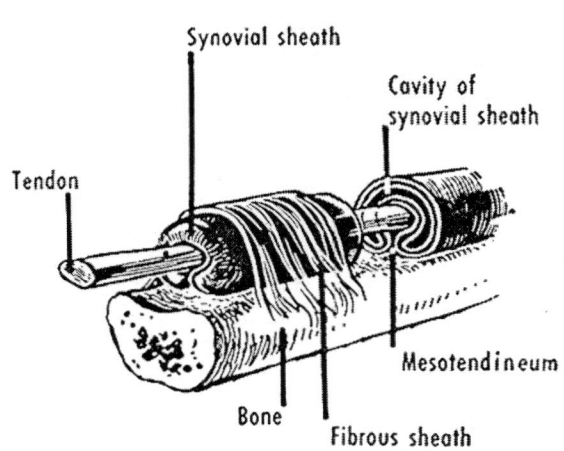

Figure 1-3. Tendon and its sheath.
© 2008 Ronan O'Rahilly,
www.dartmouth.edu/~humananatomy/index.html/.
Reproduced with permission of the authors.

Depending on their functional roles in achieving a particular movement, muscles are classified as **protagonists or agonists**, **antagonists**, **synergists or neutralizers**, and **stabilizers** or **fixators**. **Agonists** are the primary movers of a joint, while **antagonists** are those muscles that act in opposition to the agonists (e.g., the biceps is an antagonist to the triceps in forearm extension, while the triceps is the antagonist of the biceps in forearm flexion). **Synergists** help by delimiting or re-enforcing, through their action, the action of the agonists (e.g., in order to flex the elbow, the biceps needs the assistance of other muscles to keep the direction of joint motion straight). **Stabilizers** act by immobilizing other joints that would move in reaction to the action exerted on the joint we want to move, thus guaranteeing a more efficient, focused movement in the active joint (e.g., in the movement of flexing the elbow, the muscles controlling the shoulder joint must stabilize it so that the action does not affect this joint unduly).

Most frequently, muscles begin and/or end in **tendons**, which are fibrous and non-elastic cord-like bundles of tissue through which the muscle pulls on the bones.

While muscles contract, thus changing their shapes (for instance, from an elongated form to a more spherical, compact one,) tendons retain their length. Surrounding the tendon or a group of tendons (as in the long flexors of the fingers) there is frequently a **synovial sheath**, which covers all or part of the tendon(s) through its length, and protects it from excessive friction against other anatomical surfaces with a lubricating substance (**synovia or synovial fluid**).

The synovial sheath may be double-layered, as in the hand tendons, with a **mesotendon or mesotendineum** of synovial tissue between the layers. Normally, tendons slide smoothly through the sheath, but adhesions between the tendon and the sheath due to lack of lubrication or because of trauma may affect its proper functioning, causing pain or even rupture.

In the normal living organism, every muscle, when not in use, maintains a certain level of tension (this is called the **tone** of the muscle). As a muscle, or its tendon, passes over a given joint, this tone is one of the factors that keep the joint together, thus avoiding **dislocation**.

Equally important in joint stability is the presence of **ligaments** and other connective tissue, like **cartilage**, that surrounds the joint, forming a **joint capsule** that guarantees structural consistency to the articulation. Synovial fluid is also present in joint capsules, providing lubrication. It has also been demonstrated that atmospheric pressure is a factor in maintaining stability in some joints.

Nourishment

Muscles, ligaments, bones, connective tissue, etc. are nourished by the blood vessels of the **circulatory or vascular system** (Figure 1-4), whose arteries and secondary vessels bring oxygen and other nutrients to the tissues.

Residual waste substances, produced by the processing of those nutrients (**metabolism**), are then disposed of through the veins that take the used blood to the lungs for oxygenation. Muscle metabolism is directly related to the sensation of fatigue and/or pain after vigorous or prolonged exertion. The major blood vessel supplying the upper limb is the **axillary artery**, which is the continuation of a **subclavian artery** that branches off the heart's **aorta**.

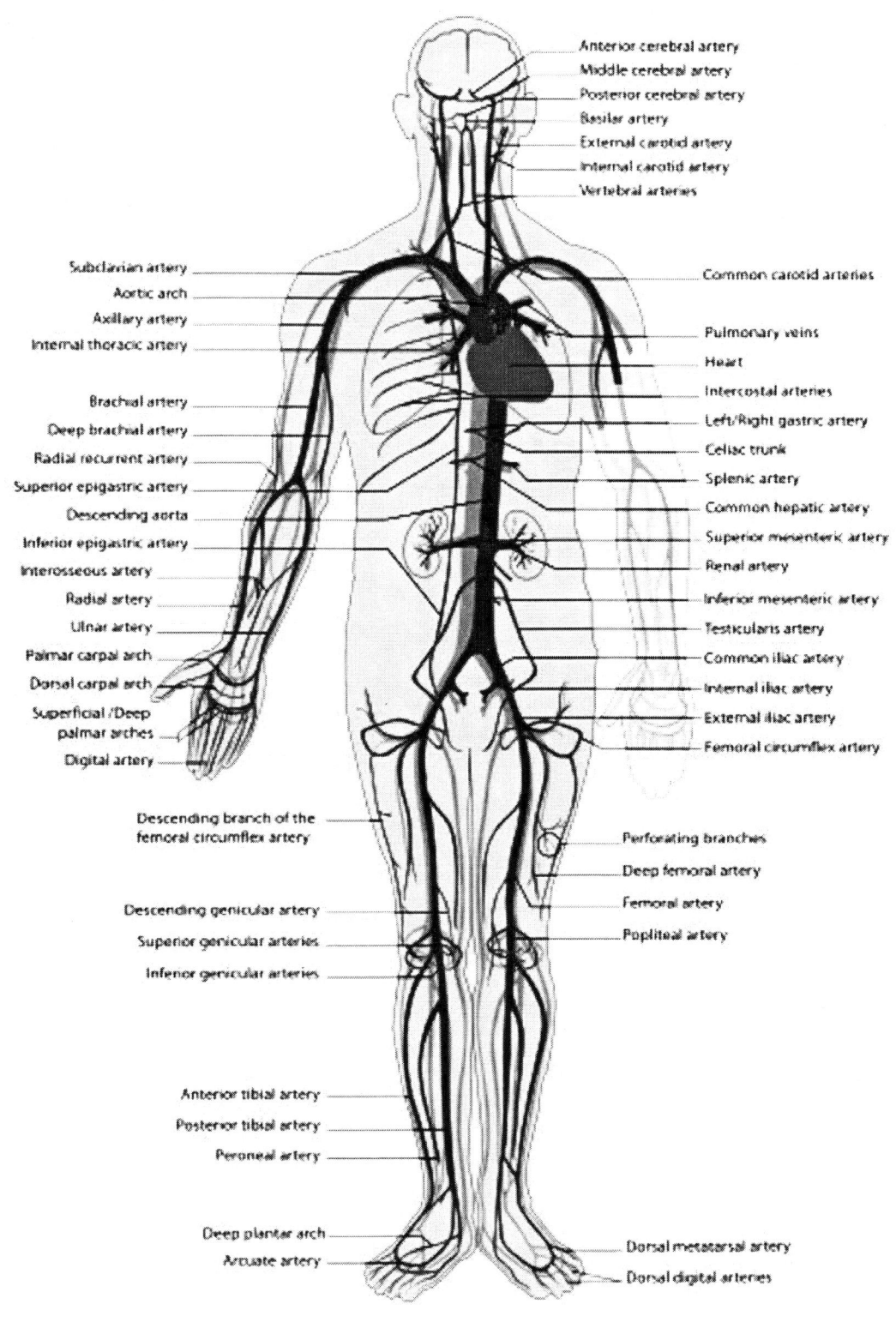

Figure 1-4. Circulatory system, arteries (dark) and veins (light). Mariana Ruiz Villareal, 2007.

The axillary artery changes name to **brachial artery** as it enters the arm, and as it reaches the forearm it divides into **radial and ulnar arteries**, running down the anterior part of the forearm to the palm of the hand. The ulnar artery gives off a branch that runs deeply on the posterior side of the forearm. Many other branches emerge from these arteries to supply the limb.

Control Systems

The **nervous system** controls the immense complexities of human movement, through the refined coordination of the **central (CNS)** and **peripheral (PNS)** nervous systems. The CNS (**brain and spinal cord**) is the major control center for the neurological components of the PNS: 12 **cranial nerves**, 31 **spinal nerves** - 8 **cervical**, 12 **thoracic**, 5 **lumbar**, 5 **sacral** and 1 **coccygeal** -, and innumerable **neurons**. The spinal nerves control muscular activity.

They are usually identified, for descriptive purposes, with the initial letter of the spinal region from which they emerge followed by a number that identifies its relative position along the length of the spine: C7 (seventh cervical nerve), T1 (first thoracic), etc.

Also part of the PNS is the **autonomous nervous system**, through which non-voluntary muscular activity, as that in the viscera, blood circulation, etc., is controlled. The ANS is, in turn, subdivided into two parts, the **sympathetic** and the **parasympathetic systems**. We will deal with the last two systems in the context of the physiology of stage-fright (performance anxiety).

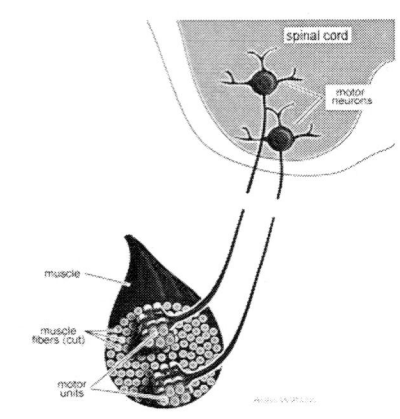

The finely coordinated motions required in instrumental performance, considered to be the most complex of all human activities in terms of senso-motor control, are managed by the sophisticated interaction of the **afferent** (sensory) and the **efferent** (motor) branches of the PNS: the afferent branch inputs sensations received, both from the outer environment and from inside the body, through **receptors (exteroceptors, interoceptors, proprioceptors)**.

Figure 1-5 Muscular control through motor unit. © 2009 Alan H. D. Watson. Reproduced under license.

Motor responses to these stimuli are then produced by the efferent branch, acting on muscles through an immensely complex neural network. It is important to realize that spinal nerves, once they leave the spine to innervate the musculature, are made up of both sensory and motor fibers.

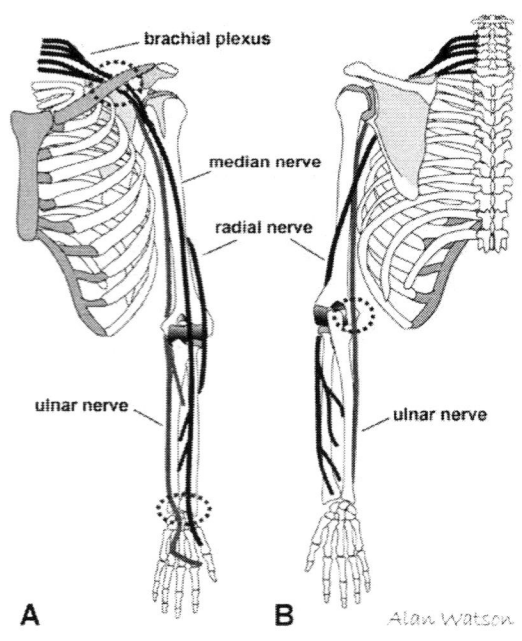

The functional unit of the system is the **motor unit**, made up of a neuron and the muscular fibers it innervates (Figure 1-5). The more motor units in a muscle, the more precision and specialization of movement will be possible.

The nerves to the upper limbs derive mostly from the lower four cervical (C5-8) and the first thoracic (T1) nerves. Through their many branches, they innervate the muscles controlling arm movement, from the chest and back, through the shoulder-arm mechanism and to the hand and fingers.

As they come into the arm they must bundle together to pass through the space in between the clavicle and the first rib (the **thoracic outlet**), forming the three main neural trunks of the **brachial plexus**.

Figure 1-6. Neural paths through brachial plexus (A: anterior view; B: posterior view). Dashed circles indicate points where nerve entrapment most frequently occur. © 2009 Alan H. D. Watson, Ph. D. Reproduced under license.

From these three trunks, anterior and posterior divisions emerge that supply the flexor and extensor musculature of the limb, respectively. Depending on their position relative to the axillary artery, the three trunks of the **brachial plexus** are described as **medial** (on the inside), **lateral** (on the outside) or **posterior** (behind).

The principal nerves running along the length of the limb are the **musculocutaneous**, **radial**, **median** and **ulnar** (the **axillary** nerve supplies muscles acting on the shoulder joint only and does not continue distally, past the upper arm).

The **musculocutaneous** nerve serves the extrinsic muscles of the forearm, while the rest continue into the hand, supplying the intrinsics.

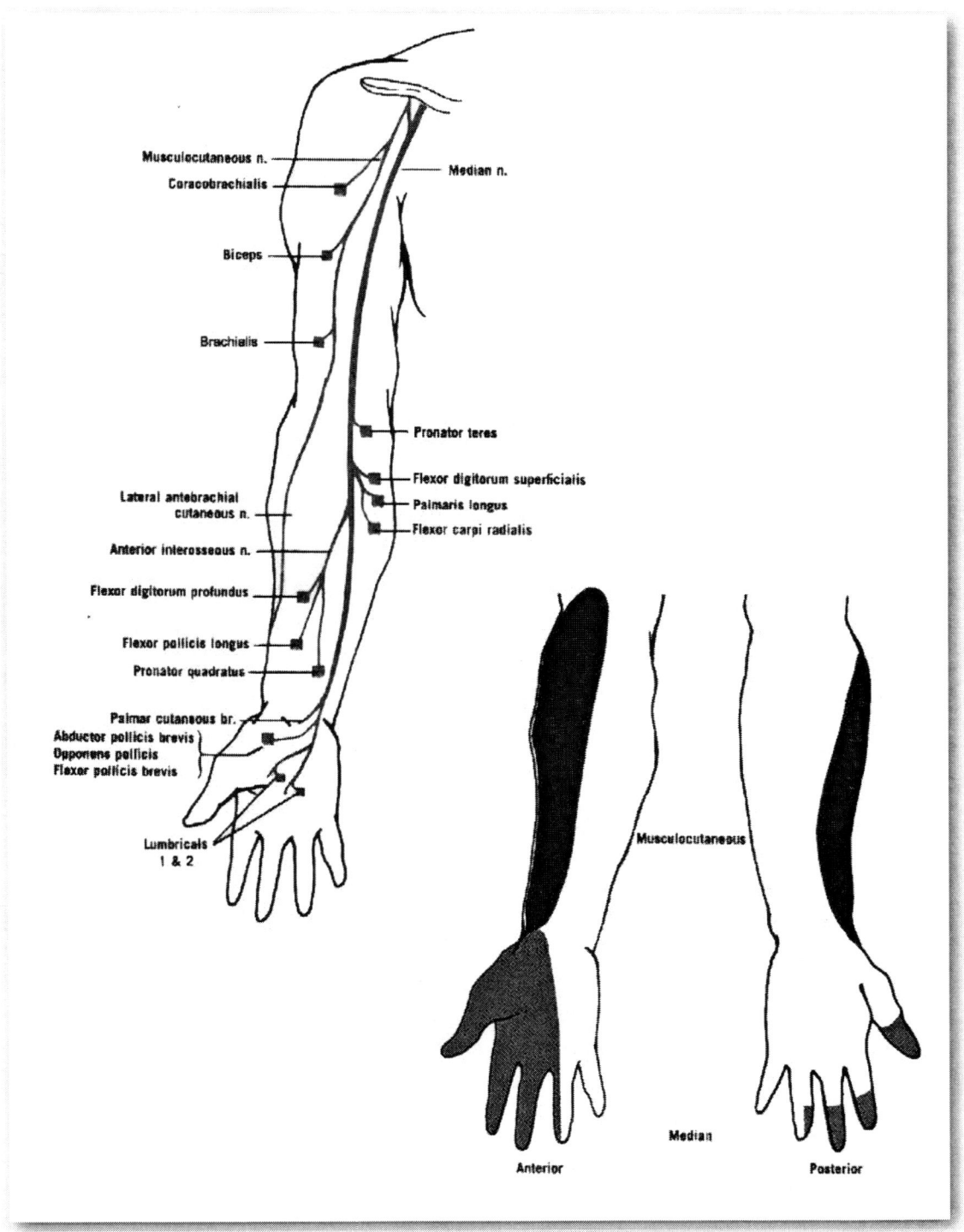

Figure 1-7. Paths of the musculocutaneous and median nerves and muscles supplied. © 2008 Ronan O'Rahilly, www.dartmouth.edu/~humananatomy/index.html/. Reproduced with permission of the authors.

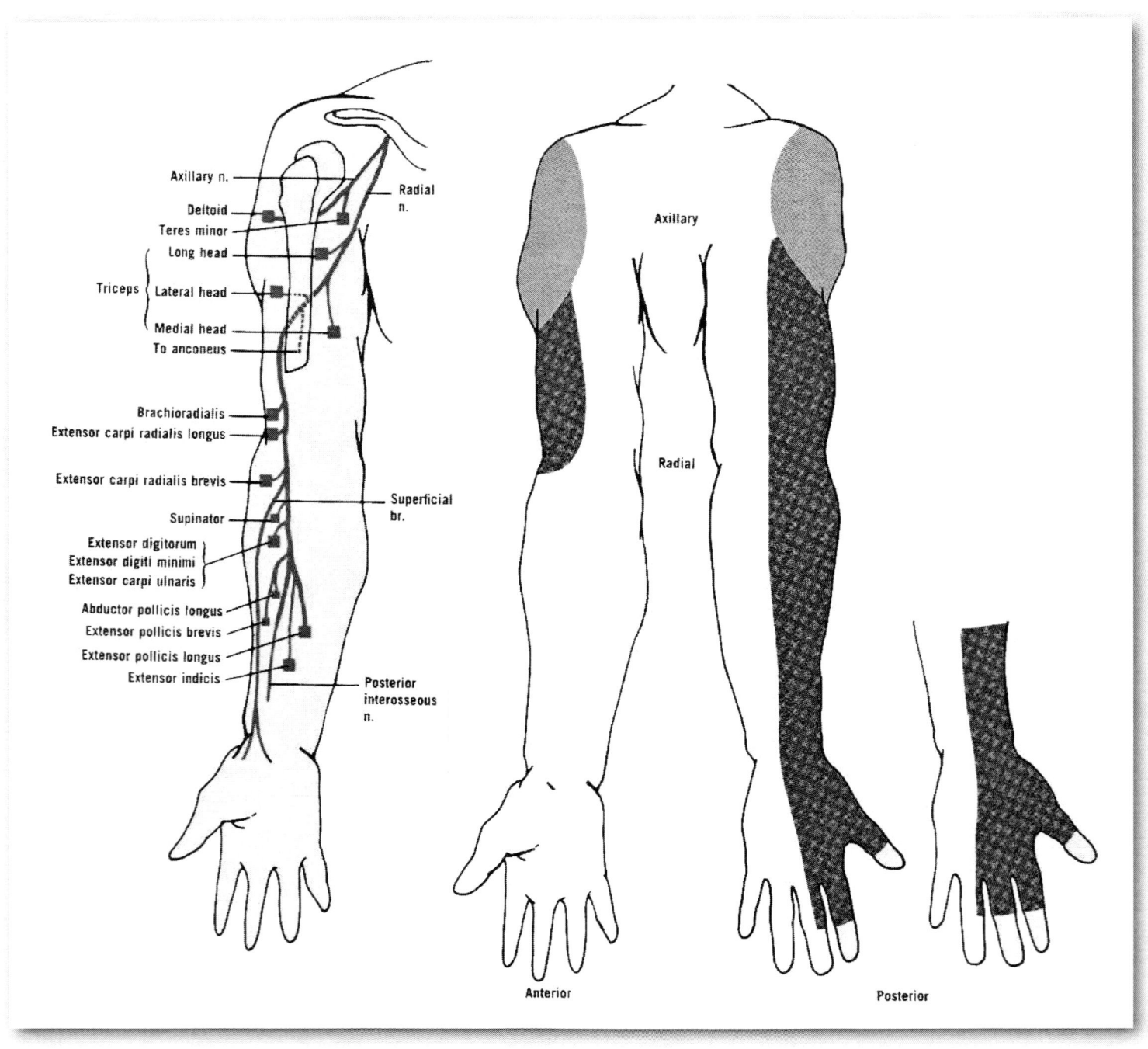

Figure 1-8. Paths of the axillary and radial nerves and muscles supplied. © 2008 Ronan O'Rahilly, www.dartmouth.edu/~humananatomy/index.html/ . Reproduced with permission of the authors.

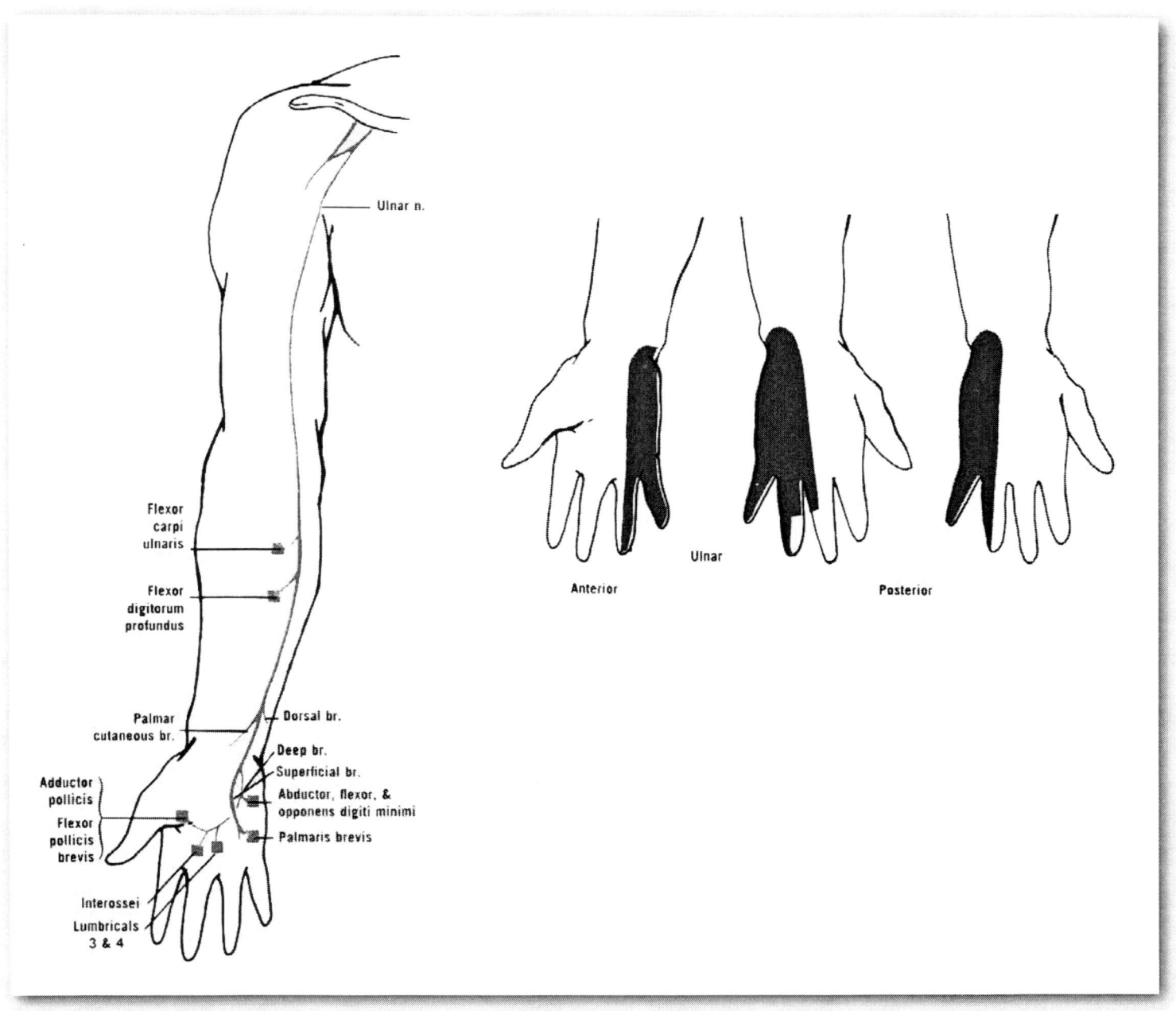

Labels in figure: Ulnar n., Flexor carpi ulnaris, Flexor digitorum profundus, Palmar cutaneous br., Adductor pollicis, Flexor pollicis brevis, Interossei, Lumbricals 3 & 4, Dorsal br., Deep br., Superficial br., Abductor, flexor, & opponens digiti minimi, Palmaris brevis, Ulnar, Anterior, Posterior

Figure 1-9. Path of the ulnar nerve and muscles supplied. © 2008 Ronan O'Rahilly, www.dartmouth.edu/~humananatomy/index.html/. Reproduced with permission of the authors.

Types of Muscle Contraction

A muscular contraction is the tensing up of muscular fibers produced as a response to a nervous stimulus. Muscles can only pull, and only towards their middle. The level of tension at their end attachments is usually the same.

There are two types of contraction: **isometric** and **isotonic**. **Isometric contraction** occurs when the muscular tension does not result in joint movement. This type of contraction is also known as **static contraction**. Holding an object still while we observe it is an example of isometric contraction. "Isometric" refers to the fact that the muscle, while developing tension, does not change appreciably in length.

Isotonic contraction occurs when the muscle contraction results in joint motion. The qualifier 'isotonic' refers to the fact that the tension level remains the same, while the length of the muscle changes. There are two sub-categories of isotonic contraction: **concentric contraction** (i.e., towards the center or axis of rotation) results when the muscular effort is greater than the resistance and the distance between proximal and distal bones is diminished. **Eccentric contraction** (i.e., away from the center) occurs when the muscular effort is smaller than the resistance and the joint movement increases the distance between proximal and distal ends. Lifting an object from a table through flexion of the elbow is an example of concentric contraction. Placing it back on the table carefully, an example of eccentric contraction.

Normally, movements in playing an instrument, or in common daily activities, are the result of complex combinations of static and isotonic contractions. Agonists are mostly involved in concentric contractions but are being controlled by the counteracting, refining eccentric contractions of the antagonists, while stabilizers and synergists may be acting isometrically to avoid interference from other muscles and joint movements while the motion takes place at the appropriate joints. And, of course, a moment later their respective functions may change so that each muscle now acts in an entirely different role. It is important to realize that every muscular contraction starts as an isometric one, until the muscle gains enough tension to overcome the resistance, at which point joint movement will begin.

Types of Movement in Relation to Muscular Contraction

Movement may be classified according to the type of muscular involvement needed, in terms of contraction. When a movement requires continued muscular involvement throughout the duration of the action, it is classified as a **tension movement**.

Tension movements are of two kinds: **Slow-tension or controlled movements** require continuous but slow coordination of opposing muscular forces. These are movements used when accuracy is more important than speed or force. **Rapid-tension movements** occur when the direction of motion has to change abruptly to the opposite direction.

A particular form of rapid-tension movement much used in instrumental playing is **repetitive or oscillatory movement**.

When a movement does not involve muscular contraction throughout its duration, it is called **ballistic**. Typically, in a ballistic movement, an initial contraction of the agonists sets a limb or object in motion. Although the muscular contraction ends, the motion continues thanks to the momentum of inertia (Newton's First Law) until the antagonists, through their eccentric contractions, end the movement or gravity, friction, or other external forces act on the projectile, gradually stopping its motion. All of these types of movement are used in guitar performance.

Section 2. Limb Joints – Anatomy and Movements

The key to understanding the complex nature of arm, hand and finger-joint movement is the realization of their inter-connectedness. Although, for purposes of description, each segment is treated individually, movement at any joint of the upper limb is produced by the coordination of muscular activity throughout the shoulder-arm mechanism. In fact, the whole muscular system could be viewed as a unified but compartmentalized mass whose activity may be managed regionally, but never in absolute isolation from the rest.

For anatomical study purposes the body's position of reference is the **anatomical position**, in which, with the body recumbent, it faces up (supine) with its segments extended.

Planes of Motion

With the body standing erect, the anatomical position serves as reference to precisely describe the position and direction of motion of the various body segments in relation to imaginary planes crossing the body (see Figure 1-10).

The front-to-back **sagittal suture** of the skull, uniting its left and right sides, is the point of reference for the **median plane**, which divides the body into symmetrical halves. Planes running parallel to the median plane are, therefore, called **sagittal.**

The **coronal suture**, linking the skull's front and back sides, gives name to the **coronal plane,** determining front or **anterior** and back or **posterior** positions. All planes parallel to it are also called coronal.

The coronal plane is one type of the **transverse plane,** the other being the **horizontal plane,** which divides the body into **superior** and **inferior** halves.

Other terms derive from more localized reference points in the body. For instance, when discussing the hand, the anterior side is also called **palmar**, the thumb side is the lateral or **radial side**, since the thumb is aligned with the radius bone in the forearm, and the little-finger side is the medial or **ulnar side**, because of its alignment with the other bone of the forearm, the ulna.

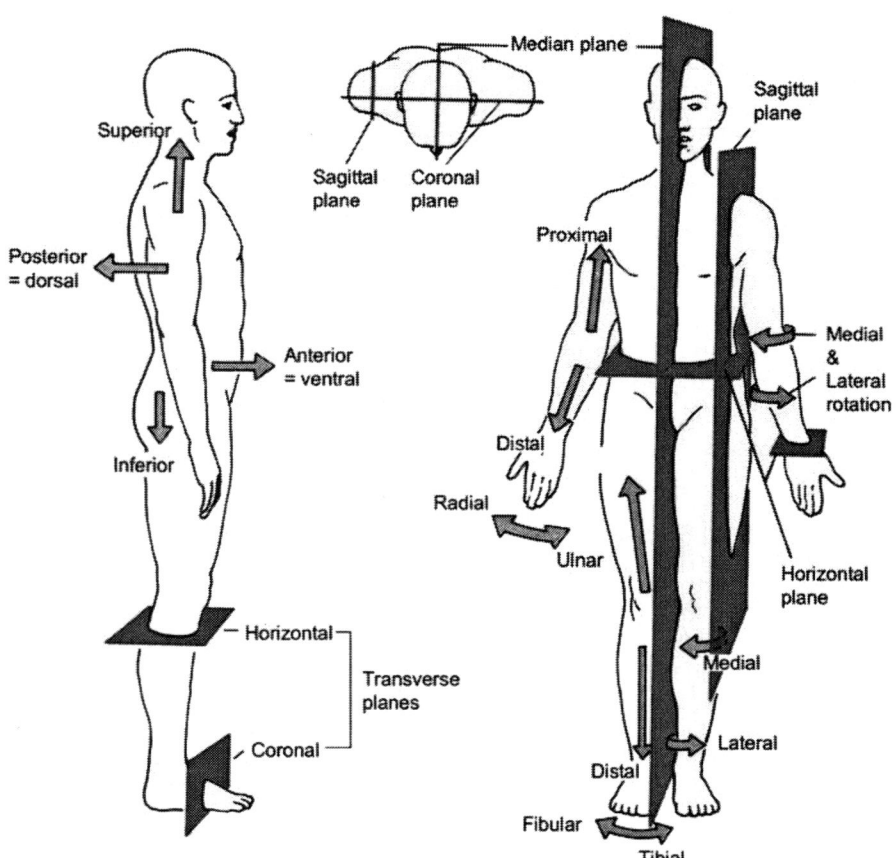

Figure 1-10. Anatomical planes and terms of position. © 2008 Ronan O'Rahilly, www. dartmouth.edu/~humananatomy/index.html/ . Reproduced with permission of the authors.

Joint Movements

These general terms are used to identify various forms of movement possible in many skeletal joints (Figure 1-11). Others, described later, identify particular types of movement that happen at certain joints only.

- In **Flexion** the angle between the two bones decreases.
- **Extension** occurs when the angle between the two bones increases.
- **Abduction** occurs when a limb or limb segment separates laterally from the midline of limb body or a body segment used as reference.
- In **Adduction** the segment approximates the midline of the body or body part used as reference.
- **Circumduction** is a compound continuous movement in which the joint goes through the four types of movement described above, thus making the moving body segment describe a circular motion.
- **Rotation** happens when the bone turns about its longitudinal axis.

Figure 1-11. Some common joint movements, from the shoulder to the digits. © 2009 Alan H. D. Watson. Reproduced under license.

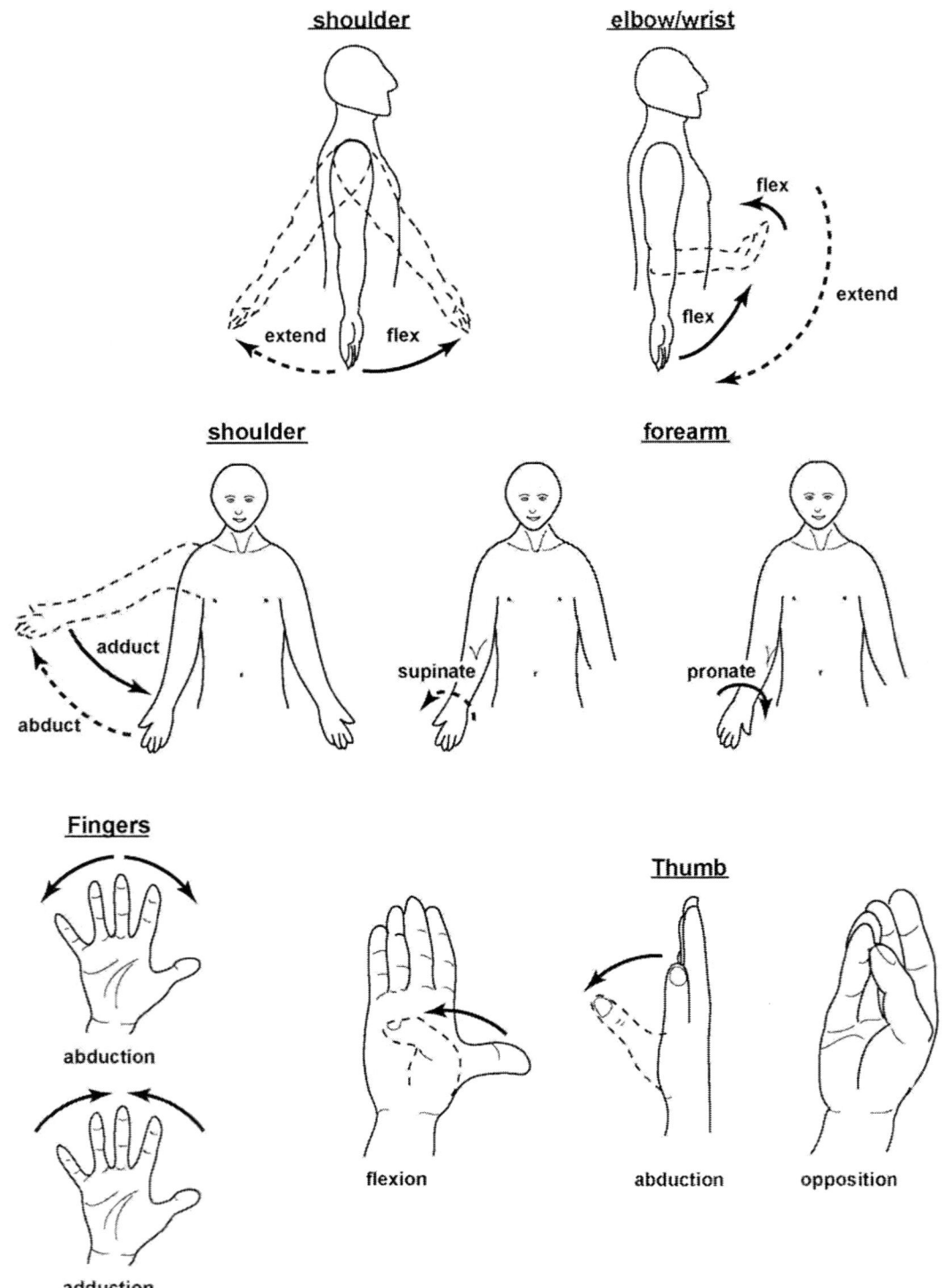

Arm Muscle Location

Flexor/pronator/adductor muscles are located in the **palmar**, **anterior** or **ventral** side of the limb and **extensors/ supinators/abductors** on the **posterior** or **dorsal side**.

20

Depending on their relative position within the arm, they are further classified as **superficial** or **deep** (in relation to the anterior and posterior sides). Muscles move all joints they pass through, from origin to insertion point, with the distal joints activated with more strength than the proximal.

 The Shoulder Girdle

The two bones of the **shoulder or pectoral girdle**, **clavicle** (collar bone) and **scapula** (shoulder blade), connect at the **acromioclavicular joint**, where the lateral end of the clavicle meets the pronounced protuberance on the superior-lateral edge of the scapula called the **acrominum**. They move as a unit, by the action of rather large muscles situated in the back and the chest, acting on the scapula, which has no other support but those provided by these muscles (see figures 1-12 to 1-15).

All movements pivot on the one articulation linking the girdle to the axial skeleton, between the clavicle, acting as a strut (Palastanga and Soames 2012), and the **sternum** or breastbone at the **sterno-clavicular joint.**

In playing the guitar, movements at the pectoral girdle are mainly those necessary to support the movements of the arm, articulated through the shoulder joint.

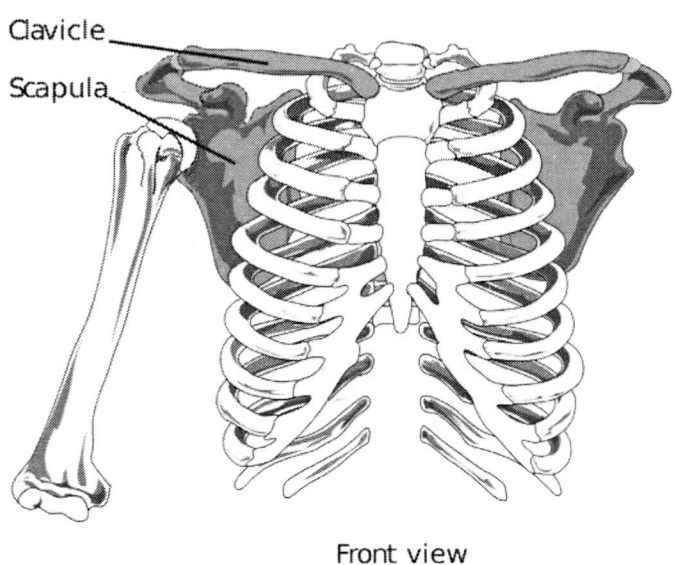

Front view

Figure 1-12. The shoulder girdle. In the middle of the chest, the sternum. Mariana Ruiz Villareal, 2007.

Adduction (also called **retraction)** is the movement bringing the lateral edge of the shoulder blade backwards and inwards (postero-medially), towards the spinal column (as in the military chest-out stance).

Abduction (or **protraction)** is the movement forward and away from the spine (antero-lateral).

These movements should not occur in the course of normal guitar playing. When they do occur, they are the result of inefficient co-ordination of arm movements, or improper support from the back muscles (slouching excessively or torsion of the spinal column).

Rotation upward moves up the scapula's superior lateral angle (where the shoulder joint is) while its lower medial edge turns laterally away from the spinal column. This movement is usually associated with hyperabduction of the arm (described later) and, again, is not relevant to guitar playing.

21

Rotation downward, the opposite move, returns the lower edge closer to the spine and levels off the shoulder joint (the movement may take it even further down), either by the action of gravity, or muscular effort, if resisted. Some players, in placing the right arm on the upper rim of the guitar, sometimes downwardly rotate the scapula ('dropping the shoulder') because of faulty positioning of the instrument. Care should be taken to maintain the line of the shoulders level.

Elevation raises the scapula, as in shrugging the shoulder. This movement, again, should not be a part of guitar technique. When it occurs, it is the product of accumulated nervous tension. In less experienced players, it is associated frequently with arm abduction in left-hand shifting, and should be corrected immediately.

Depression, the opposite move, returns the scapula to its normal position.

Track 1-2 **The Shoulder Joint**

The scapula connects to the **humerus** or arm-bone at the **glenohumeral joint:** the rounded head of the humerus fits into the **glenoid fossa** of the scapula in what is called a ball-and-socket joint, permitting movement in all directions. Muscles moving the shoulder joint are easily differentiated from those acting on the shoulder girdle because all insert on the humerus.

These muscles also originate in the back and the chest, with one exception, the **deltoid,** that covers the shoulder region proper. A **bursa**, under the muscle, provides a smooth surface upon which the mass of the deltoid 'slides', but might be prone to inflammation (**bursitis**) caused by strenuous use or trauma.

The four tendons of the muscles of the **rotator cuff** (**supraspinatus**, **infraspinatus**, **subscapularis** and **teres minor**) keep the head of the humerus in place, except no tendon supports the joint at the axilla, which explains why most shoulder dislocations happen in the downward direction (Watson, Biol. Mus. Perf. 2009, 46).

Flexion is the movement of the arm forward and upwards (antero-superior). **Hyperflexion** occurs when this movement continues beyond the frontal plane.

Extension is the return to a hanging position by the side. Continuation of this movement backwards constitutes **hyperextension**.

Upper arm flexion and extension are present in any movement of the left hand across the six strings (combined with forearm flexion/ extension; see below). It flexes in movements towards the bass strings and extends in movements towards the trebles.

Figure 1-13. Muscles acting on the girdle and shoulder (right arm front view). © 2009 Alan H. D. Watson. Reproduced under license.

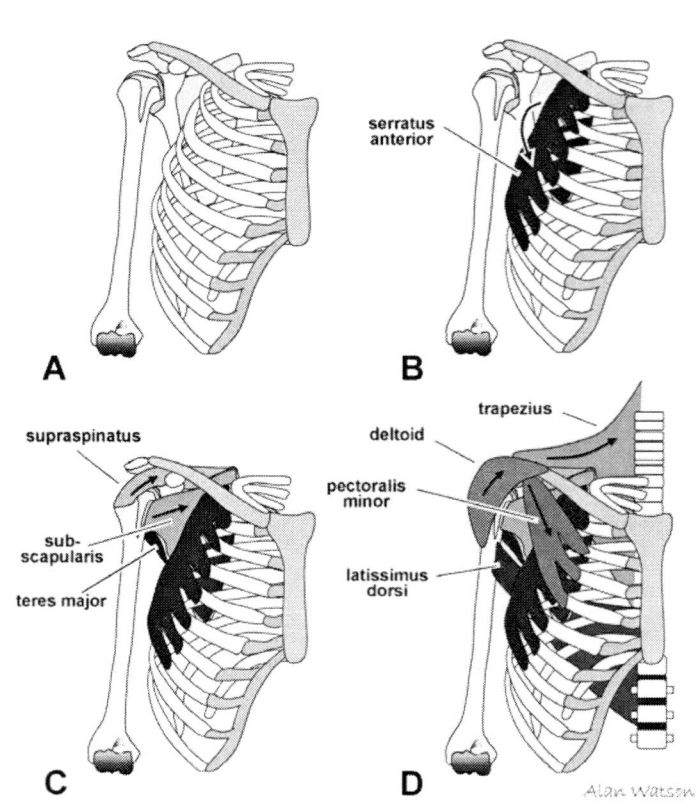

22

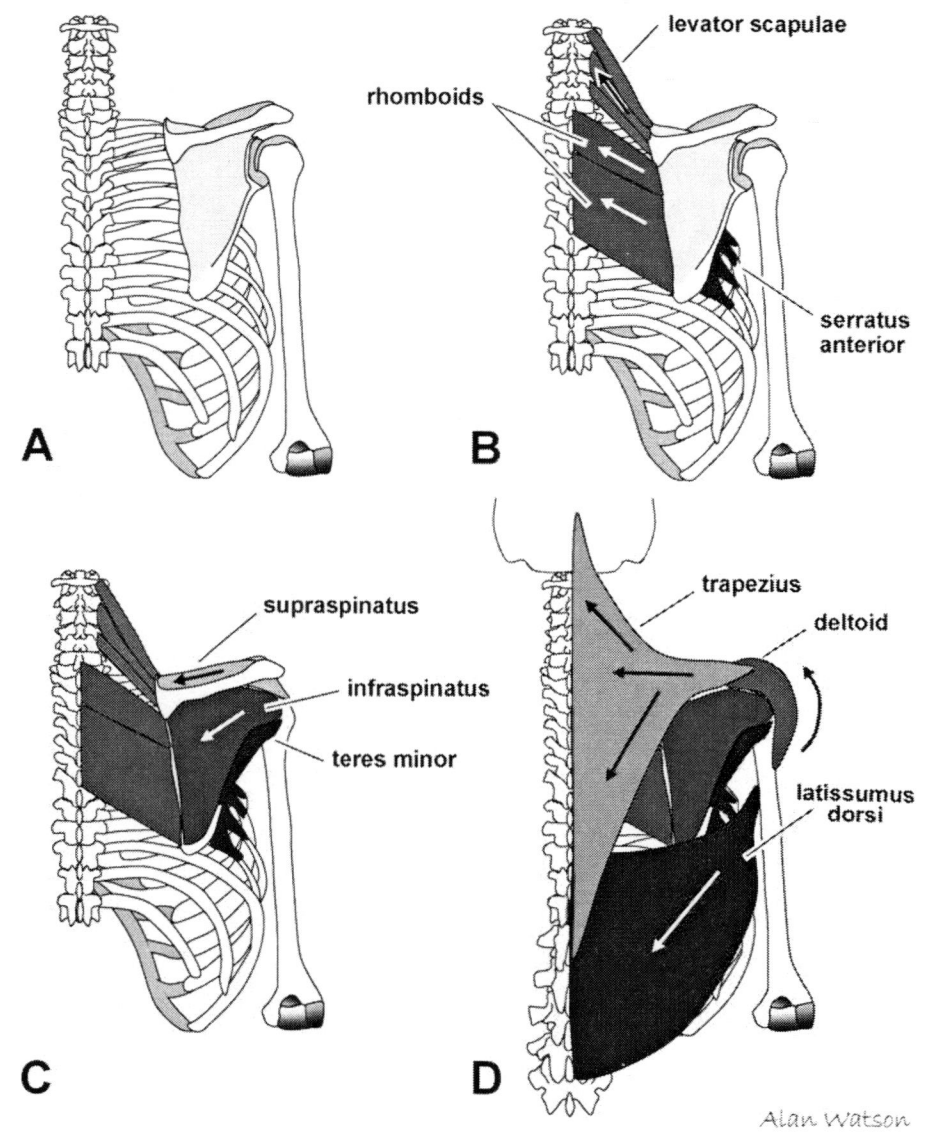

Abduction is the movement of the humerus to the side and up (latero-superior). The abduction may be along the coronal plane, or it may follow the anatomical alignment of the shoulder joint, which lies slightly antero-lateral to the coronal plane (O'Rahilly, et al. 2008).

Adduction, the opposite motion, returns the arm to the side.

Together with rotation (see below) abduction/adduction movements are present in left-hand shifting technique, as well as in the behavior of the right limb.

Horizontal flexion is the movement of the arm frontally and inwardly (antero-medial) from a position of abduction. **Horizontal extension** is the opposite movement, a backward and outwards (postero-lateral) motion in the horizontal plane from a position of horizontal flexion.

Figure 1-14. The same, back view. © 2009 Alan H. D. Watson. Reproduced under license.

In the right arm (the left, in left-handed players) these two movements are used primarily for changes in dynamics and tone color (playing towards the bridge or towards the fingerboard) and in playing artificial harmonics and other special techniques, but, as discussed later, they may also be part of a player's normal approach to shifting right-arm positions.

In **outward** or **lateral rotation** the humerus turns around its axis laterally (in a clockwise manner, for the right limb; counterclockwise in the left limb).

Inward or **medial rotation** occurs when the humerus turns around its axis inwardly (counterclockwise, in the right limb, clockwise, in the left).

Rotation of the shoulder joint is one of the fastest movements possible in any arm joint. It is the basis for arm vibrato. As mentioned earlier, it is also a component of shifting movements in changes of left hand position, in combination with abduction/adduction.

The shoulder joint is also capable of **circumduction**, in which the arm, moving forwards (flexion) or backwards (extension) continues in the same direction until it completes a circle (actually, the elbow moves circularly, while the upper arm itself draws a cone). Obviously, this movement should not be part of normal guitar performance.

The Elbow, Forearm and Wrist Joints

Track 1-3

The Elbow

Muscles acting primarily on the elbow joint are located in the upper arm and insert in the forearm (Figure 1-15). As mentioned earlier, muscles situated on the anterior side act as flexors of the elbow joint, while those on the posterior side extend it.

The **humerus** connects with the bones of the forearm through the elbow joint, which is rather complex as there are several bone surfaces articulating within a single joint cavity. The humerus links separately with the **ulna** (**humeroulnar** joint) and with the

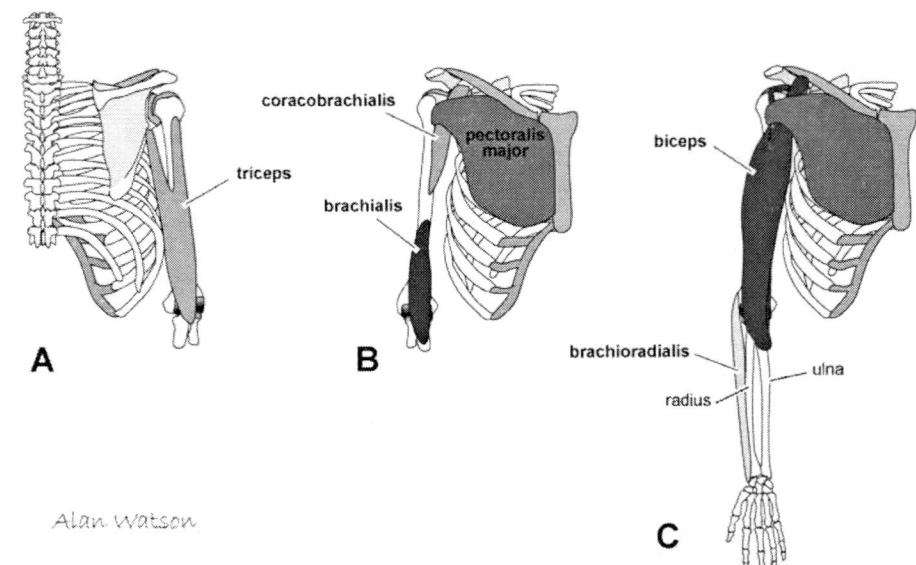

Figure 1-15. Elbow and forearm. A: Posterior view. B and C: Frontal view. The coracobrachialis and pectoralis major muscles move the shoulder joint, not the elbow. © 2009 Alan H. D. Watson. Reproduced under license.

radius (humeroradial joint), but ligaments protecting the joint make them act as one in movements of flexion and extension, while also allowing for rotation in the forearm.

Rotation occurs thanks to the way the ulna and radius themselves articulate.

They join close to the elbow and close to the wrist through pivot joints which allow a bone to rotate around or alongside another. In between the radius and ulna there exists a powerful membrane, called the **interosseous membrane**, which strengthens their articulation.

Strictly speaking, the only movements possible at the elbow joint are those of flexion and extension. The movement of rotation characteristic of the forearm is the consequence of the capability of the radius to move on top of the ulna, thanks to the aforementioned **radioulnar** joints.

Flexion is the movement that brings the forearm closer to the upper arm.

Flexors of the elbow, placed on the anterior side, include the **biceps brachi**, as primary mover, assisted by **brachialis** and **brachioradialis**.

Extension, the opposite move, increases the angle between forearm and arm. The main elbow extensor, in the posterior side of the upper arm, is the **triceps**, working together with **anconeus**, a much weaker elbow extensor but a stabilizer of this joint that acts together with triceps, almost as a fourth head of this three-headed muscle.

Flexion and extension of the elbow joint are present in any movement of the left hand across the six strings and, depending on the player's technical approach, of the right hand as well. In the left arm these movements work in conjunction with but in opposite directions to similar movements at the shoulder joint, as described earlier.

Hyperextension is possible in some arms (particularly female). It happens when the forearm surpasses 180° of separation from the upper arm.

The Forearm (Figure 1-16)

Pronation is the rotary movement of the forearm in which the palm turns inwardly (palm down). At the extreme of its range, forearm pronation may be increased by upper arm inward rotation when the elbow is extended. The main forearm pronator is **pronator teres**, originating on the anterior side of the upper arm, close to the **humeroulnar joint**, which it crosses before inserting on the lateral side of the radius.

Supination is the outward rotation of the forearm (palm up), activated by the **supinator** muscle, located by the elbow joint.

At the extreme of its range, forearm supination may be increased by upper arm outward rotation when the elbow is extended.

Many of the guitarist's problems with accumulated tension in both hands begin with improper application of pronation and supination of either forearm.

This is particularly true in the left hand, when dealing with shifting from and to lower positions, where there might be a tendency to keep an unnecessary degree of supination.

Figure 1-16. Forearm rotation. © 2009 Alan H. D. Watson. Reproduced under license.

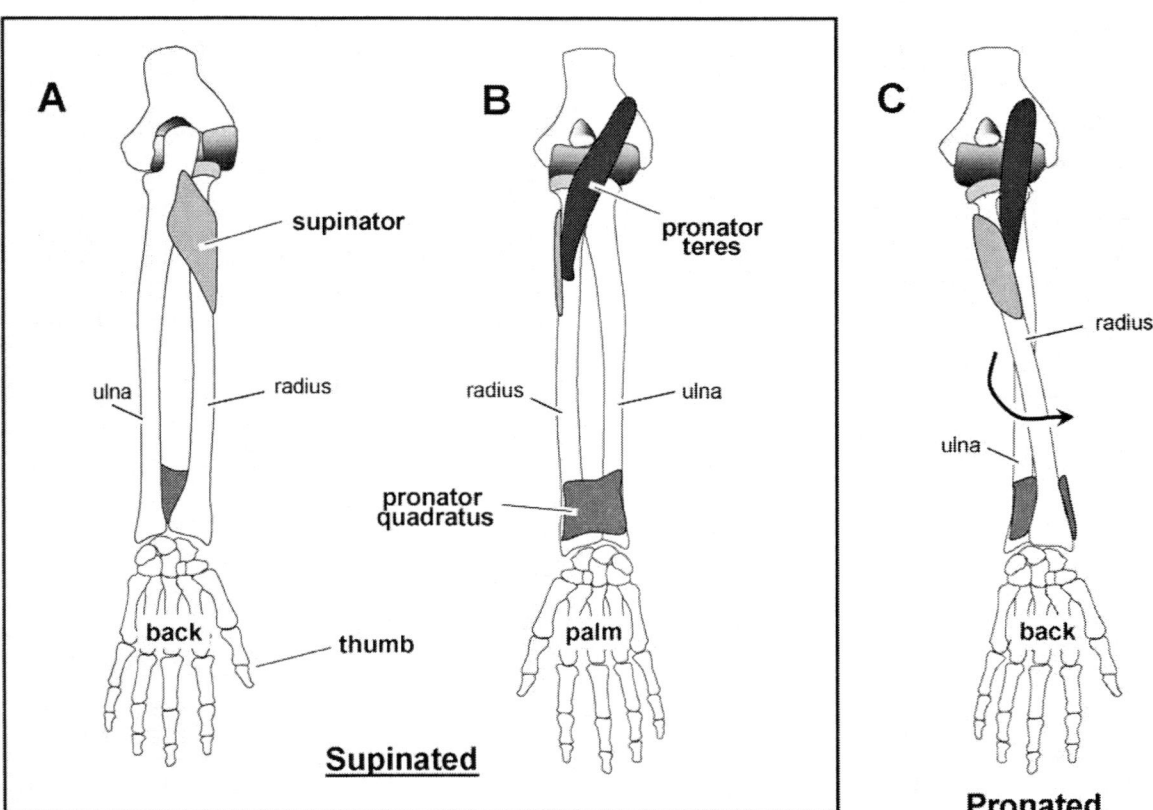

The Wrist

The eight little bones of the wrist or **carpus** are distributed in two rows of four bones each. The proximal row articulates with the concave surfaces of the radius and ulna. The major articulation uniting forearm and wrist is known as the **radiocarpal joint**.

The joints linking the proximal and distal rows of carpals form the **midcarpal articulation**. The distal carpal row joins the proximal ends of the five hand-bones or **metacarpals**, forming the **carpometacarpal articulation**.

The thumb's carpometacarpal joint allows for more diversity of movement than in any of the other digits

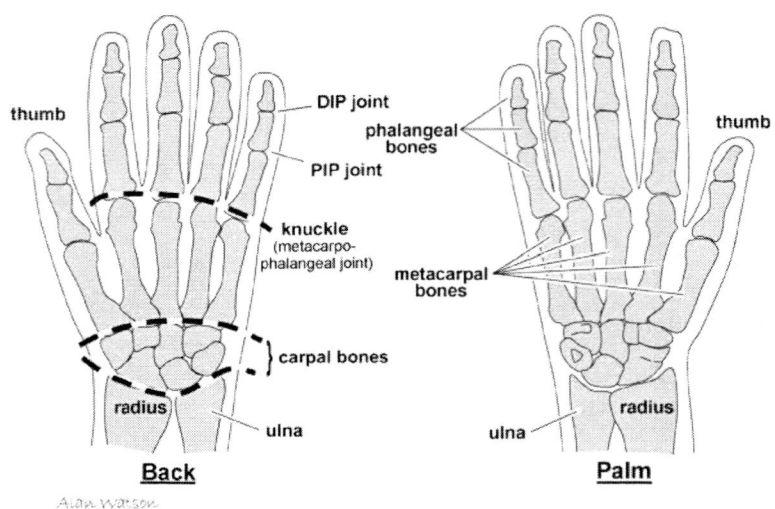

Figure 1-17. Bones of the hand. © 2009 Alan H. D. Watson. Reproduced under license.

Flexion (**palmar flexion**) is the movement of bringing the hand and fingers closer to the forearm on the palm side. The two wrist flexor muscles (**radial flexor** and **ulnar flexor**), working together (as well as the rather weak action of the **long palmar muscle**, which is, however, absent in a good number of people) are responsible for this movement. When working separately, they flex the wrist with a slight deviation to the radial or ulnar side, respectively.

Extension is the opposite movement to flexion, returning the wrist to an aligned position with the forearm. The wrist extensors (strictly speaking, three muscles: the **long and short radial extensors** – which can be considered as one, since they lie side by side and have undifferentiated functions – and the **ulnar extensor**), when working together, cause this action. When working independently, they extend the wrist also with some radial or ulnar deviation, respectively.

Hyperextension (or **dorsal flexion**) is the continuation of the extension towards the dorsal side of the forearm.

Radial abduction (or **radial deviation**) is a movement of the wrist to the thumb side. This movement is the result of *both* radial flexors and extensors working together (assisted by the thumb abductor).

Ulnar abduction (or **ulnar deviation**) is the movement of the wrist to the little-finger side. Both flexor and extensor on the ulnar side work together in this movement.

Excessive wrist deviation, to the radial or ulnar side, as well as excessive flexion and hyperextension, are some of the most common causes of technical deficiencies and even physical discomfort or injury in guitar playing.

Holding position in these extreme attitudes for prolonged periods of time will create problems for the performer.

Circumduction, as explained in the context of the shoulder joint, is a conical movement of the joint that is a combination of movements of flexion, deviation, and extension.

The wrist joint is incapable of **rotation** per se, but it partakes of the rotary movements of the forearm towards pronation or supination.

The behavior of the wrist is fundamental in all aspects of guitar technique, from left hand shifts, where it acts as a flexible 'shock absorber' smoothing out swift changes of direction, to fast scale playing, where its proper alignment and stability will guarantee effective execution in both hands.

 **Digit Joints**

The links uniting hand and digits are known as **metacarpophalangeal joints**. The distal ends of the metacarpals join the proximal phalanges. These are what we refer to as hand-knuckles.

The three **finger phalanges (first or proximal, second or middle,** and **third** or **distal)** are joined through **interphalangeal joints (proximal** and **distal)**, acting as perfect hinges and allowing for a minimum of rotation. The thumb, having only two phalanges (proximal and distal) has one interphalangeal joint.

More than 30 muscles are involved in the mechanism that controls movement of the wrist and hand digits. Typically, the muscles of the forearm taper off toward the wrist and their bellies are replaced by long tendons that continue into the hand. Many of these muscles are multi-joint muscles that may act even on the elbow joint.

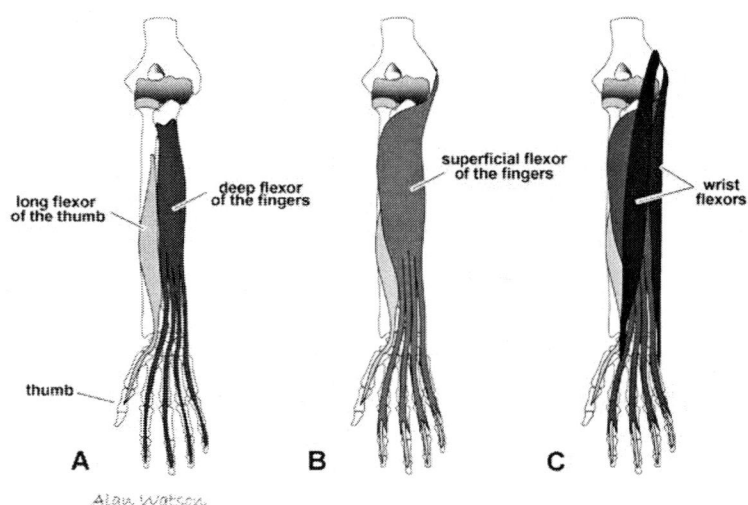

Figure 1-18. Forearm muscles, palmar view. © 2009 Alan H. D. Watson, Ph. D. Reproduced under license.

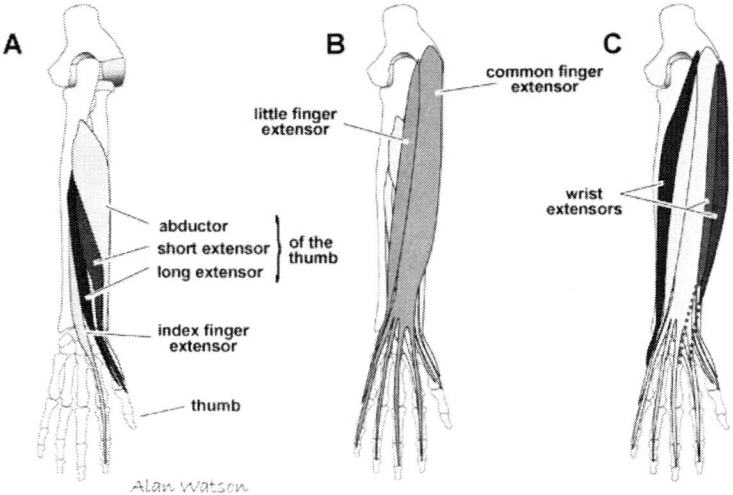

Figure 1-19. Forearm muscles, dorsal view. © 2009 Alan H. D. Watson, Ph. D. Reproduced under license.

Of particular importance in guitar technique is the role of the short muscles located in the hand proper, called **intrinsic muscles of the hand** (Figures 1-20, 1-21) as they are indispensable in individualized finger action. There are five sets of such muscles: the **lumbricals**, **palmar** and **dorsal interossei**, and those of the two muscular masses clearly distinguishable in the palm of the hand: the **thenar eminence**, the bigger of the two, situated at the base of the thumb, and the less bulky **hypothenar eminence**, under the little finger.

The thenar eminence contains short muscles controlling the thumb, the hypothenar, short muscles of the little finger.

Across the wrist, both on the palmar and dorsal surfaces, lie respective bands of thickish fibers that form the **flexor retinaculum** (palmar side) and the **extensor retinaculum** (dorsal side). The space between the flexor retinaculum and the concave surface formed by the carpals is the **carpal tunnel**, through which 9 flexor tendons and the median nerve pass to the hand and fingers.

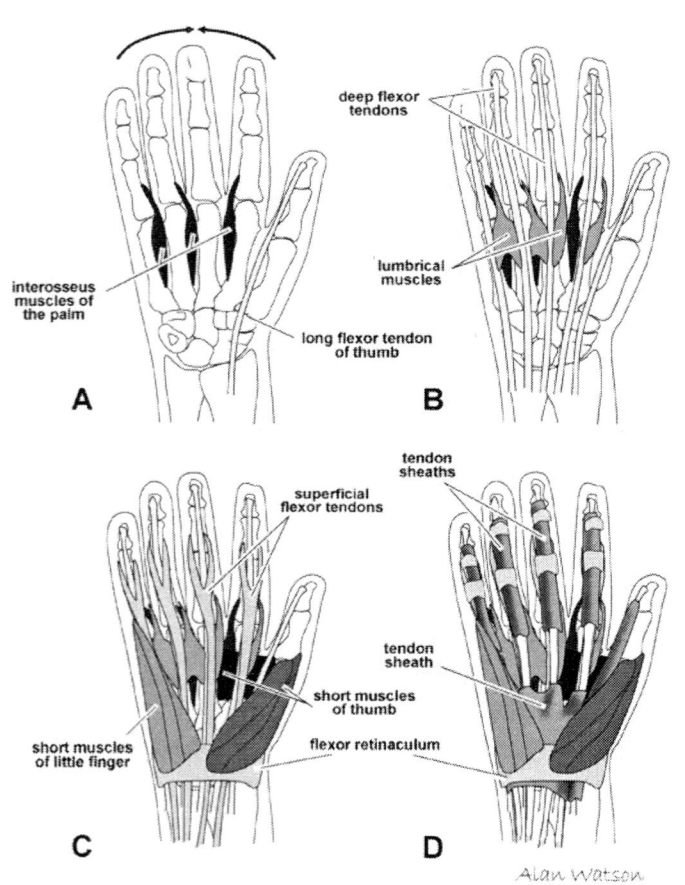 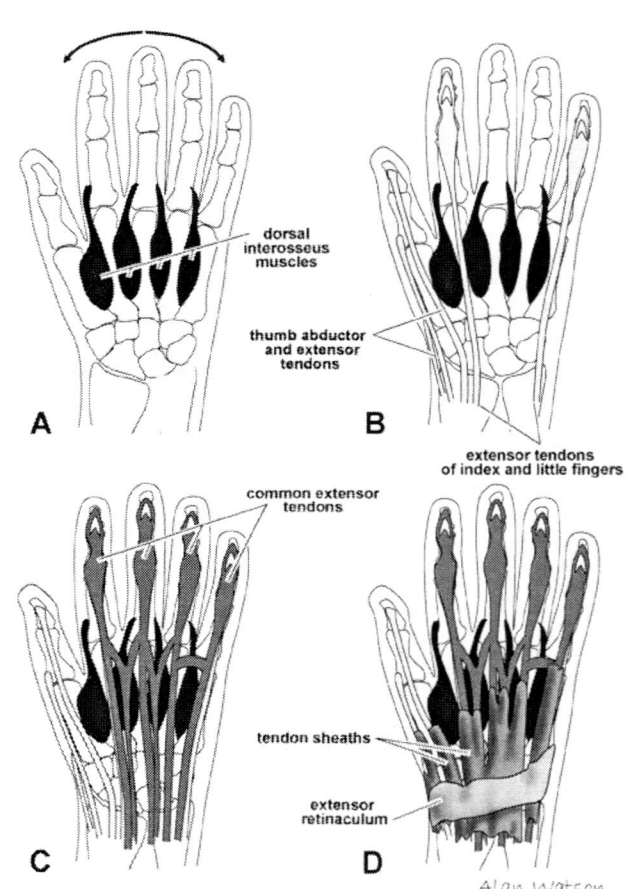

Figure 1-20. Inrinsics, palmar side (the palmar interosseous of the thumb is not shown). © 2009 Alan H. D. Watson. Reproduced under license.

Figure 1-21 Intrinsics, dorsal side. © 2009 Alan H. D. Watson. Reproduced under license.

Misalignment of the wrists, which may produce compression of these anatomical elements as they pass through the tunnel, is one of the most frequent causes of nerve irritation and entrapment (**carpal tunnel syndrome**) among guitarists and other instrumentalists.

 **Finger Movements**

Flexion is movement towards the palm of the hand, as in forming a fist.

There are two muscles located in the forearm, the **deep or long flexor (flexor digitorum profundus)** and the **superficial** or **associated flexor (flexor digitorum superficialis)**, whose finger tendons attach to the distal and the middle phalanges of the fingers, respectively.

The proximal phalanx may flex under certain conditions by the action of the previous two muscles, but the primary knuckle joint flexors are the intrinsics, primarily the **lumbricals**, muscles of the hand which originate from the tendons of the long deep flexor. When flexing against resistance, the **interossei** are also engaged.

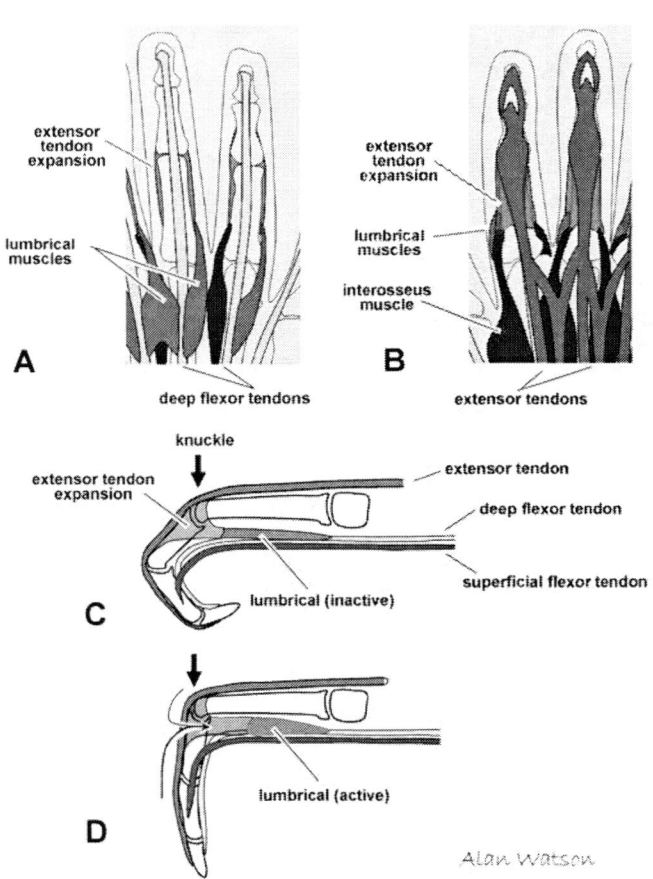

The lumbricals, in contrast with other limb muscles, originate not from a bone but from the tendon of the common long flexor of the fingers (flexor digitorum profundus). They insert on a hood-like, flattened tendonal tissue that grows out of the common extensor tendon on the dorsal side of the finger, called the **extensor expansion** or **dorsal aponeurosis**, covering the back and sides of the proximal and middle phalanges, with bands continuing to the distal phalanx. This unique design explains their capability to *simultaneously* extend the last two phalanges and flex the knuckle joints. In guitar playing, this characteristic movement, the so-called 'lumbrical effect' (Palastanga and Soames 2012), is present in right-hand finger preparatory contact with the string, for instance. It is also present, with support from the dorsal interosseous, in the left hand index finger when executing a full barré. This lumbrical action will be discussed in more detail in Chapters 2 and 3.

Figure 1-22. Finger intrinsics connection to extensor expansion (A: Palmar view. B: Dorsal view) and schema of lumbrical function (C and D). © 2009 Alan H. D. Watson. Reproduced under license.

The dorsal and palmar interossei (except the thumb's) also insert variously into the extensor expansion, thus, they can assist the lumbricals, when needed, in MCP flexion accompanied with IP extension.

Extension is the movement that brings back the fingers to align with the dorsum of the hand. A common finger extensor plus independent extensors of the index and little finger are primarily responsible for finger extension at the knuckle joint. However, the long extensors on their own cannot overcome the passive pull of the long flexors and require the engagement of the intrinsics (primarily the lumbricals), which, as explained above, extend the middle and distal phalanges, to achieve full-finger extension.

The independent extension of individual fingers may be constrained by the bands that frequently unite the extensor tendons (**intertendinous connections** or **juncturae tendinae**) on the dorsum of the hand. This is particularly true of the ring finger, whose tendon may be attached to the middle and, most commonly, the little finger tendons, respectively, by such connections. This will be discussed in more detail in Chapter 2.

Hyperextension is the continuation of finger extension beyond the plane of the hand, towards the dorsal side of the forearm.

Abduction is a sideward movement of the fingers away from the mid-line of the hand, either to the radial (thumb) or ulnar (little-finger) side. This is the primary function of the **dorsal interossei** muscles (1 for the index, 2 for the middle and 1 for the ring fingers), and of the **abductor** of the little finger (sometimes erroneously called the fifth dorsal interosseous, ignoring the fact that the word 'interosseous', meaning 'between bones,' cannot apply to a muscle which lies lateral to the last bone in the hand).

This movement is associated with finger extension: flexion of the knuckle joints will make finger abduction more difficult, and it becomes impossible when all finger joints are flexed. This is due to the increasing tautness of the **collateral ligaments** on either side of the knuckle joint, which provide structural integrity and sturdiness to the MCP articulation.

What we call extensions or stretches in guitar playing depend on finger abduction (and, of course, accompanying extension at the base joints) for their execution.

Adduction is the opposite movement from abduction: a sideward movement of the finger towards the mid-line. As the mid-line goes through the middle finger, this finger never adducts, it only abducts radially or ulnarly through the action of its two interossei on the dorsal side.

The primary adductors are the **palmar interossei** (1 each for the index, ring and little fingers. Obviously, as it never adducts, the middle finger does not have interossei on the palmar side, but has two dorsal interossei. The thumb also has a palmar interosseous, whose action is described later) but all the flexors collaborate, since, as we saw, adduction increases with finger flexion.

Hyperadduction is the continuation of adduction past the mid-line of the hand (most common in the index finger).

Circumduction (see above) is possible at the metacarpophalangeal (knuckle), but not at the interphalangeal, joints.

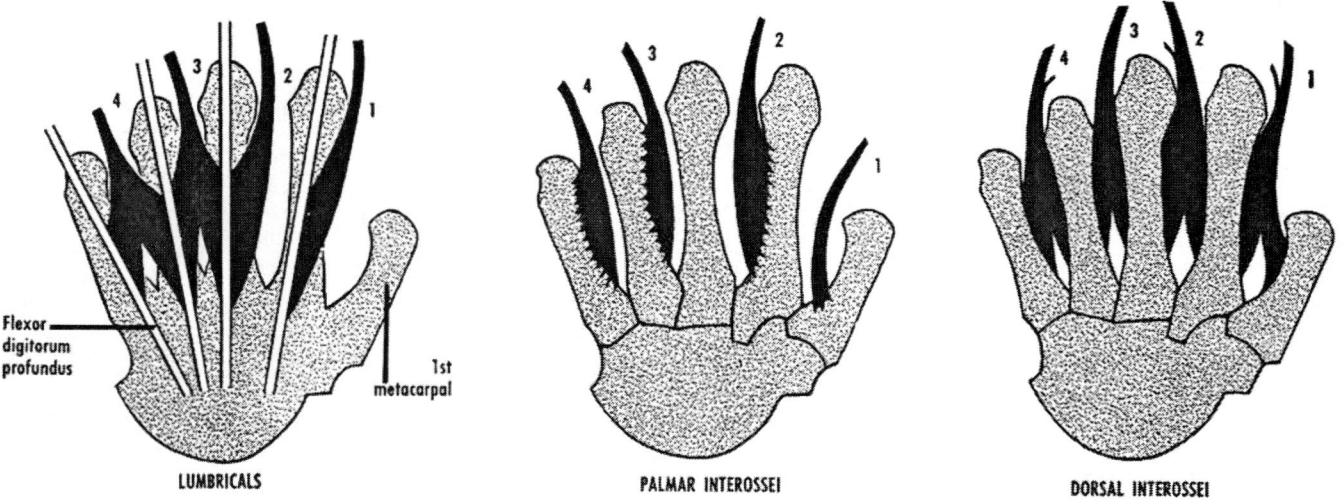

Figure 1-23. Schematic representation of location for lumbricals, palmar and dorsal interossei (right hand). © 2008 Ronan O'Rahilly, www.dartmouth.edu/~humananatomy/index.html/ . Reproduced with permission of the authors.

 Thumb Movements

Because of the position of the thumb joints, movements of this digit are at right angles to those of the fingers. The **carpometacarpal** (wrist) joint of the thumb is its most movable. By comparison, its **metacarpophalangeal** (or knuckle) joint is limited in its mobility, while its single **interphalangeal** joint can only flex or extend.

The most important and characteristic movement of the thumb is that of **opposition**, by which it comes to touch the tips of each of the other fingers. This complex movement, originating at the wrist joint, is achieved by the interaction of three muscles situated in the thenar eminence with other thumb muscles located in the forearm.

The movement of opposition is in reality a combination of several types of joint motion (flexion, abduction and inward rotation).

Flexion is the sideways movement of the thumb as a whole towards the index (**hyperflexion**, if it continues across the palm of the hand, under the fingers). It is also called **radial adduction** and involves both long and short thumb flexor muscles. Flexion of its distal phalanx only is the result of the action of the thumb's long flexor, originating in the forearm.

Extension (radial abduction) occurs when the thumb separates laterally from the hand by the actions of the thumb extensors (long and short). Extension of the distal phalanx alone is also possible, by the engagement of the long extensor.

Abduction or **palmar abduction** is the movement of the thumb away from the palm and at a right angle to it.

Adduction (palmar adduction) is its opposite, the movement of the thumb towards the palm from the position of abduction. The thumb adductor (**adductor pollicis**) is assisted by the first palmar interosseous in this movement.

Circumduction is possible at the wrist (**carpometacarpal**) joint of the thumb, while **rotation** is present as a necessary component of other thumb movements.

The movement contrary to opposition, called **reposition**, is a combination of abduction, extension and outward rotation of the first metacarpal at the wrist joint.

Almost all movements of the thumb involve the muscles of the thenar eminence, either as prime movers or assistants.

REVIEW

Forearm Muscles and Functions — Extrinsic Muscles

- **Extrinsic** muscles are located in the forearm, but some have their point of origin in the upper arm, close to the elbow joint. They control wrist and finger movements.
- The extrinsic group includes, in the anterior forearm, **wrist flexors: radial and ulnar**, and the **palmaris longus**, also a (rather weak) wrist flexor, absent in about 15% of the population (Caillet 1994); a smaller pronator (**pronator quadratus**, located close to the wrist, assisting **pronator teres** in pronounced pronation. The latter originates in the upper arm and inserts on the radius), two common finger flexors (**flexor digitorum profundus**, primary flexor of the distal IP joint, but also assisting in flexing the two proximal joints and even in wrist flexion, and **flexor digitorum superficialis**, primary flexor of the proximal IP joint, and secondarily the MCP and wrist joints) and the long thumb flexor (**flexor pollicis longus**, primary flexor of the thumb's IP joint).
- Located dorsally are the **supinator**, by the elbow joint, one common extensor of the four fingers (**extensor digitorum**), an extensor of the index (**extensor indicis**), an extensor of the little finger (**extensor digiti minimi**), the long abductor of the thumb (**abductor pollicis longus**), the two extensors of the thumb (long and short: **extensor pollicis longus, brevis**), and the wrist extensors (one ulnar, **extensor carpi ulnaris**, and the two radial extensors, short and long: **extensor carpi radialis longus, brevis**).

Hand Muscles and Functions — Intrinsic Muscles

- The intrinsic group includes dorsal and palmar interossei, lumbricals, the thenar group and the hypothenar group, all located in the hand.
- The four **dorsal interossei** (one for the index, two for the middle and one for the ring finger) are primary finger abductors and assist in MCP flexion, if resistance is present, when IP joints are extended (that is, when the extrinsic flexors are inactive).
- The three finger **palmar interossei** (one each for the index, ring and little finger) are primary finger adductors and also assist in MCP flexion, against resistance, when IP joints are extended
- The **lumbricals** have a unique double function as primary IP extensors and, when no resistance is present, MCP flexors. Against resistance, the MCP flexion is supported by the interossei.
- The **thenar eminence**, the thick, fleshy mass in the palm located underneath the thumb, includes muscles controlling the thumb: the short thumb abductor (**abductor pollicis brevis**), the short thumb flexor (**flexor pollicis brevis**), the thumb opposer (**opponens pollicis**), the thumb adductor (**adductor pollicis**) and a **palmar interosseous**, which assists in thumb adduction movement. The adductor and the index dorsal interosseus are primary muscles in the action of pinching.
- The **hypothenar** is the less prominent mass under the little finger, whose muscle group controls the little finger: the abductor (**abductor digiti minimi**), the flexor (**flexor digiti minimi**) and, like the thumb, the opposer (**opponens digiti minimi**). Also the short palmar (**palmaris brevis**), an involuntary muscle that tightens the skin of the hand in gripping action.

Summary of Basic Anatomical Terms and Abbreviations Related to the Hand

- Principal terms and abbreviations used in this text are listed below. It is a partial list, which does not pretend to be comprehensive or exhaustive:

	TERM	ABBREVIATION
JOINTS		
	Carpometacarpal joint (joint between wrist and hand)	CMC
	Metacarpophalangeal joint (joint between hand and digits)	MCP
	Interphalangeal joints (joints between phalangeal segments. Fingers have two, the thumb has one)	IP
	Proximal (first) interphalangeal joint (joint between first and middle phalanges)	PIP
	Distal (second) interphalangeal joint (joint between middle and tip phalanges)	DIP
FOREARM MUSCLES		
Anterior	Common superficial finger flexor (Flexor Digitorum Superficialis)	FDS
	Common deep finger flexor (Flexor Digitorum Profundus)	FDP
	Long thumb flexor (Flexor Pollicis Longus)	FPL
Posterior	Common finger extensor muscle (Extensor Digitorum)	ED
	Extensor of the index (Extensor Indicis)	EI
	Extensor of the little finger (Extensor Digiti Minimi)	EM
	Long thumb extensor (Extensor Pollicis Longus)	EPL
	Short thumb extensor (Extensor Pollicis Brevis)	EPB
	Long thumb abductor (Abductor Pollicis Longus)	AbPL
INTRINSICS		
	Lumbrical (Lumbricalis)	L
	Interosseous	I
Hypothenar Group		
	Flexor of the little finger (Flexor Digiti Minimi)	FM
	Abductor of the little finger (Abductor Digiti Minimi)	AM
	Opposer of the little finger (Opponens Digiti Minimi)	OM

Thenar Group

Short thumb abductor (Abductor Pollicis Brevis)	AbPB
Short thumb flexor (Flexor Pollicis Brevis)	FPB
Thumb opposer (Opponens Pollicis)	OP
Thumb adductor (Adductor Pollicis)	AdP

Further Exploration of the Physiomechanics of Digital Movement

Finger Movement

- The phalangeal joints can only flex and extend. The MCP joint can also abduct and adduct, and, in varying and limited degrees, rotate and circumduct. The MCP finger joints align with the horizontal palmar creases of the hand (the 'heart and head lines'), not with the proximal digital creases, but the middle and distal finger creases align with the PIP and DIP joints, respectively.

- The flexor tendons of the fingers maintain their functional capabilities and efficiency thanks to a system of five ring-like (**annular**) and three criss-cross (**cruciate**) **pulleys**, which are, thickened areas of the flexor tendon sheaths… of paramount biomechanical importance…, not only for accurate tracking of the tendon but also to maintain the apposition of tendon and bone across the joint and provide a fulcrum to elicit flexion and extension (Hauger, et al. 2000, 201).

- That is to say, the pulley system keeps tendon and bone together, thus avoiding 'bowstringing', gaps between the two, which makes the tendon lose its leverage functionality for flexion…a fairly frequent injury in rock climbers (fortunately, not in guitarists!)

- Two pathological conditions of the hand can help clarify the complex functional anatomy of the hand and fingers. The condition known as the **intrinsic-minus** hand is caused when the hand intrinsics are incapacitated, usually through neurological impairment (Nguyen Gillespie and Wilhellmi 2012). Without their involvement,

  > …'pure' extensor digitorum action would extend the MCP joint and flex the IP joints…
  > due to active pull of the extensors and passive pull of the flexor digitorum profundus
  > (Caillet, 53).

- This produces a 'claw' hand (**claw hand deformity**) that impedes grabbing, as the initial phalangeal extension needed to begin the grab (an intrinsic function) is absent.

- From this it follows that intrinsics are primary phalangeal extensors. As explained earlier, the long extensors, on their own, cannot overcome the passive pull of the long flexors when the MCP joint is extended. Of the two groups of intrinsics (**interossei** and **lumbricals**), the lumbricals have a more prominent role in phalangeal extension, if the knuckle joint is extended partially or fully. However, with the MCP joint flexed or near flexion, the interossei 'assist massively' (Thomas, Long and Landsmeer 1968, 109).

- In the second condition there is involuntary and unavoidable flexion of the MCP joint with full extension of the IP joints. This is known as the **intrinsic-plus** position and is due to hyperactivity of the intrinsic (Nguyen Gillespie and Wilhellmi 2012). This also impedes proper grab as the fingers cannot complete flexion around the object. A form of this position, with the wrist in dorsal flexion, is the so-called **z-position** (see Figure 1-24 below), also known as the 'safe position' for splinting the hand with minimum stress to the finger joints (Nguyen Gillespie and Wilhellmi 2012).

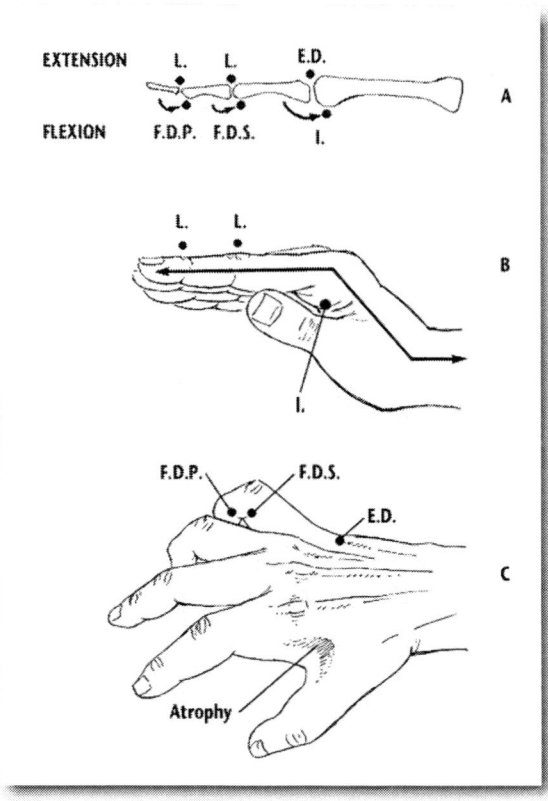

Figure 1-24. In A, diagram of finger flexion/extensor mechanism (refer to list of terms for abbreviations); B, the z-position; C, the claw-hand position. © 2008 Ronan O'Rahilly, www.dartmouth.edu/~humananatomy/index.html/ . Reproduced with permission of the authors.

- Apart from being phalangeal extensors, the intrinsics are primary MCP flexors. Lumbricals are the primary MCP joint flexors but, against resistance, the interossei are also engaged.

- The intrinsics are not extensors of the knuckle (MCP) joint. This is a primary function of ED, EI and EM, inserting dorsally in the fingers' proximal phalanges.

- The intrinsics are not flexors of the phalanges. This is a primary function of the long or deep flexor (FDP), inserting in the distal IP and flexor of all finger joints, and of FDS (the superficial flexor), inserting in the middle phalanx and flexor of the PIP and the MCP but not of the DIP.

- The intrinsics mesh with the extensor tendons in a dorsal hood-like structure (the **dorsal aponeurosis**, or extensor expansion) that expands the extensor mechanism along the length of the fingers.

- When actively working in conjunction with the extrinsic extensors, the intrinsics (lumbricals primarily) complete the action of full-finger extension by extending the phalanges through their attachments to the dorsal aponeurosis.

- As flexors of the MCP joint, when actively working in conjunction with the FDP and FDS the intrinsics complete the action of full-finger flexion, in loaded flexion (as in a power grip). In non-resisted flexion, they are essentially inactive, as is the FDS as well. FDP is the primary finger flexor when unopposed (Long 1968). However, if the DIP joint does not flex, the primary flexor is FDS.

- The eminent hand surgeon J. Wiliam Littler (1915 – 2005) showed that the finger sweep when executing full flexion-extension follows a path congruent with the **equiangular spiral**, a geometric expression of the summative series known as the **Fibonacci series**, the properties of which allow for the hand's 'limitless grasp adaptability' (Littler 1973). The same happens in the thumb movement of opposition. Dr. Littler shows in his classic article how this design allows the hand to grab an egg in such a way that even tightening the grip will not break it.

- This 'egg grip' demeanor of the hand is a good, gross reference for the normal attitude of the left hand on the fretboard when not tasked with extension/barré work.

- Within the intrinsic group, the lumbricals, rather than originating in a bone, as most muscles, originate in the tendon of the FDP at the MCP joint. As they insert as well in the extensor expansion, they are unique in being able to simultaneously slacken ('pull forward') the FDP as they 'pull back' on the ED expansion, producing IP joint extension as they mechanically flex the MCP joint (Watson, Biol. Mus. Perf. 2009, 57, Thomas, Long and Landsmeer 1968, 108).

- However, they cannot flex the MCP further once the IP joints reach maximal extension. Flexing the MCP joint while the IP's are kept extended is a combination of both lumbrical and interossei contraction. The lumbricals keep the IP extension while the interossei flex the MCP (Long 1968, 977).

- With the IP joints in the natural resting attitude (slightly flexed), flexion and extension of the MCP joint can be easily achieved by the extrinsic mechanism of flexion/extension (FDP and ED), without active intrinsic involvement:

  > We have observed clinically that it seems relatively effortless to perform metacarpophalangeal (MP) flexion or extension when the MP joint is neither fully extended nor flexed and the interphalangeal (IP) joints are allowed to remain in their rest position without either flexing or extending… In this particular motion, only the extrinsic muscles are active… (Thomas, Long and Landsmeer, 108).

  > In the same article the authors show that though inactive, the lumbricals' "unique mode of origin and insertion" are responsible for the 'stiffness' factor that keeps the IP joints mostly in their resting attitude during the unimpeded MCP flexion/extension movement.

- Although it is a single-belly muscle, FDP subdivides in two 'bundles', a smaller radial mass whose tendon inserts in the index DIP, and a bigger ulnar mass controlling the three ulnar fingers through tendons inserting in those fingers' DIP joints. This gives the index more autonomy in terms of independent flexion and extension than its companions (Wheeless 2008). In contrast, FDS, inserting in the middle phalanx, is a primary flexor of the PIP, and secondarily the MCP as well, but does not flex the DIP. In all-joint single-finger non-loaded flexion (described above), it is essentially inactive but contracts to support the FDP in resisted finger flexion (Gonzalez, et al. 2005). Apparently, its recruitment depends also on the speed of movement (Nikanjan, et al. 2007).

- According to Tubiana, in normal flexion activity, as in gripping, the joint flexion sequence begins at the PIP joint, followed by MCP and DIP joints, to complete the grip (Tubiana 2000, 40). This would indicate a protagonist role of FDS, followed by FDP. Other authors have reported that, in tests done on the intrinsic-minus hand, MCP and IP joints flex simultaneously (Srinivasan 1976), which probably points to a tandem engagement of both FDS and FDP, compensating for the absence of the intrinsic musculature.

- Understanding the interaction between the two long flexors, FDS and FDP, is an important factor in determining the behavior of the finger joints. The FDP, inserting in the distal phalanx, is a flexor of all three finger joints as well as being a wrist flexor but with decreasing degrees of strength (stronger at the distal IP joint, and weakest at the wrist). It is the main phalangeal flexor. However, its flexing effect over the MCP joint can be easily overcome by antagonistic ED contraction. This is the case, for instance, in a hook or briefcase grip, in which the MCP joint is extended while the two IP joints flex.

- It has also been shown that in index finger flexion the FDS tends to be as active as, or more, than FDP. The reasons for this seem to be related to the index' frequent work as thumb opposer in strong pinch (which requires FDS involvement to maintain the stability of the PIP), although anatomists are not in total agreement (Long 1968, 981).

- The FDS is really a group of four muscle bundles, two controlling middle and ring fingers, located superficial to a deeper pair controlling index and little fingers. This explains why it can act individually on each finger, but only if FDP is inactive (Wheeless, Wheeless Textbook of Orthopedics 2008).

- In about 20% of hands, FDS tendon to the little finger is absent, and it is relatively underdeveloped in most hands in comparison to the other three fingers (Shrewsbury and Kuczynski 1974). The FDS acts synergistically with FDP when needed for full-fisted grip strength or to flex the wrist, however, it has been shown that its absence from the little finger does not affect grip strength (Puhaindran, et al. 2008), which confirms the role of FDP as the main gripping muscle in the hand.

- Adduction is finger movement toward the imaginary mid-line of the hand, running through the middle finger, and abduction movement away from it. The middle finger only abducts, laterally or medially. These are functions of the hand intrinsics as well, primarily the palmar and dorsal interossei (finger adductors and abductors, respectively). The extrinsics act as secondary agents: the flexors in adduction, the extensors in abduction. Adduction and abduction are movements usually associated with flexion and extension.

- Both active abduction and adduction are possible with extension. However, finger flexion makes finger abduction gradually more difficult and in full flexion (as in the power grip) impossible. This is due to the increasing tautness in the MCP joint's strong collateral ligaments (Tubiana 2000, 28).

- The extensor mechanism is always active in powerful finger flexion as a stabilizer of the knuckle joint, which could dislocate in the action of forceful gripping, and to enhance the MCP collateral ligaments' stabilizing role against finger abduction. In this, the extensor apparatus is helped by the connections (**juncturae** and **fascia**) linking the tendonal structure in the dorsum of the hand.

- Coordination of muscular engagement in movements of the fingers is very variable and entirely task-oriented. Although it has been proven that the full anatomical range of movements in both flexion and extension can be controlled by just three muscles, one flexor, one extensor and the interossei (Landsmeer 1955, cited in, Thomas, Long and Landsmeer 1968), the system's redundancies (i.e. various muscles performing similar functions) allow for motor equivalencies in the execution of a task that provides for many possibilities for control:

The presumed value of exploiting such redundancies is that movement goals can be achieved nonstereotypically, and thus the control process may more easily accommodate changes in load, changes in muscle status (e.g., fatigue), or errors from any source that develop during the evolving movement (Cole and Abbs 1986, 1419).

- As the ultimate prehensile tool, the hand is primarily designed to allow for a variety of gripping actions, categorized by anatomists in two major types: precision or pinch grips, and power grips, with various sub-types: tip-to-side, tip-to-tip or pad-to-pad (for pinch grips); hook or briefcase grip or full-fisted grip (for power grip), etc.

- Obviously, in guitar playing one is not concerned with actual 'gripping' activity, but fingerwork is essentially founded on the same types of muscular engagements present in the various grips. This narrative incorporates references to gripping attitudes in the hand as they become relevant to the discussion.

- The following table summarizes the functional anatomy described above in a very simplified way, showing primary functions only. Most normal joint movements require multi-muscular involvements much more complex than those showed by the chart.

Muscular Activity	Resulting Joint Movement
'Pure' extensor (ED, EI, EM)	Active MCP extension and passive IP flexion (intrinsic-minus position; 'claw' hand). Refer to * below
'Pure' long flexors (primarily FDP)	(Non-resisted) Flexion of all finger joints.
'Pure' lumbricals	IP extension and mechanical MCP flexion (as in a pointing, uncurling movement.)
Combined lumbrical and interossei	Active MCP flexion with IPs extended
Combined action of extensors with intrinsics.	Full finger active extension/abduction.
Combined action of both long flexors with intrinsics (the interossei only, lumbricals are not involved)	Full finger resisted active flexion (power grip)
Combined action of intrinsics with FDS	Active flexion at MCP and at PIP, but no flexion at DIP
Combined action of ED and long flexors	Active MCP extension, active IP flexion (forceful hook grip)*.

*   Although these two positions resemble each other, they require very different muscular activity. In the former, the apparent clawing of the hand is a passive outcome of the extensor engagement, while in the second *both* the extensor and the long flexors engage simultaneously, producing a physiomechanical tug-of-war, so to speak, between the two opposing elements.

- As reference, the table below shows typical ROM (range of motion) for the finger joints. Different authors present different average standards for digital ROM, as there is a substantial amount of individual variability. Sources used for this and subsequent ROM tables are Eaton 2007 and Magee 2008. ROM is an important factor in determining whether limb attitude during playing is optimal or not for the task at hand. Following the conclusions of anatomists, kinesiologists and hand specialists, modern guitar pedagogy has established that mid-range of joint motion is the ideal norm for fingerwork. Mid-range is defined as the middle two-fourths of total ROM (Shearer, Learning the Classic Guitar 1990, 10).

Finger DIP joints	Extension/Flexion	0/80
Finger PIP joints	Extension/Flexion	0/100
Finger MCP joints	Hyperextension/Flexion	45/90
	Adduction*/Abduction	0/30

* Hyperadduction is also possible, as in the action of crossing fingers. In guitar playing, the old traditional recommendation to overlap the fingertips (*a* over *m*, *m* over *i*) as a way of properly placing the right-hand fingers on their strings is an example of hyperadduction of both *i* and *a* (while *m* abducts towards the index).

Thumb Movement

- The thumb lacks a middle phalanx. Its only IP joint is equivalent to the DIP in the fingers, but has more flexion/extension ROM than that of the fingers' DIP. The thumb's CMC joint, also called the basal joint, has mobility not possible to the fingers' CMC. This compensates for the more limited range of motion of its MCP joint, typically more limited than that of the fingers', although it is the most variable joint, in terms of range of motion, among individuals ("The MP joint may flex only a few degrees in some individuals and bend to 90 degrees in others" (Colditz 2002, 1859)). The IP range is in part determined by the range at the MCP: the bigger the range of the latter, the smaller it is at the IP, and vice versa. However, with the CMC joint fully extended/abducted, neither the IP nor the MCP can achieve their full range of flexion (Colditz 2002, id.).

- The following table shows normal ROM for thumb joints:

Thumb CMC (basal) joint	Palmar Adduction/Abduction	Contact/45
	Flexion/Extension (Radial Adduction/Abduction)	Contact/60
Thumb IP	Hyperextension/Flexion	15/80
Thumb MCP	Hyperextension/Flexion	10/55

- As described earlier, the thumb joints lie at a right angle, approximately, to the fingers, and so are their motions.

- This means that while flexion and extension of one of the fingers are movements toward or away from the palm, in the thumb they are movements toward (flexion) or away (extension) from the radial side of the index (when originating at the basal joint, they are also called radial adduction/abduction, rather than flexion/extension.)

- Likewise, abduction and adduction of the fingers (sideways movements of separation or approximation to the middle finger axis) become, for the thumb, movements away or towards the palm but at 90° to the palm's plane (palmar abduction/adduction.)

- Abduction and adduction can be visualized best by imagining the behavior of the thumb on the piano when depressing and releasing a key: palmar abduction, when pressing down, and palmar adduction, when releasing.

- The normal behavior of the thumb on the guitar relies primarily on flexion/extension, or radial adduction/abduction, with varying degrees of palmar adduction/abduction. An important factor in determining the degree of involvement of one or another movement type is the angle of the thumb relative to the plane parallel to the string, requiring less or more palmar abduction/adduction depending on the more or less angled alignment anterior to the string plane. This is discussed in detail in Chapter 2.

- The thumb's muscular mechanism is the most independent and versatile of the digits in the hand, thanks to the interaction of the extrinsic longer muscles lying in the forearm with the smaller intrinsics, located in the thenar eminence.

- Both muscular groups participate, to greater or lesser degrees, in movements involving all three thumb joints, allowing it a range and variety of motion not possible to other digits (for instance, the 'opposing thumb' movement, by which it can meet and touch the fingers' tips).

- The following chart summarizes the effect of some primary movers in thumb joint motion. As with the fingers, this is a gross simplification of the muscular coordination required for most thumb activities:

Muscular Activity	Resulting Joint Movement
Long flexor	IP flexion, secondary MCP flexion
Long extensor	IP extension, secondary MCP extension
Combined long and short flexors	Full-thumb flexion (as in full-fisted power grip. Also present in tip-to-side pinch grip. In the hook grip the thumb is not a major actor)
Combined long and short extensors	Full finger extension
Long and short abductors	Palmar abduction
Adductor and short flexor	Palmar adduction (as in a pad-to-pad pinching grip.)
Combined and sequential activity of flexors, extensors, abductors, adductors and oppose*.	Thumb opposition (as in tip-to-tip precision grip)

* The start of the opposition movement involves most of the thumb intrinsics plus the long extensor: "The abductor pollicis brevis, adductor pollicis, flexor pollicis brevis, extensor pollicis longus and extensor pollicis brevis all contribute to the extensor mechanism of the thumb. As these muscles begin to abduct and flex the CMC and MCP joints, tension is transmitted to the extensor pollicis longus via the extensor hood creating IP joint extension until additional effort is placed to flex the IP joint in the last phase of opposition." (Li and Tang 2007, 506) The mechanical extension at the IP, caused by the abduction/flexion of the proximal phalanges, is an important factor to keep in mind when studying thumb stroke on the guitar, as shall be discussed presently.

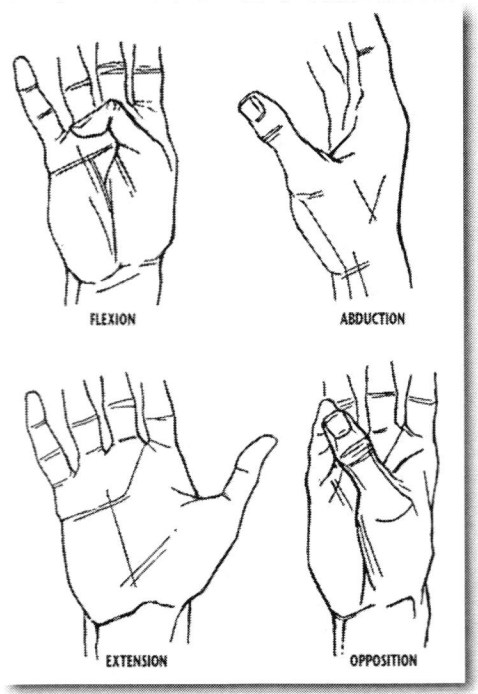

Figure 1-25. Basic thumb movements.
© 2008 Ronan O'Rahilly,
www.dartmouth.edu/~humananatomy/index.html/ .
Reproduced with permission of the authors.

Anatomical Constraints to Digital Movement

The anatomical design of the hand as well as other factors place natural constraints on finger and thumb mobility.

Lateral Extensor Attachments

The most important of these concerns the ED tendons and, hence, movements of extension in the fingers (except for the index and the little finger, possessing additional extensors of their own).

In order to reinforce the hand's support for its gripping capabilities (primary function of the hand), the ED tendons have lateral attachments linking the middle to the ring and the ring to the little finger (also present between ED tendons to the index and middle finger.)

These intertendinous connections (also called *juncturae tendinae*) limit the extension ROM (range of motion) in all fingers when a finger tries to extend against flexion in their neighbors, but mostly the ring finger, as it is the one most firmly attached on both sides. Index and little fingers are quite free, and, to a somewhat lesser extent, the middle or long finger, which, in some individuals, may even have a separate extensor tendon of its own (as index and little normally have).

Particularly when the little finger is flexed, the ring's capability to extend is greatly compromised. Freeing up the little finger and allowing it to move sympathetically with the ring solves this difficulty.

However, extension at the MCP joint and extension of the IP joints are, functionally, different: the former is the primary responsibility of the ED tendons, while the latter are extended through lumbrical engagement. Hence, the ring-finger IP joints can extend fully if the ED remains unengaged, that is, without extension at the MCP joint, even if the middle and little fingers are held in flexion. In this case, the MCP joint, rather than extend, will flex slightly, as is typical of the aforementioned 'lumbrical effect' (O'Rahilly, et al. 2008).

Finger Flexion Constraints

Flexion in all fingers is freer of impediments, as normally flexor tendons do not have juncturae. However, the individual bellies of the two long flexors and the common extensor partially fuse, so a contraction in one will have some impact on the others. The degree of interconnectivity varies substantially among individuals (Watson, What Studying Musicians 2006).

As discussed earlier, 'curling', by the pronounced engagement of the deep flexor, will cause problems with finger mobility, as it produces a simultaneous flexing of the adjacent fingers, in particular, between *m* and *a*. When planting both middle and ring fingers, for instance, forcefully flexing either one in such a way as to engage FDP (flexion at the DIP) will produce this reflex flexion in its companion, which would interfere with finger independence.

Equally constraining is the excessive engagement of the palmar intrinsics (primarily, lumbricals) in certain circumstances where a rapid return to the string is required of the fingers, for instance, in the typical six-note arpeggio *p-i-m-a-m-i*: the ring and/or middle finger tends to 'push-in' on the string (the lumbrical engagement that produces simultaneous MCP flexion and IP extension) before the stroke in such a way that it makes the stroke too 'deep' (too much into the palm), thus requiring an extra amount of energy in the recovery extension of the digit, which, as a consequence, feels heavy and unresponsive in speedy playing.

In more general terms, finger intrinsics, particularly lumbricals and dorsal interossei, are frequently closely interconnected with other anatomical elements of the fingers (bones and tendons), with possible constraining effects on finger independence and mobility. Again, individual variability is substantial (Beauchamp, Anatomical Variations).

An example of this may be seen in forceful MCP flexion with extended IP joints in a finger, which may cause one or both neighboring fingers, if inactive, to extend their IP joints and flex the MCP joint as well.

In guitar playing, this phenomenon is most evident when executing the full barré, and will be discussed in Chapter 3.

With some frequency the little finger either lacks a tendon from FDS, or has a weak slip, which means that finger flexion is the responsibility of the deep flexor and its own intrinsic short flexor. In these circumstances, little finger phalangeal flexion will produce also flexion of the ring finger's DIP joint. This fact is important primarily for five-finger players, but may affect four-finger players as well in certain activities when the little finger may flex sympathetically in response to ring-finger action.

Linburg-Comstock Syndrome
In some hands a linkage between the long thumb flexor tendon, responsible for tip-joint flexion, and the deep flexor tendon to the index, responsible for DIP flexion, exists through a lateral slip, a *junctura*, connecting the two tendons (Watson, Biol. Mus. Perf. 2009, 62). This condition, known as *Linburg-Comstock syndrome*, produces an involuntary flexion of the index IP joints every time the thumb's IP joint flexes in a pronounced way (the reverse does not happen). The reader can test herself by supinating the hand, with fingers and thumb extended, and flexing the tip joint of the thumb fully into the palm.

In a small number of cases the condition becomes pathological and is so extreme that dysfunction or even pain may exist, although usually the condition is not severe. Nonetheless, the articulation of the thumb stroke from the tip-joint may lead to subtle forms of mishaps in the course of playing if the player is unaware of the presence of this condition in her or his hand.

Joint Hypermobility ('double-jointedness'")
Many musicians have what is erroneously labeled as "double-jointedness", the capability of a joint to hyperextend. The causes for this condition can be very varied: laxness in the joint capsule ligaments, cartilage that does not cover the joint surface sufficiently, bones with excessively well-rounded articular ends, or a combination of these. These conditions are frequently associated with **Ehrlers-Danlos syndrome**, a condition that modern researchers have speculated might have affected Paganini, or **Marfan's disease**, which affected Rachmaninoff. Some of the extreme demands imposed by certain repertoires can be explained, at least partially, by studying the health conditions of particular composers, as is the case with these two. In both conditions, extreme joint hypermobility is present, and the typical physiognomy of Marfan's is that of Rachmaninoff, tall, long-limbed, arachnodactylic (elongated and easily spreadable digits and toes) (Andrews 2005).

In the guitarist's right hand, hypermobility is most frequently found in the CMC joint of the thumb. Like Paganini or Rachmaninoff, many musicians have exploited the peculiarities of hyper-mobility to great advantage, but it is not good pedagogy to encourage students who show it to rely on it, since there are serious risks of future joint problems, like arthritis. Since in these cases the normal structural limits to movement are missing, the only remedy is muscular training that counteracts the tendency towards hyper-mobility in the joint. In guitar playing, the most common forms of hyper-extension occur at the MCP joint of the thumb, the first IP joint in the ring and little fingers and the tip joints in all digits.

Students can be taught to use the method of **opposition**, discussed later (section 4), by exerting effort on the loose joint with their free hand and making the musculature of the affected hand work against it isometrically. Of course, the student must realize that the effort must be exerted *in favor* of the double-jointedness so that the opposing muscles can learn how to work against it.

Although strengthening exercises of the flexion/extension mechanism of the fingers are of dubious merit for performing artists (Taubman 1988, 147), careful manipulation of solid-core rubber balls, of different degrees of elasticity, small enough to fit in the half-fisted hand but big enough not to allow total closing of the hand, may help improve the condition. When some progress has been achieved (but not at the beginning of treatment) manipulation of Chinese "energy" metal balls may also be beneficial. Attention must be paid to whether the affected hand is free from other ailments, like tendonitis or carpal tunnel syndrome, which may be exacerbated by these exercises. Keen observation of proper alignment, avoidance of excessive finger extensor activity or overall levels of tension in the limb, are required of the teacher treating a "double-jointed" hand.

Stiffness

When the range of motion in a joint is limited beyond conventional standards, we speak of a "stiff joint". Of course, at the initiation of training all hands are incapable of achieving the degree of motility that training will later impart, but we are dealing here with those situations when training does not produce the developmental evolution that one would normally expect. The causes of abnormal stiffness are the opposite of those causing double-jointedness: bone endings that are flat or have irregularities that act as obstacles to smooth contact among articular surfaces, bones that are too thick (therefore limiting the space for the muscular or tendinous tissues to move around), tight joint capsules, thickness of tissues, etc.

If the stiffness is bone-related, there is not much anyone can do, except, in some cases, work with alternative attitudes, in terms of joint angles, so that muscular work may become more effective.

An extreme and rare form of this type of joint stiffness is the condition known as **symphalangism**, in which the finger joints either fuse (**anarthrosis**) or show great limitations to their flexion range, even if structurally normal. This infrequent condition tends to affect the distal IP more than the proximal, and there seems to be correlation with the absence of visible IP joint creases, on the palmar and dorsal sides (Fried and Mundel 1976).

Joint stiffness demands the utmost of the teacher's powers of observation and versatility of methods. If soft-tissue is suspected as the main reason, regularly applied massage and stretching may, over time, improve the condition. Lacking x-rays as diagnostic tool, passive stretches and flexions of the joint done carefully can indicate if the stiffness is soft- or hard-tissue related. In the latter case, there will be very little or no "give" in the joint. Extreme care must be taken not to overdo these manipulative techniques. The assistance of an expert in physiotherapy or massage therapy is always preferable to well-intentioned but improvised approaches.

Individual idiosyncrasies in the design of the hand play a vital role in determining a player's potentialities from the physical standpoint. These variations are, in fact, so common that it is difficult to determine what would constitute the anatomical 'norm' for the hand.

Personal differences in factors such as finger length, joint flexibility and stability, alignment of MCP joints, interdigital folds (webs), etc, play a determining role in establishing a player's physiomechanical profile.

The teacher must learn to work within the physical characteristics of each student, not with an abstract standard that is applied to all. As Otto Ortman pointed out many years ago (Ortmann 1929), what we identify as a performer's "style" has to do with these individual characteristics of the player's body that, coupled with other intangible cognitive and emotional factors, constitute the sum-all of what we perceive as the individual's "talent".

Anatomical constraints to finger movement in piano playing have been studied thoroughly from a biomechanical perspective (J. N. Leinjse, et al. 1992, J. N. Leinjse, et al. 1993). The conclusion in a major study is worth remembering for anyone involved in the teaching of instrumental performance:

> ...Anatomical variations in the hand are systemic parameters, more or less invariant to exercise. ...Each hand has unique functional characteristics, determined by its unique anatomical built (sic). This perception cautions against too strict a concept of the 'ideal' instrumental technique. ...Many attempts have been made to formulate such a codex (of the 'ideal' key stroke, the 'ideal' hand position, etc.). Within the view of the hand as a constrained and invariant system, the purpose of exercise can only be the selection and assimilation of the most functional movements compatible with the (anatomic) constraints, and paedagogic (sic) models should be flexible enough to be of guidance at the level of the individuals' possibilities (J. N. Leinjse, et al. 1993, 1179).

Section 3. Motor Function, Proprioception and Muscle Metabolism

When humans act, motor activity frequently originates with a willful decision implemented through an unconscious process that takes care of the specific details of achieving it. We are not, nor should we be, aware of the specific muscles, joints and nervous connections involved in the action. We are concerned with *what* to do but not with *how* to do it.

This hierarchy of function is possible thanks to the integrated structure of the **afferent** (sensory) and **efferent** (motor) branches of the nervous system, described earlier, whose feedback mechanisms allow not only for infinite gradations of response to sensory stimulation, but for an enormous capacity for learning new ways of doing things and improving the old ways through training based on correct practice. In this way, the neuromuscular system becomes an extremely versatile tool of our will, capable of self-selecting its own methods to achieve our motor goals.

All our motor functions are classifiable according to the level of control operating in the nervous system: spinal cord level, lower brain level, and higher brain (or cortical) level. Motor activities known as "reflexes" do not involve higher brain function, but are controlled locally by the sensory-motor nerves coming out and into the spinal cord at a given point. An example of this is the 'knee-jerk' reflex. Other unconscious motor activities are controlled by lower brain structures, like the cerebellum or the basal ganglia. Vital functions like heart beat, breathing, blood circulation, etc., belong to this category, as well as certain neuromuscular functions related to balance and equilibrium. Cortical or higher brain activity controls those motor functions that depend on cognitive or intellectual processes. The cortex receives a vast array of sensory information that is then processed and distributed to other areas of the brain and the brain stem. Memories are stored and compared with current circumstances, providing a foundation for decision-making related to motor activity.

Motor skill learning relies on the interaction between these three levels. Some innate reflexes serve as foundation for more complex, willfully controlled movement. For instance, the reflex mechanism known as **reciprocal**

innervation automatically controls the relationship between agonists and antagonists that act on the same joint: when the former are stimulated, the reflex inhibits action of the opposing muscles to facilitate the movement. The **stretch reflex** causes an involuntary contraction in any muscle that is suddenly stretched. This mechanism is at the basis of the body's capability to maintain upright posture. The phenomenon of the **conditioned reflex** makes possible the assimilation of learned actions, through cortical processing, to the extent that, in time, they can be controlled through lower brain function and, therefore, automatized. The cerebellum seems to be a fundamental structure in the control of these acquired reflexes. Although the physiology of movement is too complex to be treated in any detail in a text as basic as this is, the following is an elementary summary description of its fundamentals.

Muscular Innervation

The means of communication of the nervous system is the **neuron** or nerve cell, through which nervous impulses are transmitted and received. A neuron has a **cell body**, a stem-like structure called the **axon**, through which impulses are transmitted away from the cell body, and other fibers through which impulses are received by the cell body, called **dendrites**. Depending on their functional role, neurons are classified as: **sensory** or **afferent**, if they receive information in the form of sensations that is communicated to the spinal cord and the brain; **motor** or **efferent**, when they carry impulses from the brain and spinal cord to the muscular fibers, producing contraction or relaxation; and **internuncial**, contained within the brain and spinal cord, that act as connectors that integrate the functions of the sensory and the motor neurons.

Neurons communicate with each other only at the **synapse**, where the axon of one cell is in close proximity to the dendrites of another. They create a tree-like network of connections which provide multiple paths for impulse transmittal. Synaptic connections are of two types: **excitation** or **inhibition**, depending on whether they favor or stop the transference of impulses from a neuron to another.

The point at which a motor nerve cell fiber meets a muscular fiber is called the **end plate**, a specialized end structure of motor neurons. Although the majority of skeletal muscles have thousands of fibers, it does not mean that each one of them is stimulated by a separate nerve cell but, rather, the axon of a motor neuron divides into many branches (**collaterals**) that connect individually to a number of muscle fibers, all of which simultaneously respond to the impulse sent from the spinal cord and transmitted through the motor neuron.

The neuron and the muscle fibers that it innervates through its axon's collaterals form what is known as a **motor unit** (refer to Figure 1-4). Both neurons and muscle fibers respond to stimulus according to the so-called **all-or-nothing** principle, i.e., a neuron unavoidably will transmit an impulse, and a muscle fiber will contract maximally, if the stimulus received is above a threshold level. The contraction of a muscle will therefore depend on the number of motor units it needs in order to achieve its task. Lifting a light weight will need a smaller number of motor units than lifting a heavier one. By the same token, a well-conditioned muscle will use less motor units than a weaker one. Generally speaking, the fewer the number of muscle fibers per motor unit, the more apt the muscle is for precision movement.

For instance, some muscles in the eye, whose movements are the most rapidly changing in the body, may have as little as 5 to 15 fibers per motor unit. Motor units, in turn, are classified as **alpha** or **gamma** motor units, depending on the type of muscular fibers its neuron stimulates. Alpha and gamma units differ in the rate and intensity of their impulse firing.

Types of Muscular Fiber

A muscle fiber stimulated by a nerve impulse above a threshold level will contract, after a brief period of no response (called the **latent period**), and will then relax. This response to a single nervous stimulus is called a **twitch**. Single-twitch responses are unusual in the normal living body, since nervous stimulation occurs usually through volleys of repeated impulses. When nervous impulses reach the muscular fiber before the previous contraction is relaxed, **summation** occurs and the fiber will tense up even further. This process, if continued for some time, will keep the level of tension in the muscle at a higher level than any one twitch would produce, until fatigue occurs.

Within the muscle there are different types of fibers, some of which are innervated by alpha motor units, and others by gamma units. Depending on the duration and intensity of their twitch response, alpha neurons and the fibers they stimulate may be classified as **fast-twitch** (or **pale**) or **slow-twitch** (or **red**). The colors associated with these types of fibers have to do with the metabolic processes taking place during contraction, as discussed later.

The distribution of fast—and slow-twitch fibers in the musculature is very variable. Some muscles have approximately equal numbers of fast and slow-twitch fibers (like the deltoid and the biceps) while others are predominantly slow or fast (the triceps, for instance, may have as much as 80% more fast-twitch fibers than the other arm muscles). Fast-twitch muscle fibers are stimulated by the larger axons of the alpha fast-twitch neurons and respond with a rapid rate of contractions (**phasic** contractions), but fatigue more easily than slow-twitch fibers, stimulated by smaller neurons, that respond with more prolonged contractions (**tonic** contractions). Therefore, muscles whose main function is the sustenance of prolonged effort will have a higher number of the latter, while muscles whose function is achieving quick movements of short duration will be primarily fast-twitch.

These relationships, however, may be altered through training, since muscle fiber is one of the most adaptable tissues in the human organism. Also, the greater incidence of one type of muscular fiber over another may vary from individual to individual thanks to hereditary or even ethnic factors. This might explain individual predispositions towards or against certain types of physical activities.

Muscle Spindle

Gamma motor units have smaller and slower neurons than alpha units. They act on small groupings of fibers that are different from the fibers described above, being smaller and therefore weaker. A grouping of such fibers is known as a **muscle spindle**. Muscle spindles lie parallel and in between the other muscle fibers, surrounded by a **capsule** which is a sheath of connective tissue. Fibers within the sheath or capsule are called **intrafusal**, those outside (the ones described previously) are called **extrafusal**. Intrafusal fibers in the muscle spindles are not numerous nor strong enough to produce movement, even if all of a muscle's intrafusal fibers contract at once.

Their role is to serve as monitors of changes in the degree of stretch in the muscle, both receiving and transmitting information from and to the central nervous system and serving thus as coordinators of muscular activity in any movement. Muscle spindles are, therefore, part of the refined sensory-motor servomechanism that controls the intricacies of human motility.

The Body's 'Sixth Sense': Proprioception and Kinesthesia

A motor activity is the response to a change in the environment (internal or external) which is sensed by specialized nerve fibers whose endings, known as **receptors**, are designed to respond to specific kinds of stimuli. These receptors are the starting point of the nerve impulses that will eventually reach the motor units that contract the musculature. Sight, sound, smell, taste and touch are the result of the impulses received by the cerebral cortex from sensory receptors (**exteroceptors**) placed in the tissues of the eye, ear, nose, mouth and skin that perceive changes in the outer world. These sensors are specialized: eye sensors sense changes in light; ear sensors, changes in sound, etc.

Other sensors receive information from the internal environment within the body. Those that respond to changes in the viscera are known as **interoceptors**. A third type of receptors, of which the muscle spindle is an example, have as their primary role the monitoring of changes in the structures of the musculoskeletal system. They are present within the muscle mass, in tendinous attachments to muscle, in the joints and in the skin. These sensors, known as **proprioceptors**, are discussed below.

Muscle spindles, described above, after receiving information about the level of stretch or contraction in a muscle, may influence the activity of the same and other muscles near or far by transmitting an impulse to the spinal cord that may be distributed to a greater or lesser extent through the cord's vast network of synaptic pathways. They are, together with the Golgi tendon organs (see below), responsible for triggering the mechanism of the stretch reflex response.

Golgi tendon organs (GTO) are located in tendons close to the point where they originate in the muscle, as well as in the muscle's connective tissue. GTO's act as protectors of the integrity of the muscle by inhibiting motor neuron activity, thus relaxing the muscle that, when contracting excessively, forces the level of stretch in its tendon to the point where the GTO can sense it. Because GTO's are located close to body joints, they also serve as providers of information about body positions to the central nervous system.

Other important proprioceptors are the **Pacinian corpuscles** and the **Ruffini endings** spread widely in the fascia or sheath that surrounds the muscles, at the point where a tendon inserts at the joint, as well as in the deeper layers of the skin. They respond to pressure stimuli due to joint position and muscular contraction and stretch. It is primarily through the combined sensations read by these receptors that we become aware of limb movements and positions.

Other receptors located in the skin, known as **cutaneous** or **skin receptors**, respond both as extero and proprioceptors, while still other receptors, located in the inner ear and the neck, control the orientation of head and balance movements as well as the maintenance of normal posture and alignment of the body.

The information received by the central nervous system from these proprioceptors is the basis for the so-called **kinesthetic sense** (also called "motor sense" or "muscular sense"): awareness of our body and its activities in the space surrounding us. Both volitionally controlled and reflex actions are based on the proper functioning of these sensors as kinesthetic control mechanisms. The fine motor skills needed in instrumental performance depend on a highly developed kinesthetic sense for their successful application.

Muscle Metabolism

As far as muscle activity is concerned, the air we breathe and the nourishment we ingest have the goal of producing the two basic ingredients of muscle metabolism: oxygen and glucose. Glucose, a form of sugar and the raw material for the cells, is transformed into the necessary chemicals utilized in the metabolic cycle which culminates, through a combustion-like process of oxygenation, in the production of **ATP** (adenosine triphosphate), the true fuel of muscular contraction. The amounts of ATP needed by a muscle are directly related to the intensity of the work it delivers when contracting. The more ATP is needed, the more nutrients (oxygen and glucose) have to be consumed by the cells.

This need explains the changes in breathing rhythm and pulse rate when we engage in vigorous physical exercise: as the need for oxygen and other nutrients increases, both the intake of air and the flow of blood have to increase. However, the muscle's contraction itself produces a constriction in the tissues and capillaries through which blood circulates, thus making more difficult the delivery of the necessary nutrients to the cell. This is why sustained muscular contractions are more demanding and tiring than contractions that allow for phases of release between motions.

This provides the physiological foundation for one of the most important skills in technical instrumental training: *the ability to relax the muscular contractions in between exertions.*

ATP may also be produced through an anaerobic process (i.e., it does not use oxygen). This process, known as **anaerobic glycolysis**, is more "expensive" than the former, in terms of glucose consumption, and produces more metabolic wastes, like lactic acid, whose toxicity cause irritation and discomfort in the muscle tissue. Red or slow-twitch fibers depend on high rates of oxygen delivery, because their function is sustenance of tonic activity. Therefore, they are profusely supplied by blood capillaries.

Pale or fast-twitch fibers, on the contrary, are less dependent on oxygen and more on glucose to feed their anaerobic metabolic process, for they are responsible for high-energy phasic activity. Hence, the diminished presence of blood vessels.

Generally speaking, the red fibers are capable of less energetic but more prolonged effort than the pale fibers, which can exert more energy but fatigue more easily. It should be remembered, though, that most muscles possess both types of fibers, to a greater or lesser extent, since both endurance and vigor are part of many motor activities.

Leverage

In the study of human movement, a basic understanding of leverage is fundamental to analyze, correct and improve a particular move or pattern of moves. A lever is any rigid body that is moved around a fixed pivot or axis through the application of force. It is a tool through which energy is transmitted and allows one to do work.

There are three elements in any lever: a point of support (the axis or fulcrum), a point where force or effort is applied (effort) and a point where resistance is applied (be it the weight of the lever itself or another external resistance). Apart from the point of application, other important elements of the force are its intensity and its direction of motion. How they relate to the position, the intensity and the direction of motion of the resistance defines the effectiveness of the lever system for the work to be accomplished.

In the musculoskeletal structure of the body, the bone is the lever (resistance), the joint is the axis or fulcrum, and the point of insertion of the muscle is where the force or effort is applied. The intensity of this effort is controlled by the muscle contraction, and the position of the muscle defines its direction or line of motion.

Types of Levers

There are three types or classes of levers, classified according to how the axis, the resistance and the force or effort are positioned. In short, the type of lever can be identified by which of the three components lies between the other two:

Type 1: The Axis or fulcrum is in between the Effort and the Resistance (**E-A-R**).

E ————————————— R   **First-class lever**
—————————————
      A

Example: the see-saw, scissors, elbow extension.

Type 2: The Resistance is in between the Effort and the Axis (**E-R-A**).

E ——————— R   **Second-class lever**
—————————————
          A

Example: the wheel-barrow, nutcracker, tip-toeing, push-up.

Type 3: The Effort is in between the Axis and the Resistance (**A-E-R**).

      E ——————— R   **Third-class lever**
—————————————
A

Example: draw-bridge, golf club, shovel, elbow flexion.

Mechanical Advantage

The distance between the resistance and the axis is called the **resistance arm** of the lever, while the distance between axis and point of application of force is called the **effort arm** or **force arm**. The concept of **mechanical advantage** is used to evaluate leverage, and is expressed as the ratio of the lengths of the effort and resistance arms:

Mechanical Advantage (MA) = Effort Arm (EA)/Resistance Arm (RA)

In a type-1 lever the mechanical advantage changes according to whether the fulcrum lies closer to the effort or to the resistance. When both are equidistant to the axis, there is balance (no movement) if both effort and resistance are equal in value.

In second-class levers the effort arm is always longer than the resistance arm, while the opposite is true of third-class levers. This means that the type-2 lever has a mechanical advantage over a type 3: given the same resistance to overcome, the former will need less effort than the latter.

While a type-3 lever is less efficient in lifting loads, it has an advantage in terms of range and speed of motion: given the same resistance, and an effort intense enough to overcome it, a third-class lever will move it farther and quicker. The most common leverage type in the musculoskeletal system is type 3. Our bodies are designed primarily for swift action and range of movement, and not for power.

Point of Application of Force

In third-class levers the position of the applied effort is fundamental in increasing or decreasing the mechanical advantage. In terms of muscular work, this means that the point of insertion of a muscle conditions, to a great extent, its effectiveness to act on the joint. All other things being equal, an insertion closer to the axis (the joint) than the resistance (an object being lifted, or the center of gravity of the limb) will be less powerful than an insertion closer to the resistance.

Direction of Force (Angle of Pull)

As mentioned before, another factor in determining the power of a lever system is the line or direction of force. The more perpendicular the direction of the application of force is to the lever arm, the more power there is. The power diminishes as the angle diminishes. In terms of muscle work, this means that a muscle will be at its most efficient in terms of power when the angle of pull formed between its origin and its insertion is closest to being perpendicular to the resistance arm.

The opposite holds in regards to speed. The speed increases as the angle of pull diminishes. A muscle will move a limb segment quicker when its direction of pull is closer to being parallel to the resistance arm (of course, if it were parallel, there would be no movement whatsoever, as there would be no power acting on the resistance).

The combination of these factors (type of lever, intensity and point of application of effort, and direction or line of effort) permits for any gradation of force- or speed-effects. A lever system favoring speed rather than power will improve its mechanical advantage if effort is increased, or if its point of application, angle of pull or both is made more favorable. An effort applied at an unfavorable point in the lever may overcome this by acting in a proper direction. A weak effort may be strengthened by being applied at a more favorable point. A thorough understanding of leverage is an important element in developing best practices in the application of technical procedures in guitar playing.

Section 4. General Pedagogical Considerations

Tension and the Experience of Mastery

The student's path to mastery in the art of playing is, more often than not, filled with conflict, doubt and ambiguity. This conflict is exteriorized through misapplied tension. This tension, if left unsolved, creates a self-perpetuating vicious circle in which inner tensions give rise to outer tensions that, in turn, increase the level of internal turmoil, and so on *per aeternum*. The applied music teacher's first responsibility is the elimination of this vicious cycle and its substitution with a *virtuous* one, in which the student's progress builds on experiences of mastery, rather than on failed struggle to achieve unrealizable goals.

Mastery, then, becomes the measuring-rod of progress. Properly defining mastery, though, is the crux of the matter, for the conventional usage of the concept, as the ultimate level of accomplishment, won't do. Mastery is the achievement of levels of performance in which the task and the skills needed to accomplish it are perfectly matched, thus securing execution that provides effective control with an overall feeling of ease.

The teacher's methods must help advance the sensory-motor learning process with minimal risk in tension build-up caused by the student's confusion and/or frustration. Individualized procedures, which apply only to a specific student, are more the norm than the exception. However, there are certain principles of work that can be used as a general foundation from which to devise more particularized procedures of instruction. The learning of motor skills depends on the integration of sensory input received, primarily, through sight, sound and touch. Therefore, the best teaching tools will combine the three approaches that address those sensory needs: **demonstration**, **explanation** and **manipulation**.

In the initial stages of learning, demonstration, followed by manipulation, are more important than explanation. Explanation becomes an important tool for more advanced levels of development. The stimulation of the student's proprioception is one of the most important challenges in instrumental teaching. The most direct way to start this process is through discrete manipulation of limb activity. Demonstration is a secondary complement in this regard and will work more or less well depending on the student's eidetic imagination and mimetic powers (i.e., how developed his/her capability to convert visual and aural information into kinesthetic sensation). In manipulation, **opposition** to the movement being taught is much more effective than passively moving the student's limb. Through opposition, the neuromuscular system learns the sensations related to the muscular effort needed to accomplish the move, while the sensors are not properly stimulated if the teacher does the movement for the student.

An exception to the method of opposition is when teaching passive movements, in which Gravity and not muscular effort is the prime mover. In these cases, a very light touch or pressure in the direction of movement may be sufficient for the student to allow the limb or limb segment to relax enough for gravity to have its effect.

Alternatively, the teacher may ask the student to rest the limb or limb segment on her hand (for instance, if there is tension at the shoulder, placing the hand under the student's elbow and asking the student to release the weight of the arm on the teacher's hand).

In demonstration, showing not only the proper way of moving, but also the incorrect ways is a valuable approach. Contrast of references is a powerful learning tool. This is important also for the student: once a move has been corrected, s/he will greatly benefit from doing it in both the corrected and the incorrect forms, to solidify proprioceptive references. Repetitive practice, though, should obviously involve only the correct form.

Performance anxiety and **stage fright** may affect students of performance not only while on stage but in the lesson studio. In explanation, the language used by the instructor should avoid wording that implies obligation, prohibition ("should's" and "don'ts"), or judgmental statements of value about the student. Every statement should be open to discussion, and every instruction must be verified in application. In explanation, details pertaining to the anatomo-physiomechanics of motor activity better be reserved until the student has reached very advanced levels of development. These details, if provided prematurely, may be a hindrance for the unimpeded acquisition of motor skills by involving the intellect too much in the details of how the motor system achieves its functions. Words are not the best tool for motor learning. Sensations are.

The clear differentiation between **static** and **dynamic work** is one of the first goals of motor training. The student should be guided to recognize the difference in sensations between the effort of holding position and the effort of moving from position to position, and how the former may be happening, in some parts of the body, while other parts are moving.

A complementary aspect of this issue is the identification of **active** and **passive states** or **attitudes**, which may be either static or dynamic. An active state is achieved through muscular effort. A passive attitude happens when the limb or limb segment moves or keeps still by the action of an external force, most commonly Gravity. This is equivalent to saying that the student must learn to distinguish between sensations of **effort** and sensations of **weight**.

The four basic principles of efficient muscular work, as defined by Shearer (Shearer, Learning the Classic Guitar 1990, 10), are important guidelines to keep in mind:
1. **Natural alignment**. Muscles work best when their lines of pull follow their natural alignment from origin to insertion.

2. **Mid-range of joint motion**. Muscles work best when the joint they move does so within the mid-range of its motion capability (mid-range is defined as the middle two-fourths of the total range of motion).

3. **Uniform direction of (finger) joint movement**. Finger muscles work best when all joints of a finger or of the thumb flex or extend together.

4. **Follow-through**. Muscles work best when there is enough follow-through in the movement they produce to avoid a build-up of opposing tension.

No movement is intrinsically wrong. Only its effectiveness and its *feel* determine its value.

Sitting Down to Play the Guitar

The traditional sitting position adopted by classical guitarists, with a footstool used as a raised platform for the left leg, requires certain adjustments in the spine and/or hips to counteract the force (backwards and to the right side) that the raised leg imparts to the sitting body. Either the spine flexes and rotates to the left, or the right thigh is abducted so that the splayed leg will bring the right foot to an angle of support that counteracts the push of the raised leg. In either case, the continued static flexion of the left hip, and the counteracting muscular effort in the back and/or the right limb, causes strain to the surrounding musculature. It is, therefore, not surprising that many guitarists that use this sitting position end up with lower back pain problems, sometimes of a paralyzing intensity.

A number of support mechanisms, to be placed over the left thigh or across the lap, have been created to eliminate the use of the footstool, thus allowing for a sitting position in which both feet are in contact with the ground and the spine and hips can maintain a more organic attitude. However, many of the lap-supports available in the market have not yet achieved a level of satisfactory ergonomic quality. The generic **cushion supports** are usually lower than most guitarists would need, to the point that many guitarists that use the cushion end up using a footstool *as well*, a rather puzzling compromise.

Other types of support have the advantage of being adjustable, but ignore the ergonomic requirement for a naturally relaxed and forward-curving spine (see below), forcing the body into a rather stiff sitting stance that creates problems for some players. Other players are beginning to use **body straps** that allow, perhaps, for a more ideal combination of stability and naturalness in body attitude. These, however, run the risk of producing discomfort in the neck, shoulder and/or upper back if not adjusted properly.

Perhaps it is time to reconsider the merits of Dionisio Aguado's **tripod** or **tripodison**, an adjustable legged artifact that supported the guitar without any need for body effort (Aguado, Method 1981 , 6-7, 13-15). Be it as it may, the footstool is still the norm for many guitarists and, as such, we must deal with the problems its use presents.

Static Effort and Dynamic Work When Using the Footstool

Despite the problems of alignment presented by the footstool, it should be understood that it is the prolonged static (i.e., non-moving) effort of maintaining this sitting position while playing that results, over time, in physical injury or discomfort. Movement is a releaser of tension and should be incorporated frequently even within the frame of our basic sitting position. We can change the instrument to the right leg when we tune, we should take breaks when we practice during which we stand and stretch or walk a bit, we will release this static tension during our public performances when we acknowledge audience applause, and we can incorporate, over time, a nice fluidity of body motions which will involve head, torso and even leg movements, as a direct uncontrived expression of the inner rhythms which the assimilation of the music we play will develop within us. Hip flexion/extension and other stretching exercises done regularly as part of one's daily routine will also be of great help.

Good, erect back posture, without rigidity, but avoiding slouching or hunching, is, of course, indispensable.

Anthropometrics and Guitar Playing

The height and positioning of footstool and chair are matters that have to do with the more general topic of **anthropometrics**. **Anthropometrics** or **anthropometry** is the study of the measurements of the human body. It is one of the branches of the science of **biomechanics**, which is the combination of biology and mechanics in the study of human action. It is also a fundamental factor in **ergonomics**, the science that studies the fit between worker and work environment and tools. There are several anthropometry issues that affect the guitarist.

The proper height of the chair can be determined, with the player standing by the chair, by measuring the distance between the edge of the seat and the hollow of the knee joint. The latter should be at a distance somewhere in between two and five finger-widths above the edge of the sitting surface. The footstool height depends on the length of the player's torso. It should bring the guitar (its upper bass-side arch) to about the mid-point of the sternum. In cases when the chair is higher or lower than ideal, the footstool height has to accommodate this difference, but the right foot will probably end up tip-toeing, if the chair is too high, or, if too low, the right leg will have to open up excessively.

Scale-size

In the last 20 years, more attention has been paid to the issue of matching the player's measurements with the scale length of the instrument. Dr. Richard Norris, former medical director of the National Arts Medicine Center in Bethesda, Maryland, USA, recommends that the instrument's size should be such that the angle of separation of the upper arm from the body, when the left hand is in first position, should not exceed 20° (qtd. in Kopfstein-Penk 1994, 5-7, 11-14). Other anthropometric relationships indicate that the span between the first and fourth finger of the left hand (i.e., index and little-finger) should be able to encompass the distance from the first to the sixth fret on the sixth string, without strain or discomfort (Kopfstein-Penk, ibid.).

This is a fundamental issue that must be carefully monitored by teachers and parents of young players. It is of importance also to more advanced players who might discover that many of their technical and musical problems are caused by playing too big an instrument. On the other hand, some players who possess longer-than-normal arms are constrained by playing instruments that, even at scales of 660 mm. or longer, are small for them.

The problem is reflected principally in the right hand: these players are forced either to support the right arm at a point much closer to the wrist than it would be desirable or to bend the wrist in an exaggerated angle of flexion and/or ulnar abduction, detrimental to agile fingerwork.

A detachable armrest, designed to fit an individual player's arm length, would allow the player to find a point of support more appropriate to his/her anthropometric dimensions, thus ameliorating a problem that is more common than we might think. A good model of this type of arm rest is the Janssen Support, patented by a former student of the author, distributed (as well as other support paraphernalia) through guitarest.com.

Associated to this might be an idea proposed by Norris: a beveled bout (Kopstein-Penk, ibid). The idea of the beveled bout is recommended by Norris to avoid the impingement on the forearm musculature caused by the bite of the edge of the guitar (or the armrest) into the player's arm. This will also make possible a full range of arm displacements associated with color nuances that would be limited if the armrest ended at an edge.

Nails

Although important historically, since the majority of vihuelists, lutenists and guitarists up to the mid-XIX century played this way, no-nail approaches to the right hand have all but disappeared from the current concert scene. This is a natural development caused by the increasing demands for loudness, brilliance, agility and tone-color palette of the repertoire.

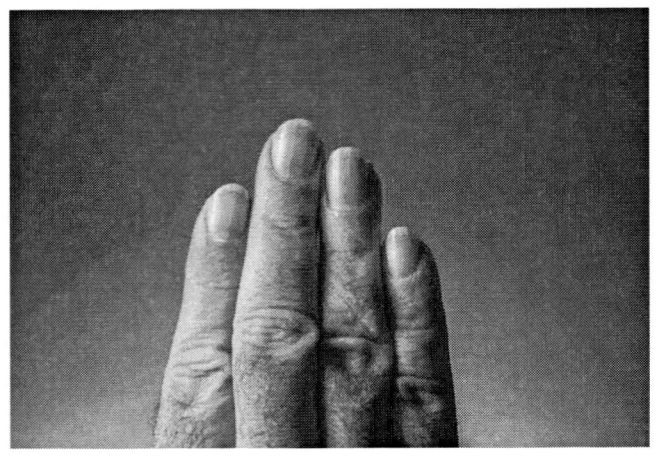

Photo 1-1. Finger nails, dorsal view.
Photo Wayne Armstrong.

While the flesh method tends to emphasize the fundamental of the harmonic series, the nail method is richer in upper partials and thereby offers more versatility of color nuances (and, hence, dynamics: one does not go without the other in guitar playing), since it can be manipulated with more fluency than the thick finger tip in changes of its angle of attack on the string. By providing a thinner surface from which the string departs after the stroke, the nail also allows for quicker responsiveness and a more penetrating tone. In addition it produces fewer noise factors, when properly filed, than the flesh, thus creating a cleaner, purer musical sound.

The shape and length of the nails are areas of individual concern. Many factors influence the player's decision in this context, from thickness of the tip pad to curvature of the nail shape on the dorsal side of the finger.

In general, the old advice, following Segovia (Segovia and Mendoza 1980, 27 (illus.). 29), to follow in parallel the curvature of the finger tip holds for most normal nails, taking care not to let them grow too long, not to overlook the risk of shaping in such a way that two points of contact, instead of one, are present (this may occur easily with fingers with very dorsally curved nails), and not to make the arc of the distal clear edge too pronounced, thus making the nail travel against an 'uphill' resistance (Tennant 1995, 32).

Nail shape, length and care have been well described and explained in various popular methods (Shearer, Learning the Classic Guitar 1990, Romero 2012, Tennant 1995).

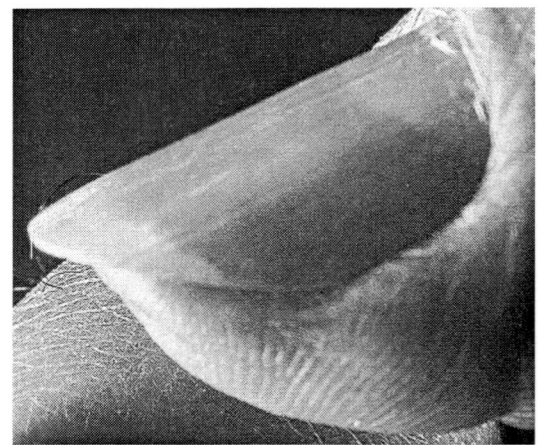

Photo 1-2. Lateral view of (right) thumb nail.
The distal end of the lateral fold may end
where the nail and the hyponychium converge
or continue distally for a short distance.
Photo Wayne Armstrong.

An important feature of the nail, for guitarists, is the location where the clear or free edge of the nail originates. Assuming we are studying a right-handed guitarist, this point coincides, location-wise, with the lateral (radial) origin of the quick of the nail, or **hyponychium** (the distal border of the pinkish, fleshy bed under the nail plate). Adjacent to these nail elements, and protecting them, lies the lateral skin fold bordering the nail, the **paronychium** (Phillips 2013, Haneke 2006).

The paronychium may end at this point, with the fleshy tip immediately turning medially, towards the center of the nail (as in photo 1-2), or it may continue distally for a small distance *before* the tip-flesh curves.

This difference will be a factor in determining where the 'ramping' of the clear edge should begin: if the edge is allowed to go straight beyond the point where the paronychium ends, the nail will probably have problems clearing the string after the stroke, particularly in rest stroke mode. In fact, it could be hypothesized that this factor might be a frequent reason why some players give up on their rest stroke technique, without realizing theirs is not really a technical problem per se, but a nail problem.

Whether the player contacts the string more or less on the nail itself or on the 'gulley' between the nail and flesh (Biberian 2012, 58) is also a determinant factor. The former placement can afford more protruding straight nail edge than the latter.

Beginners usually feel more comfortable with longer than shorter nails, but it is pedagogically sound to start all beginning instruction on the guitar without nails, so that the mechanics of fingerwork are well-assimilated without their influence (Romero 2012, 44). This is an invaluable resource even for more advanced players, to recover some of the possibly lost sensitivity of touch, the intimate rapport, between finger (or thumb) and string, that, over time, might occur.

In general, players will prefer shorter nails as their technical know-how progresses to advanced levels.

Problems with hooks and brittleness need specialized attention. For the former, local application of a modicum of heat with a hair curler, after showering or bathing, can be an effective remedy. Care must be taken not to burn the delicate flesh under the nail or in the tip.

Weak and brittle nails can be strengthened by appropriate diet, rich in minerals and vitamins, and by local application of certain products that provide the nail with organic nutrients, but never by using the commercial cosmetic hardeners which will, in time, deteriorate or even kill the nail because of the presence of formaldehyde and other noxious chemicals in their composition.

For exceptional cases, or for nail breaks, artificial nails might be indicated. Again, the shaping and length of the artificial nail has to fit the individual finger size and shape. Some prominent players favor using shaped pieces of ping-pong balls instead of the commercially available false nails. In recent years, new products have become available that provide reliability and durability, without the harsh consequences that old nail glues used to produce in the past.

Apart from the issue of shape and strength, the polish of the nail is of great importance. Filing should be done in at least three stages: a first stage that shortens the length, if needed, preferably with a diamond-dust file, not emery boards or scissors. A second, smoothing stage done with a fine grade sanding material (the material used in polishing optical lenses is ideal), and a third, polishing stage utilizing the finest grade possible. No roughness, dirt or irregularity in the nail surface should be allowed, for these will affect both the quality of the tone and the fluency of technique.

Leverage Conditions in Holding the Guitar

In the traditional classical guitar sitting position, four points of contact are used to sustain the guitar: two between the lower arch of the guitar and the two thighs, one between the back of the guitar and the chest, and another between the right forearm and the bass-side bout of the sound box. Without the latter, the weight of the guitar's neck and tuning machine-head will tilt the instrument until it falls to the left.

The holding in position of the guitar is, therefore, a class-1 lever system in which the left thigh is the axis of rotation, the resistance is the weight of the neck, and the force is the weight of the soundbox together with the projected weight of the right arm when supported by the bout.

The support given by the back and the right thigh act as secondary fulcra that limit the direction and amount of motion in the leverage, but do not alter its nature. The left arm can hold the instrument, without needing the right-arm's support, and simultaneously maintain fingers acting on the fretboard statically (like in holding a chord or sustained notes). In this case, the leverage will be a type-3 system, with the left thigh as fulcrum, the left hand applying the force at the point where it holds the neck, and the weight of the neck (whose center of gravity lies in the machine-head) as resistance.

Were the left hand to sustain the neck at the extreme of the machine-head, then the leverage would be a class-2 system (resistance in between force and fulcrum). The right-arm/sound box point of contact is indispensable for the proper execution of any dynamic activity of the left hand (some fingerwork, in position, is possible, but not shifting).

The amount of weight projected at the right-arm point of contact is a functional issue: if there is no left-hand activity, all that is needed is enough weight to balance the counteracting weight resistance of the neck (in this case, purely theoretical and not functional, the lower bout of the instrument does not need to touch the right thigh at all! The guitar would, then, be suspended in perfect balance, as a see-saw). Depending on left-hand activity, different degrees of weight release will be needed to balance it. This coordination of left-hand activity with appropriate right-arm balancing weight release is one of the most disregarded issues in guitar training.

A Kinesiological Approach to Motor Training on the Guitar
In kinesiology (the science that studies human motion), motor skills are classified in a variety of ways. This classification helps in the analysis of applied skills activities and, hence, is a good tool in the development of training and practice methods for guitarists.

Skills are **open**, when the environment in which they take place changes continuously and the actions are unpredictable and not patterned. These conditions are typical of team sports and individual competitive sports, like tennis. Skills are **closed** when the environment does not change and the patterns of motion are pre-established and can be improved through correct repetition in practice. Golf, gymnastics and musical performance (including playing the guitar) are examples of closed skills.

Skills are **discrete** when they begin and end in self-contained gestural units, like in throwing a projectile, hitting a ball, etc. They are **continuous** when they do not end abruptly but continue in a series over a more or less long period of time, with repetition as a main characteristic. Playing the guitar is a continuous skill activity.

Finally, motor skills can be classified as **gross**, when they require full-body motion and depend primarily on the activity of large muscle groups, as in running or jumping, or **fine** if they require movements of precision and delicacy, involving smaller muscles, as in manual activities. Many skills combine elements of both, so a subcategorization into **large** or **small muscle** involvement and **coarse** or **refined performance** is also convenient. Guitar playing is a fine motor activity.

Given the above classification we can define guitar playing as being primarily a **closed, continuous, small-muscle** and **refined motor skill activity**.

Learning by Doing
Skills can only be learned by trying them out. The process of learning is based on the continuous feed-back received from the body's proprioceptors, combined with the maturation process taking place as a consequence of growth, knowledge of proper principles of movement, supervised performance and developing kinesthesia.

An important psychological factor is that of intentionality or goal-orientation, through which the performer has a clearly defined mental picture of the task.

The Mind-Body Connection

As the skill learning becomes more advanced, mental practicing becomes more and more important. This takes the form of visualization or imaging, mimicking of the activity and, in the case of musicians, vocalization of the musical lines with the naming of the notes through their letter names or syllables. As explained by Havas and Shearer, among others, the naming of notes, while visualizing their performance, acts as a powerful abstraction of all the sensory-motor and intellectual data gathered, in the course of practicing, about that musical entity. It is a particularly useful tool in building up speed in agility passages (Havas 1978, Shearer, Learning the Classic Guitar 1990).

Simple to Complex

Skills training should begin with simpler tasks and gradually increase the level of complexity, building on the acquired skills. From a physiological stand-point, movements involving bigger muscles are simpler to learn and control than refined precision movements. In simplistic terms, one should learn big movements before learning small movements.

However, there are certain procedures that require a combination of bigger muscle work with precision movements (like in long-distance shifting). This complexity of functions makes it indispensable that shorter shifts, a smaller movement, be learned before larger shifts be attempted.

Poppelreuter's Law of Practice

PLP, named after German neuropsychiatrist Walther Poppelreuter (1886–1939), is a theory of practice in skills training that advocates developing accuracy of movement before working on speed, in the belief that once the proper form of a movement pattern is well-assimilated, the knowledge will transfer to higher levels of speed in the execution of the pattern.

This principle holds only in those types of skills where the speed is a variable that can be altered and is not an intrinsic element upon which the skill itself depends. For the latter, insistence on both accuracy *and* speed, simultaneously, is necessary (as in training for a correct tennis serve). In guitar playing, speed is mostly a variable that can be altered without affecting the essential nature of the movement, although the muscular coordination will vary to some extent as the speed increases.

However, building speed requires practicing procedures at speed. Although slow practice is an indispensable preliminary step before we train for speed, it will not, by itself, teach us how to play fast and accurately.

Specificity of Practice

This relates to the fact that not much of the skills learned in one activity transfer automatically to another. In other words, playing the violin or the piano are not necessarily helpful in learning to play the guitar, although many of the fundamentals concerning fingerwork are similar in these various activities. By the same token, exercises away from the instrument, except for those recommended for general physical fitness and flexibility purposes, are of no great use in training for the specific skills required in playing the guitar.

Practicing the Whole vs. Practicing the Parts

In athletic training opinions are divided about how to best teach and train complex skills. Breaking down the pattern into its constituent elements may not be the best way to train for the timing and speed requirements of the activity, while practicing the whole pattern may provide for less-than-ideal accuracy and attention to the form.

In guitar playing, a flexible approach that uses both as needed is best. Specific gestural components may be isolated and taken out of context before attempting a more general and contextual execution that integrates the steps into a seamless sequence, i.e., what the author has called elsewhere "spotting" (Iznaola, On Practicing 2000, 14).

However, the integrative phase of practice is indispensable. Play-throughs of big sections in pieces and entire pieces to attain peak performance levels of mastery are as much a part of good practice as are fragmentation and "spotting" in the early, formative stages of training.

Length and Intensity of Practice Periods

Kinesiologists recommend the use of what they call **distributive** practice (i.e., practice over shorter periods of time with frequent breaks) for activities that require high intensity of effort, that are particularly complex, that are repetitive in nature and/or that may produce boredom. They recommend **massed** practice (i.e., continuous practice for longer periods of time) when the skill level is high and peak-performance levels in execution are sought.

Massed practice requires high levels of motivation on the part of the performer and this is usually associated with the meaningfulness of the activity. In guitar playing, distributive practice would be indicated in the beginning stages of learning new skills, in the practice of repetitive technical exercises, in fragmentary practice of spots in pieces, etc.

Massed practice seems to be appropriate when doing integrative practice in repertoire preparation, particularly when all the preliminary technical work is well-assimilated and the performer is readying him/herself for a public performance situation.

It is important to note the risks inherent to massed practice approaches, in which the enthusiasm and motivation factors might blind the performer to symptoms of tension build-up or sensations of struggle and difficulty. An intelligent balance between these approaches is, of course, the ideal.

Practicing strategies for the guitarist are well described, from various viewpoints, in a good number of publications (Duncan, The Art of Classical Guitar Playing 1980) (Isbin 1999) (Iznaola, On Practicing 2000) (Klickstein 2009) (Shearer, Learning the Classic Guitar 1990) (Romero 2012) (Tennant 1995).

Somatic Training

Under this generic term we subsume those methods that deal with postural and movement re-training and enhanced awareness of the body and its motor functions. These may be important complements to one's instrumental practice. These methods have contributed to our understanding of the role of noxious tension in our daily lives, and how to free ourselves from it. The importance of massage therapies in this context is also universally recognized.

For the performer, familiarity with one or more of these methods will be of great importance, for through their influence one will acquire a better sense of self and a deeper communion with one's own sensory-motor capacities, all to the benefit of one's artistry. We will not deal with other methods, founded in the spiritual traditions, which depart somewhat from the main thrust of our discussion. Among these, the techniques of **Yoga** and **Transcendental Meditation** have gained in popularity in the last few decades.

The Alexander Technique

The method devised by Australian actor F. M. Alexander (1869-1955) has proven of great benefit to many musicians. Its emphasis is in the correction of erroneous postural and motor habits through increased awareness and the application of simple movement patterns designed to develop more control in our physical activities. It underlines the importance of spinal alignment from the neck down, and, in general, well-balanced postural stances when standing, sitting or in motion (F. M. Alexander 1932 (2001)) (Alexander and Fischer 1996).

Another key concept is **inhibition**, not in the psychoanalytical sense of repressing an emotion, but rather as a mental reminder to check and focus positively on specific movements, in order to ensure that they are each anticipated and enacted correctly. The concept is utilized, as well, in training practices like **Dalcroze Eurhythmics**, and is closely associated with Aaron Shearer's concept of **Aim Directed Motion (ADM)** (Shearer, Learning the Classic Guitar 1990, 1:4).

The Feldenkrais Method

Moshe Feldenkrais (1904-1984) was a Polish-born engineer who emigrated to Palestine before settling in Paris in 1929. After suffering a debilitating knee injury, and being diagnosed as irreversibly handicapped, he taught himself to walk again and, in the process, developed his method, defined as **Awareness Through Movement**, or **Functional Integration** (Feldenkrais 1990).

The emphasis is in understanding and improving or eliminating movement patterns that may be interfering with other motor activities, unbeknownst to the subject. While the approach, as in the Alexander Technique, underlines awareness and conscious re-education, it is implemented from a more dynamic standpoint than the postural emphasis of the latter.

Arthur Lessac's Body Wisdom

Although not as established a formal somatic training method as either Feldenkrais' or Alexander's, the work of Arthur Lessac (1909 – 2011) offers an intriguing and inspiring alternative to re-educating the body for enhanced motor performance and overall well-being.

A prominent voice teacher and coach, Lessac developed a unique method, known as **Kinesensics**, integrating the human voice with sensory-motor procedures designed to re-connect the individual with her intuition about her body's potential (Lessac 1981).

Bodywork

Various forms of massage and other manipulative therapies have long been recognized as invaluable tools in the elimination of dysfunctional tensions and psycho-somatic ailments. Deprivation of body touch has been linked to the expression of physical violence as well as emotional dysfunctions in the individual (Juhan 1987).

Among the many methods of bodywork, those involving deep-tissue manipulation have sparked great interest in recent times. "**Rolfing**", nickname of the method of soft-tissue manipulation called "structural integration" by her founder, Dr. Ida P. Rolf, works by re-aligning muscular and connective tissue masses in accordance with gravity (Rolf 1989). Other massage therapies offer many benefits to musicians when implemented by experienced practitioners. Among them, **Shiatzu**, **Aromatherapy** and **Reflexology** are worthy of mention.

The Pathology of Guitar Playing

Performance Anxiety

The source of all problems possible in the execution of a skilled performance activity is the accumulation of dysfunctional tension, that is to say, the exertion of effort without a functional goal. And the simple cause for this to occur is fear, based on a more-or-less ill-defined sense of insecurity in facing the challenges posed by the performance task. The insecurity is nothing else but the absence of a sense of personal mastery, which means that one is doubtful of one's capability to match skills and goals.

The immediate result of this doubt is the development of a state of stress, which is what we call **performance anxiety** or **stage fright**. This stressful state, initiated consciously or, more frequently, unconsciously, by an intellectual process of self-evaluation, produces an emotional response (fear) which in turn triggers a somatic chain-reaction of symptoms, characteristic of what is known as the "fight-or-flight" syndrome.

Dr. Hans Seyle, the pioneer who introduced and first described the concept of stress, says in his classic *The Stress of Life,* "Only in the rare instance where you really succeed in totally disregarding a potential source of trouble, without even having to force yourself, do you avoid tension" (Selye 1978, 116).

This tension may take one of three forms: retreat or recoil (flight), advance against the perceived danger (fight), or stand on one's ground (static tension). The chemistry and neurology of stress reactions is controlled by the complex interaction of the sympathetic and parasympathetic divisions of the ANS (autonomous nervous system). The former "acts out" involuntary physiological changes as response to emotional states, triggered through the nerve fibers that arise from the thoracic and lumbar areas of the spinal cord that innervate our internal organs. It, thus, changes heart rate, blood pressure, digestive function, breathing patterns, kidney function, and secretion in the adrenal, salivary and sweat glands.

Some of the typical manifestations or symptoms of intense performance anxiety, like dry mouth, sweaty and/or cold hands, pounding heart, dizziness, hyperactivity, drowsiness, nausea and hunger, are the byproducts of these sympathetic responses. There is also general hypertonicity in the musculature and an increase in the production of lactic acid, waste product of muscular metabolism, which is, as well, an anxiety-producing chemical.

The parasympathetic system, trying to reestablish the normal state in the internal environment, is momentarily superseded, until the chemical changes brought about by the stress reaction subside (**adrenaline** and the adrenaline-like neurotransmitter **norepinephrine** are important chemicals in these reactions).

The presence of performance anxiety in young students is an indicator either of excessive or of premature demands for public demonstrations of their capabilities, or of a mismatch between skills and repertoire.

In older students, the situation can be more difficult to diagnose, especially if they are adolescents. In this period of their lives, the pressures of socialization, the onset of puberty, parental influences, etc., may all contribute to a state of stress which might not be necessarily related to issues of artistic competence.

In any case, the moment of performance must be prepared for and perceived as a wondrous culmination to a joyful, exciting process of discovery, not devoid of challenge, but free from frustration, obligation or any consideration of competitiveness.

In this context, it is worth emphasizing that, no matter how well-intentioned the teaching and how psychologically nurturing, if the physical training imposed on the student does not follow guidelines of efficient, well-coordinated and easy action, it will lead to situations of distress and self-doubt that will produce performance anxiety.

The phenomenon of performance anxiety does provide a glimpse of a higher truth: as it is produced by one's imagined reality (the perception that one's capacities are not enough), it points to the indivisible unity of mind and body, and how the one, intangible and indefinable as it still is, very definitely influences our body's very physiology.

The power of ideation, visualization, imagination, can then be trained to assist and accelerate the process of achieving mastery, the only definitive remedy to the problem.

Breathing

Shallow breathing, or lack of breathing for more or less long periods of time, may occur in performance situations when the level of anxiety is high. This becomes a factor in the vicious cycle of stage fright, since good respiration is indispensable to the proper oxygenation needed by the musculature to perform its motor duties efficiently.

However, it is unwise to advise the player to train himself/herself to "breathe normally" during performance, for this cannot happen. There is research evidence that shows that breathing patterns are substantially altered during motor activity by factors such as accent, upbeat/downbeat relationships, movements at the shoulder girdle, pauses in the music, etc. In fact, it seems that the breathing patterns match the gestural language of the motor activities through which the expressive content of the music is realized (Szende and Nemessuri 1971, 98-121).

This does not mean that breathing patterns in oneself or one's students can be ignored. A well-placed deep inhalation/ exhalation will do a lot to relieve nervous tension and provide the necessary rhythmic energy to start the next phrase or piece. It is also important to use breathing exercises whenever one feels the need to stimulate general relaxation. All meditation practices underline the importance of focused breathing as a tool in their methods.

CTD (Cumulative Trauma Disorders)

This generic expression encompasses a series of motor dysfunctions of the upper limb, caused by a combination of stress-factors, mainly: force, repetition, bad posture and lack of rest (Putz-Anderson 1994, 4).

Force, in our context, refers to such physically demanding procedures as extensions, barrés, sustained 'hovering' right-hand fingerwork, or, in general, any procedure demanding sustained effort. This static contraction-type, as we have seen, leaves metabolic wastes that fatigue and irritate the muscle fibers.

Repetition produces oxygen deprivation in the muscle mass by the overlapping of phasic contractions, without proper release of tension in between them. It also produces tendon and nerve irritation because of the exacerbated localized friction, particularly through the narrow sheaths of the wrist/hand mechanism. Cumulative trauma disorders due to repetitive movement are sub-categorized as **Repetitive Strain Injuries (RSI)**.

In guitar playing, procedures such as rasgueados, tremolos, arpeggios, slurs, scales, can lead to RSI if not well-developed technically.

Bad posture refers both to static positions and to movements at the limits of a joint's range of motion. This makes muscles work at disadvantageous angles of pull, thus creating unnecessary tension in their fibers, and forcing extreme levels of stretch on tendons.

61

The teacher must be very aware of students' personal ranges of joint motion, as the ideal mid-range depends on the individual's joint motility. A stiff-jointed student may seem to be within mid-range when in reality she is, because of the joint's limitations, closer to an extreme than one might think. Visual appearance alone can be deceiving.

In guitar playing, excessive wrist abduction (radial and ulnar), hyperflexion, hyperextension (dorsiflexion), finger-joint collapse, thumb's retraction, can all lead to problems over time.

Lack of rest refers both to the pacing of one's practice on a daily basis and to the balance of periods of work with periods of rest. Highly motivated, competitive players may fall in the trap of what has been termed "neurotic practice", through which the needs of the body are ignored in the pursuit of ill-guided goals (Holmquist 1994, 93). In this context, it is important to understand that, as in other forms of physical training, musculo-skeletal groups should be alternated during training, so that one does not overwork any one particular group.

Guitarists, and other musicians, must also be very aware of other repetitive activities they may get involved with, especially computer-related: manipulation of computer keyboards and mice are among the biggest culprits in the current high-incidence levels of RSI.

Immediate medical and/or physiotherapy treatment must be provided for any of the dysfunctions described below. Among the most important disorders that may affect players are:

Tendinitis or **tendonitis**, inflammation of the tendon in its sheath. An associated problem is **tenosynovitis**, in which the tendon and the sheath develop adhesions due to the inflammation and consequent dryness of the internal synovial lining. Pain with movement and swelling in the surrounding tissues will require medical treatment and complete rest until the condition subsides.

A particular form of tenosynovitis, known as **stenosing tenosynovitis** or **De Quervain's syndrome**, produces fibrous bands around a tendon sheath to the thumb or finger (felt as lumps in the palm, if affecting the fingers, or on the radial side of the wrist, if on the thumb), making actions of bending and stretching possible only through forcefully snapping the digits. It is also known as **trigger finger**.

Tennis elbow (lateral epicondylitis) and **golfer's elbow (medial epicondylitis)** are less common among guitarists but may also occur. These are localized points of pain, caused by overuse or trauma at the point of origin of the finger and wrist extensors and flexors, respectively.

Neural Entrapment
Nerves supplying the limb's musculature may suffer from various forms of entrapment at different points.

Thoracic outlet syndrome is a neuro-vascular disorder that affects the nerves and arteries that supply the upper limb (the brachial plexus) through constriction caused by the pressure of the muscular masses that control arm movement, or other inflammatory processes. Its symptoms may resemble those of carpal tunnel syndrome, but it may affect all of the musculature of the arm and hand.

Cubital tunnel syndrome is a nerve condition affecting the ulnar nerve as it passes through and gets trapped at the ulnar groove of the humerus at its distal end. Pins and needles sensations affect the ulnar side of the forearm and run down to the ring and little fingers, with consequent weakness of the intrinsic hand muscles.

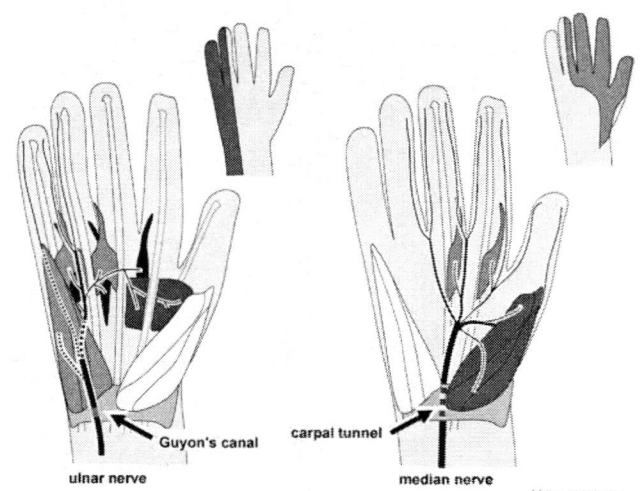

Figure 1-26. Nerve entrapment at the wrist. Hand areas affected are shown by shadowed contours in the little hands on top of figure. © 2009 Alan H. D. Watson. Reproduced under license.

Carpal tunnel syndrome is a nerve injury caused by pressure on the median nerve, produced by inflammation due to overuse or arthritic tissue growth in the narrow cavity of the carpal tunnel (between the flexor retinaculum and the carpal bones). Pain, weakness in the finger and thumb movements (all flexors go through the retinaculum), pins and needles sensations in the palm and fingers, are symptoms that will justify immediate medical attention. The ulnar nerve may get compressed as well as it crosses the retinaculum through **Guyon's canal**, a narrow passageway (Watson, Biol. Mus. Perf. 2009, 65).

Focal Hand Dystonia

This serious ailment is a neuro-muscular disorder whose causes and mechanisms are only partially understood. It shows in the form of involuntary movement distortions and abnormal contraction patterns in one or more muscles, causing dysfunction and, sometimes but not always, pain.

Focal dystonia in the hand and fingers is known also as writer's or pianist's cramp. It seems to affect the proper functioning of the reciprocal inhibition reflex, thus allowing opposing muscles to keep their respective contractions in an abnormal antagonistic struggle:

> The later stages of dystonia are sometimes characterised (sic) by a fierce simultaneous contraction of antagonistic flexor and extensor muscles of the digits that causes fatigue and pain (Watson, What Studying Musicians 2006, 17).

Recent brain imaging research done with dystonic monkeys trained to perform specific repetitive hand movements to gather food shows evidence of "a marked degradation of the sensory map of the hand… In both musicians and non-musicians with focal dystonia of the hand, maladaptive changes are also seen in cortical mapping." These investigations have lead to new therapeutic techniques based on sensory-motor retraining, rather than drug treatments, with variable levels of success (Watson, What Studying Musicians 2006, 19).

These recent research outcomes point to an important pedagogical issue: when training technically, one's initial perception of how things work in one's hand may have a profound effect on how healthy, from the physical standpoint, one's technical development will be. (Mis-) perception may become an ugly reality.

Other Pathological Processes

Among many possible illnesses affecting the upper limb, the following occur with some frequency:

Rheumatoid and **osteo-arthritis** are inflammatory processes in the joints. In the guitar world, a well-known case was that of the great Cuban guitarist, José Rey de la Torre (1917 – 1994), a victim of rheumatoid arthritis, because of which he had to stop his concert career in the mid-1970's (Danner 1994). Nowadays, though, joint inflammation, pain and dysfunction may be controlled through appropriate medical treatment to a degree that was unimaginable a generation ago.

Dupuytren's contracture begins as a thickening of the fascia of the palm, eventually developing into the formation of a fibrous cord, which pulls on the fingers, producing an involuntary bend mainly affecting the ring and little fingers (almost never the thumb and index, and the middle finger with less frecuency), until they cannot be straightened out completely. There is no known cure, but there are treatment options that may slow down the progression of the illness over the course of many years.

Ischemia is the lack of proper blood circulation in a local area, and may affect guitarists either through excess muscular tension, or pathological vaso-spasms that constrict the flow of blood in the small arteries, producing cold, bluish hands. Avoidance of cold conditions, gloves, and other common-sense measures (including adopting a more effortless technique) will help with this situation, unless it is a side-symptom of a more serious health condition.

All of the pathological processes briefly described above require expert medical assessment, diagnosis and treatment and should not be dealt with by the teacher, other than by making the student (or oneself) aware that, if suspicious symptoms are present, immediate attention by a qualified practitioner might be necessary.

Training for Virtuosity

The sections on the pathology of, and the anatomical constraints to, playing may lead to a distorted viewpoint of the realities of teaching and learning to play the guitar, because they underscore those things that can go wrong. Thankfully, the normal course of events is not one that leads to injury and precaution, but to fulfillment and exhilaration. It is a course that leads to virtuosity.

Earlier, mastery was defined as the perfect match between skills and task. This continued trajectory through successive stages of masterful achievement has as its natural culmination the complete unfolding of the player's ultimate potentialities.

This is what we now define as virtuosity. As in the case of mastery, conventional wisdom has understood virtuosity based on a comparative scale of levels of achievement in performance, which of course still applies when dealing with the professional realities of the social environment.

Pedagogically, though, the concept refers to the *unburdening* through which individuals break free of psycho-physiological obstacles that impede the blossoming of their unknown capacities in a given discipline (Iznaola, Unleash. Talent 1994)

If accepted, this view of instrumental pedagogy would demand an attitude of self-propelled curiosity and a commitment to continuing exploration and experimentation on the part of both student and teacher, because the unknown potential of an individual is only developed through the discovery of unique ways of expression and unique things to express. This sense of curiosity and risk-taking will succeed if founded on solid knowledge, unhindered by any sense of defensive self-preservation.

There is a way with our body, and our soul, through which we can reach the ultimate echelon in our path to whatever glory might await us if we know just exactly how and when to stretch, and how far.

The chapters that follow consider some of these possibilities.

Chapter 2

I see no more than you, but I have trained myself to notice what I see.
Sherlock Holmes
(Conan Doyle 2005, 132)

THE TALENTED HAND

Section 1. Physiomechanical Aspects of Right-Hand Technique

The genius of the long-standing oral tradition in guitar playing has produced results that are as unpredictable as they are surprisingly effective. It could be argued that the achievements in technical development in guitar playing throughout its history can be traced back, *ad ovo,* to 'discoveries' made by folkloric and popular players, across time and geographies.

One is tempted to say that if there is such a thing as 'innate talent,' speaking of guitar playing, it certainly has its best proof in the right-hand virtuosity of Gypsy, Flamenco, South American and other popular practitioners.

This chapter explores the physiomechanics of right-hand technique in the hope of finding a way through which the intuitive and the highly formalized, the ardor of spontaneity and the rigors of method may be integrated within an all-encompassing vision of what constitutes great mastery in playing the instrument.

As described earlier, the guitar can be conceived as a balanced see-saw whose tendency to collapse to the left is counteracted by the weight of the right arm. Apart from its support function for keeping the instrument in place, the positioning of the right-arm has to favor free and unimpeded motility in all its joints, from the shoulder to the phalanges. Generally speaking, the point of support of the forearm on the upper rim will determine the type of muscular involvement needed to achieve a sensation of poise and balance, without excessive rigidity or weightiness. If this point of support is close to the elbow, the forearm and hand weight will be free to fall, with the hand drawing an arch of a circle whose radius is the length of the forearm.

As the point of support moves away from the elbow, more distally, towards the wrist, the tendency to fall is counter-balanced by the weight of the part of the arm lying posterior to the support point. When the pivot point where perfect balance is achieved is reached, the leverage is that of a balanced see-saw (class-1 lever). In this position the hand cannot play, because it lies too far above and forward of the strings (if the wrist is relaxed at this point, it will be fully flexed). Therefore, some type of arm involvement will be needed in order to establish a starting attitude of poise that will position the hand and fingers in optimal playing demeanor.

This arm involvement can be of two types: a) the upper arm slightly abducts and rotates medially (inwardly), bringing the hand into appropriate playing alignment. We will call this the **short-arm approach**. Or b), the upper arm moves slightly forward (flexion), allowing some more forearm weight to project. The hand and fingers are kept in playing position at this point through the action of the elbow flexors. We will call this the **long-arm** approach.

A.

Photo 2-1. Short-arm position.
Photo by Wayne Armstrong.

B.

Photo 2-2. Long-arm position.
Photo by Wayne Armstrong.

The leverage type in each case is different. In A. (photo 2-1), it fluctuates between lever types 1 and 2, depending on whether the two segments of the forearm (antero-medial and postero-lateral to the fulcrum) are in balance (type 1) or leaning posteriorly, towards the elbow side (type 2). In this, the resistance (weight of the arm behind the point of support) lies in between the force (the upper arm's abduction/rotation) and the fulcrum (the support point). Case B. is a class-3 lever, with the resistance (the forearm and hand weight) at one end, and the effort (the insertion of the elbow flexors) in between resistance and axis (the elbow joint) (Iznaola, Rest and Free 1990).

The anthropometric issues discussed earlier may condition a player's decision as to which type of leverage to favor: longer-limbed players, unless they adopt a larger instrument or some type of armrest, will tend to favor a short-arm approach over a long-arm, while the opposite will be true with shorter-limbed players. Some sitting positions, however, pre-determine the arm's alignment: players who hold the instrument over the right thigh (like Flamenco players frequently do) have to use the long-arm approach, while guitarists who prefer a very steep angle of inclination are short-arm players. A full discussion of the issue of neck angle follows later in this chapter.

In actual practice, it is not unusual for many experienced players to mix approaches, applying them according to their appropriateness for the musical or technical context at any given moment.

The different weight distribution in one and the other has a bearing upon many other aspects of right-hand technique, from type of finger stroke to color and dynamics. Hence, apart from the technical advantages or disadvantages determined by the context, the musical characteristics intrinsic to each approach must be clearly understood.

More detailed analysis of leverage conditions in the right arm will be presented later on in this chapter.

Arm Support and Stroke Type

The long-arm support projects more weight distally than the short-arm approach. This means that when the fingers are not in contact with the strings, the flexors of the forearm need to work eccentrically to keep the hand and fingers in playing attitude, hovering over the strings. Therefore, in free strokes with the long arm approach the muscular effort will be slightly greater than for rest strokes, because the weight of the arm has to be controlled muscularly so that the hand does not lose its playing position. In a rest stroke, however, this weight is transferred from the initial string contact of the finger, through its stroke, to its final resting contact on the adjacent string.

The situation is the opposite in the short-arm support. Here the weight does not hang distally from the point of arm rest, but rather it is balanced or even projecting proximally from the point of support, falling towards the elbow. The weight of the forearm is not a factor interfering with maintaining the hovering hand position, which is actually achieved by the abduction/rotation of the upper arm. Free strokes become less cumbersome and easier to control than in the long-arm approach, especially for shorter-limbed individuals. In contrast, rest strokes will tend to be slightly more forced, more emphatic, of a type sometimes known as a "snap" rest stroke, in which the finger, after the stroke, momentarily comes in contact with the next string and quickly bounces off to a hovering attitude, as there is no arm weight being transferred.

Of course, there are many degrees of intermediate weight-release situations that allow for minute, exquisitely refined control of the relationship between arm support and stroke type, which good players with a well-developed technique intuitively apply in the course of a performance.

Physiomechanics of Right-Hand Fingerwork

Free Stroke

It is nowadays usual to define a 'normal' stroke (a misnomer: it should be called, more appropriately, a *pluck*) as consisting of three phases: preparation (understood as pre-stroke contact with the string, generally called 'planting' or 'touching'), pressure, and release (Tennant 1995, 35-36, Romero 2012, 43). To this, of course, must be added the recovery phase that brings the finger to an optimal attitude to restart the cycle. However, the 'prepared' stroke described here has not always been considered the norm (Quine 1990). The unprepared, 'swinging' stroke is discussed later in this section.

Some methods describe the guitar as a percussion instrument (Pick 1992) and, indeed, the instrument has percussive potential, as in the special effect called the *tambora*. The confusion seems to arise when one compares a prepared versus an unprepared stroke (discussed later).

The second mode, in which the finger plucks the string without anticipatory placement, may be interpreted by the casual observer as a 'strike' of the string, which it is initially. What defines it as a plucking action, however, is what happens afterwards: a true percussion would require the finger to bounce off the string (as it does in the *tambora*), rather than engage it and displace it as its trajectory moves 'through' it.

A comparison with left-hand action in slurring may be useful: the ascending slur (the 'hammer-on') is a percussive stroke; the descending slur (the 'pull-out') is, normally, a pluck. Of course the most obvious analogy is with the respective mechanisms of the harpsichord (plectrum pluck) and the piano (hammer percussion). A categorical difference.

Phase One: Preparation

The concept of preparation may be made comprehensive by defining it broadly as the action of readying a digit to pluck a string. This can be done either through contact with the string or by closely hovering over it.

Contact preparation itself can be more or less passive, depending on the amount of arm-weight release allowed to be supported by the digit after having contacted the string. In this text, the term *placing*, borrowed from harpists, will be used to differentiate contact preparation that is muscularly active, when the weight is not released, from passive preparation, with weight released on the support-point of one or more digits on the strings. The term *planting* will be reserved for the latter.

In summary, the following three terms will be used to describe the various types of preparation: **hovering** (for non-contact preparation), **placing** (for muscularly active anticipatory string contact), and **planting** (when this contact supports passively part of the hand and arm weight released on the string). In very general terms, planting is most frequent and practical in chordal and arpeggio fingerwork, since these textures allow for a more passive anticipatory contact with the strings, as in the so-called **full plant**, in which all fingers involved in the arpeggio or chord are placed and allowed to rest before their turn to play comes.

In most other cases and depending on tempo primarily, the fingers don't plant, but either hover, as in melodic, legato passages on a single string, where anticipatory placing is not possible, or they may be placed on the string subsequently to be plucked, without weight release, as in scalar passages across strings.

The thumb, however, is very frequently placed and planted as support for its companions' fingerwork. This allows not only for a point of stability for the hand, but also diminishes partially the workload of the support musculature that keeps the arm in steady alignment with the strings (Romero 2012, 43). This is particularly vital in prolonged free stroke work, where there is little opportunity for weight release other than through the thumb's planting on a string superior to the ones being acted upon. The fingers fulfill the same role when one or more plant to support the thumb's work, in passages where the latter has 'solo' responsibilities. More about planting will be discussed later on in this chapter.

It is important to realize that hovering occurs before placing, and this precedes planting (when the latter is possible), in other words, the initial contact with the string in actual playing is always active, the weight release occurs later, if allowed.

The primary movers for placing are the intrinsics of the hand, mainly the lumbricals, which, as described earlier, extend both PIP and DIP joints as the MCP joint flexes mechanically. *This phase of the stroke cycle is fundamental in differentiating the free- and rest stroke*, the difference being the alignment of the PIP joint relative to the string: perpendicular or antero-inferior to the string plane for the free stroke, antero-superior to the string plane in the rest stroke (Shearer, Learning the Classic Guitar 1990, 1:56).

Some players, though, primarily Flamenco guitarists, emphasize a more perpendicular alignment for their scale *picado* rest stroke, to increase the string resistance and enhance its characteristic brilliance. This is also the case, although for different reasons, for players who follow the so-called 'flat-hand' technique, in which the MCP joint is kept extended (thus producing a flatter profile to the dorsum of the hand) in order to equalize the movement trajectories in both free- and rest stroke, now entirely dependent on the engagement of the IP joints only. The most notable practitioners of this approach are disciples or followers of the distinguished Argentinian-born Mexican guitarist Manuel López Ramos (1929 – 2006) and his school.

In most other cases the alignment of the PIP joint determines whether the arc of the stroke's path completes its flexing trajectory towards the palm, in the free stroke, or is stopped by the adjacent lower string, in the rest stroke.

Changing stroke types on the same string can be achieved either: 1. by extending the IP joints frontally (more precisely, in an antero-superior direction), without changing the arm's alignment relative to the string. This movement will raise them slightly superior to the plane of the string and increase flexion at the MCP joint but without affecting the position of the hand relative to the strings in the vertical axis. Or 2: by shifting the arm upwardly, which will also extend the PIP joint without necessarily causing flexion at the MCP joint.

These two approaches are sometimes known as the Open- and Closed-Hand positions, respectively (Glise 1997, 26). In either case, the difference in the stroke type depends on the change in the flexion angle of the PIP joint, more pronounced in free stroke, less in rest stroke.

The initial alignment of the MCP joint relative to the string to be plucked is an important consideration as well. Some authors recommend a lower alignment, closer to the horizontal string plane (Duncan, The Art of Classical Guitar Playing 1980, 37ff.), while others advise it be higher (Shearer, Learning the Classic Guitar 1990, 1:56-57).

In either case, in free stroke the angle of flexion at the PIP joint should remain the same or become more pronounced, lest the stroke-type becomes a rest stroke or brushes through the adjacent string.

Phase Two: Pressure

Pressure is the action of pushing on the string. This is a continuation against string resistance of the same intrinsic (primarily lumbrical) activity responsible for placing, through which the degree of string displacement prior to the pluck (hence, the dynamic level,) can be controlled with great precision. The duration of this phase, of course, depends in great part on the tempo requirements of the passage, but is also influenced by the initial alignment of the MCP joint.

The open hand approach tends to prolong the 'pushing down' phase (more accurately, 'pushing in') before the stroke is completed, almost as a triggering release, while in the second (the closed-hand) the IP flexion starts earlier and the release phase feels more like a scratching movement through the string (Shearer, Learning the Classic Guitar, 1:55, Glise 1997, 47ff.).

As an aside, in his excellent book on guitar pedagogy Mr. Glise describes the 'scratching' movement as being a 'knuckle movement' throughout. In fact, his 'scratching exercise' (pp. 50-51) seems to be the combination of two different movements: the finger begins the scratching with the long flexors (otherwise, the IPs would not flex) but, in order to continue contact with the scratched surface (in his description, a table or any flat surface) after PIP reaches its maximum angle of flexion, the intrinsics need to become engaged in order to *extend* the phalanges while the MCP continues to flex, so that the finger does not curl towards the palm and lift from the table, as it would if the PIP were allowed to complete its flexion arc without the interference of the intrinsics.

In summary, the well-trained hand is, indeed, capable to be in a closed-hand attitude one moment and in the open-hand demeanor the next.

Phase Three: Release

The third phase, release, is the outcome of the pluck after the finger escapes from the string. The finger's middle-joint (PIP) flexion seems to be responsible for getting the finger 'through' the string, if arm position is to be maintained.

The degree of DIP joint flexion during the release is, again, a function of the initial MCP joint alignment: almost non-existent in the lower alignment, more pronounced in the higher alignment.

The specific muscular coordination in finger movement is a debated topic not only among guitarists but even among anatomists and other musculoskeletal specialists:

The precise details of lumbrical and interosseous movement and their correlation with the actions of the long flexors and extensors of the digits are still not clear (O'Rahilly 2008, Chapter 10: The Hand).

In particular, the role of the MCP joint in right-hand technique is a topic of substantial confusion and debate among guitar players and teachers.

Nonetheless, based on the known facts, one can safely state the following:

MCP joint flexion may begin in two physiologically distinct ways,
1. As a consequence of extrinsic-flexor contraction only.

As described in Chapter 1, with the finger joints in a normally resting state, unresisted finger flexion and extension can be easily controlled with the extrinsic musculature only. FDP can flex all finger joints: DIP, PIP and MCP. Given the stabilized state of all finger joints, the finger moves as a single entity, rather than as a multi-jointed lever, with the axis of rotation at the knuckle joint. However, upon arriving at the point of contact with the string, the resistance of the latter is too big to be overcome by this mode of finger flexion, and the proximal IP joint needs to flex in order for the movement to displace the string. The action of plucking, itself, cannot be completed otherwise. This points toward an engagement of FDS as well as FDP.

2. As a consequence of intrinsic involvement.

This movement (what is usually understood as 'moving or pushing from the knuckle') produces *extension* of the phalanges as well as flexion at the knuckle joint, as it is driven by lumbrical contraction. When phalangeal extension reaches its limit, the MCP joint stops flexing. Therefore the finger cannot get through and release the string by continued lumbrical involvement only, as there is no possibility to move the finger further.

Against string resistance, at this point the interossei may continue flexing the MCP joint further while lumbricals maintain the IP extension, *but the flexion trajectory would unavoidably take the finger to rest on the adjacent string*, given the degree of IP extension.

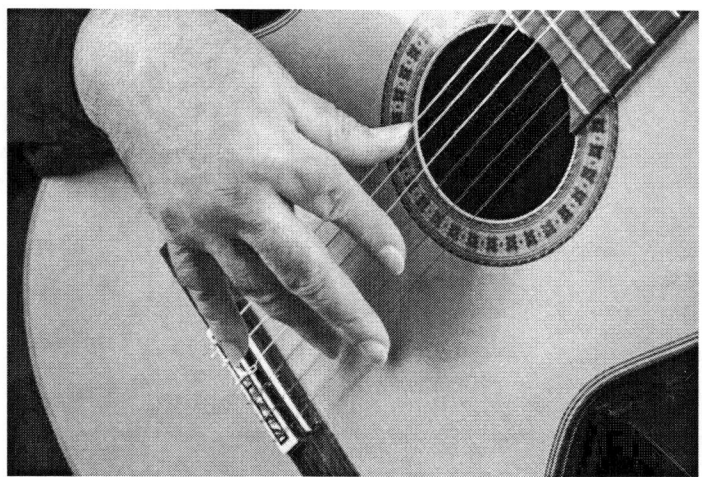 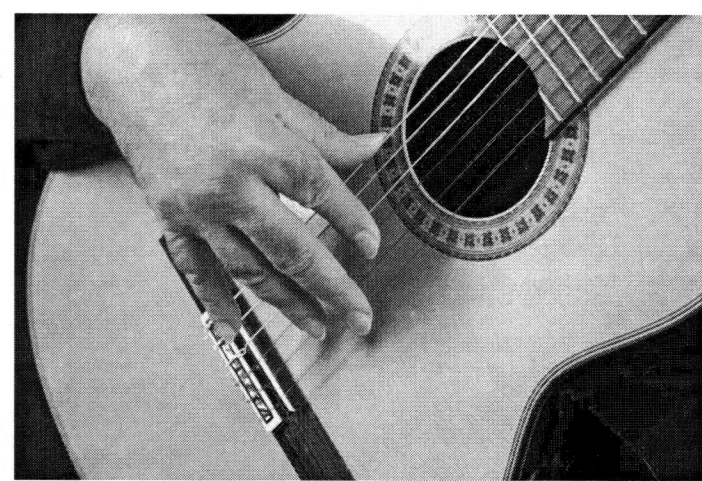

Photo 2-3.   **Photo 2-4. Photos by Wayne Armstrong**

Photos 2-3 and 2-4 show this stroke. Note the high alignment of the hand: the lower the alignment, the closer the MCP joint would be taken to its range-of-motion limit for flexion, eliminating the possibility for further interossei activity.

In fact, even in this highly unusual and cumbersome attitude of finger extension, the player would need to overcome the strong tendency to finish the rest stroke with PIP flexion, rather than continued and exclusive MCP flexion.

Engagement of both extrinsic flexors and the interossei happens only in very forceful flexion, with the interossei acting *after* the extrinsics have contracted maximally (taking the fingers to a fist-like attitude). The interossei, again, can continue the MCP joint flexion to increase the gripping force (as when one tightens the fist to the point that it leaves nail marks on the palm). Of course, this movement is inapplicable to guitar playing.

Given these facts, it seems that in order for the release phase of the free stroke to take place, one of two things need to happen: either the PIP flexes, a function of FDS contraction, or a hand- or arm-supported stroke takes place, by which the straightened and stabilized finger is moved across the string by some type of arm movement discussed later on in this chapter. Absent PIP flexion, or an arm movement, it appears to be mechanically impossible for the finger to release the string through continued movement from the knuckle (MCP) joint exclusively, without changing stroke type, and even this falls somewhat beyond what would be considered normal functional finger behavior on the guitar.

It seems to be an inaccurate description of what really happens in free stroke playing.

It is characteristic in lower hand alignment of the open-hand variety, with a pronounced initial MCP joint flexion, to see the finger follow-through produce a more or less flexed PIP joint but an extended DIP joint.

Although the actual coordination is hard to pinpoint at sight, this seems to be caused because the FDP tendon, responsible for DIP joint flexion, is slackened by the action of the lumbricals during the MCP joint flexion in the preparation and pressure stages of the stroke, thus liberating the distal IP joint from the influence of FDP.

FDS, flexor of the PIP joint but not of the DIP, is, then, responsible for completing the stroke by lightly flexing the PIP joint. The DIP joint remains unaffected. This is an instance of what the great anatomist J. M. F. (Johann Matthijs Frederik) Landsmeer (1919 – 1999) described as the 'phenomenon of the loosened distal phalanx' (Landsmeer, The Coordination of Finger-Joint Motions 1963).

It should be noted that it is also possible for the player, unawares, to engage the intrinsics anew, during the follow-through, producing further MCP flexion and IP extension. This may be misinterpreted as meaning that the release phase of the stroke was the consequence of continued intrinsic involvement ('moving from the knuckle'), when, in fact, this happens right *after* the release phase.

In a higher alignment (closed-hand), with a less pronounced 'pressure' phase of the stroke, thus an early engagement of the long flexors, the flexion of both IP joints would be more pronounced than the flexion at the MCP at the end of the follow-through.

This indicates an involvement of the FDP. Here, again, the player may also unintentionally prolong the follow-through by engaging the intrinsics as described above, *after the release*, thus producing a proprioceptive sensation that could lead to an inaccurate identification of the exact muscular engagement involved in the release phase of the stroke.

A factor of importance may alter the functional behavior of the muscular engagements described above: the finger's approach to the stroke may be more or less 'pointed' towards the nail. Simply stated, the more the pluck is a nail stroke, the more the tip joint will flex (FDP involvement); if the stroke is more 'padded' (more of a flesh/nail approach), the movement will be middle-joint driven (FDS engagement).

Each approach brings with it technical and esthetic consequences whose exploration will bring heightened awareness of some of the uncounted possibilities that can become part of the catalogue of artistic resources available to the expert hand.

Phase four: Recovery

Contrary to what would happen in normal finger extension away from the guitar, the recovery phase *starts* with ED extending the MCP joint, *followed* by lumbrical activity to lightly extend the still flexed IP joints, as MCP flexes, thus starting a new preparation phase (the phalangeal extension coincides with relaxation of the ED contraction, thus allowing for the MCP joint flexion).

In other words, the recovery phase involves the passive and very slight clawing of the hand that occurs whenever the MCP joint is extended by the ED without any involvement of the intrinsics, a movement form described in Chapter 1.

The passive pull of the FDP keeps the IP joints flexed throughout the brief extension movement of the MCP joint.

In day-to-day, normal finger extension movement, the reverse sequence occurs: initial phalangeal extension (intrinsic involvement varies according to degree of MCP joint flexion), followed by MCP joint extension (due to ED contraction). On the guitar, this sequence would make the finger strike the vibrating string with the back of the nail, since it just retraces in reverse its arc trajectory when executing the pluck.

In fact, this is what the finger does in downward strokes in rasgueado technique.

Some Clarifications about the Role of the FDP

This muscle acts on the distal joints of the four fingers simultaneously, although flexion of the index DIP joint does not affect the other fingers in any major way because its *profundus* tendon branch is partially separated, and therefore independent, from the other three tendons. By the same token, full phalangeal flexion of the other fingers does not affect the index to the same degree.

However, middle and ring fingers' FDP tendons are closely bundled, so these fingers show a more or less marked parallelism in flexion movements whenever the FDP is engaged (that is, whenever the DIP joint is flexed), particularly the ring finger, which is quite constrained on both sides.

Whenever finger independence needs to be enhanced, for instance, in alternation between *m* and *a*, the more 'padded' stroke described above (more pronounced in *a* than in *m*), that is, a 'brushing' stroke led by FDS instead of FDP, might be useful, since the flexion of the distal joint through the FDP involvement would impede their full independent motility.

The distinguished piano pedagogue Dorothy Taubmann (1917 – 2013) discussed the issue of 'flat' versus 'curled' fingers in piano playing in various publications and forums through which she described her path-breaking approach to piano playing (the Taubmann Approach. A good summary can be found at wellbalancedpianist.com/bptaubmann.htm. Accessed July 30, 2013).

Although the key-stroke on the piano is percussive and not a pluck, the basic concept still applies: curled fingers move with more difficulty than lightly curved fingers, as the reader can easily verify by trying alternating movements between *m* and *a* with and without flexion at the DIP (Taubman 1988).

This is an important consideration in determining right-hand positional placement, since more extended fingers require to be aligned carefully in order not to accidentally engage adjacent strings in free stroke mode, as shall be explained in detail in the next section. In any case, the differentiation of flexion function between the index and the other fingers has very important implications for the theory of positional framing proposed later on in this book.

Rest Stroke

In rest stroke mode, phase one (preparation) is implemented as in free stroke but with less flexion of the PIP joint. While in the free stroke this joint aligns perpendicularly to or even below the string plane, in the rest stroke it aligns above the string plane, more diagonally (antero-superior), on the extension side of its mid-range, in Shearer's terminology. The degree of extension in the joint may vary greatly, depending on the player's particular 'school' of playing (open- vs. closed-hand). It also varies in relation to finger reach: by necessity the middle finger will flex more than the index or ring fingers.

Assuming an initial placement of the finger on string x and in free stroke alignment, if the next stroke is a rest stroke to be executed on a string inferior (higher in pitch) to this string, the difference in the PIP joint angle of flexion between free- and rest stroke is achieved by extension of the IP joints, without any shifting of the arm position. In the next section of this chapter, dealing with a positional framing theory of fingerwork for the right hand, we will see how this finger behavior serves as the foundation for the 'mixed stroke framing' approach there described.

To change the stroke type on the same string without moving the position of the arm, two approaches may be identified for the short-arm alignment: the player 'pushes up' from the contact point of the finger on the string (Glise 1997, 29), moving the hand frontally, increasing the MCP joint flexion and the PIP extension, allowing the wrist slightly to extend (dorsal flexion) passively. Or, if the wrist remains fixed, the MCP joint flexion and IP joint extension will cause the forearm to 'lift' ever-so-slightly, the result of passive adduction of the upper arm.

The difference between these two behaviors can be easily discerned by either letting the thumb slide on its string or not: in the first instance, the arm will lift; with the thumb anchored at its point of contact, the wrist will extend.

For some players, with particularly flexible IP joints, the 'push' would allow the distal joint to slightly hyperextend, which would permit the execution of the rest stroke without noticeable change in hand or arm demeanor. This is the 'perpendicular' rest stroke referred to earlier, not uncommon among flamenco players.

Changing stroke type on the same string can also be accomplished by having the forearm pronate as the elbow minimally flexes thus causing the finger phalanges to achieve the necessary extension for the rest stroke, but without pronounced MCP joint flexion. (In short-arm position, the upper arm may slightly adduct from the point of support, if needed. Long-arm players will pronate and flex the elbow more markedly, with more or less ulnar deviation of the wrist, but no upper-arm adduction will happen.) Or the upper arm may extend horizontally, achieving the same result, but without the possible arm adduction that may happen in the first instance. In this case, the weight of the forearm segment posterior to the support point is not released, an action that requires continued isometric engagement of the upper-arm abductors, deltoids and supraspinatus. Both short- and long-arm players may do this.

In either of these movement choreographies involving arm shifting, the resulting finger extension is *passive*, as it happens when the arm changes positional attitudes through active engagement of the arm's musculature, by pivoting on the fingers resting on the strings. In contrast, with no arm movement, it is *active*, as it is the outcome of the engagement of the intrinsic musculature of the fingers, MCP flexors and IP extensors, while the arm responds passively.

Phase three (release) brings the finger tip to rest on the adjacent lower string, since the path of the stroke once released from phase two, given the initial flexion angle of the PIP joint, will not allow this string to be cleared, as in the free stroke. As is the case in the free stroke, the level of DIP joint extension is variable, depending on whether the stroke is nail-oriented or pad-oriented, although in rest stroke the latter is a more natural behavior.

However, for beginners with extremely flexible joints, this last approach may have to be managed carefully, allowing some involvement of the FDP to overcome the tendency of the tip joint to collapse in hyperextension as a result of the string resistance, until the player's technical know-how allows him to manage well this advanced technical procedure. Especially with younger players this is a matter of some concern.

For more experienced players, nonetheless, the 'collapsed tip' stroke can be used profitably for special nuancing of the attack on the string, in melodic, *cantabile* playing.

As mentioned before, in players who flex considerably the PIP joint in fast scalar playing, the DIP joint 'gives' somewhat to the string resistance, particularly in the middle finger. If the FDP resists the string, the finger will get 'stuck'.

The more pronounced the PIP flexion, the more resistance from the string is produced, and the more natural a free stroke would feel. That is why the more perpendicular *picado* rest stroke is difficult to master, as it requires stronger contraction of the FDS, a more powerful but less agile muscular engagement than the one occurring with a more moderately flexed initial finger alignment, which imposes less of a load to the extrinsic flexor mechanism.

On the other end of the spectrum, and as was described earlier, in the rest stroke there is the possibility, extreme but real, to release the string from a fully extended finger attitude, that is, a real MCP joint stroke, by the continued activity of the interossei once the lumbricals have completed the IP extension.

This is possible thanks to the smaller trajectory of the rest stroke once released from the string into contact with the adjacent string. Because of the finger-length factor, it is easier to achieve in the ring finger and almost impossible (unless the player adopts an extreme hand position requiring excessive wrist flexion) in the middle finger. But, as already mentioned, this type of stroke would have very limited application in the normal course of guitar performance.

In rest stroke mode, the recovery phase is, again, slightly different than in the free stroke, but only as a matter of degree, not of process: given the initial angle of flexion, the finger in fact curls just a little upon recovery, a mechanism that is, indeed, the same as in the free stroke (active extension of MCP joint, passive flexion of IPs), but within a shorter range of motion, so that it would seem to the casual observer that the finger just goes in and out of the string straightened. Were this to happen, though, the finger would unavoidably strike the string on the back swing. Some passive 'clawing', so minuscule as to be imperceptible to the casual observer, is always present.

The 'Unprepared' Free Stroke

Frequently in the course of playing, fingerwork, either by necessity or by willful decision, consists of plucking the string without anticipatory contact preparation of the alternating finger. For instance, a speedy passage of notes on the same string may give the impression of freely swinging, alternating strokes between the fingers involved.

The transition between phase one (preparation) and phase two (pressure) in the 'normal' stroke is, in fact, the key issue: in the 'unprepared' stroke, also named by Shearer the 'continuity' stroke (Shearer 1990, 1:41, 53, et al.), the hovering pointing motion (phase 1) does culminate in string contact (placing), but, since it is not placed ahead of time, it is followed, without establishing a real pressure phase (phase 2), by the release phase, the final swing-through pluck energized by the extrinsic flexors.

The 'unprepared' stroke is, more accurately, an 'unpressured' stroke. This means active MCP joint flexion simultaneous with IP joint extension in phase one, getting the finger-tip to its string, followed by IP joint flexion to pluck the string without further engagement of the MCP joint, except by its passive follow-through flexion at the outset of the stroke.

Although the whole action may seem, to the untrained eye, as a single action, it is, in fact, a complex coordination of different digital joint movements, beginning with a controlled-tension movement, in the approach to the string, and ending with a ballistic movement, as the plucking motion swings through.

The possibility of antagonistically opposing the momentum of the ballistic follow-through, of course, exists and has, in fact, been recommended as the proper way to return the finger to an attitude of readiness by some authors (Carlevaro 1984, Biberian 2012). This matter will be discussed at some length later.

The placed or planted stroke by necessity has a pressure phase before releasing the string, since the finger sits on the string for a time before initiating its plucking action, unless the player momentarily lifts it before plucking, which is another possibility. The 'prepared' (contact) stroke, although also ending in a ballistic movement at the follow-through, is more of a controlled-tension movement at the *onset* of the plucking motion.

Role of the Extensors

As pointed out by some authors, the under-training of the extensor musculature is one of the main causes of technical deficiency in the classical guitarist's right hand since the recovery phase in fingerwork is the key to developing speed in finger alternation:

> ...why is it that flamenco players in general have so much faster articulation than their classical counterparts?...It occurred to me some time ago that right-hand finger reflexes and general speed of articulation can be much improved by carefully practising [sic] outward movements of the fingers...". (Crosskey 1990, 48)

In contrast with their flamenco counterparts, who train early and persistently in extensor-intensive fingerwork, like rasgueados, classical guitarists focus for the most part in flexor-intensive techniques, not always aware that the main factor in the development of speed and power is how well-conditioned the mechanism responsible for the recovery phase of the fingerwork, the extensor mechanism, is, from a gymnastic stand-point.

In this context, it is important to recall that the finger extensor mechanism includes an extrinsic component (the long extensors in the forearm) acting on the MCP joint, and the intrinsics, primarily the lumbricals, phalangeal extensors. Their well-developed coordinated response is fundamental to achieving high levels of speed and power in fingerwork.

The Role of Forearm Rotation and Upper-Arm Motility

As pianists discovered relatively early (Matthay 1947 (rev 1997), Ortmann 1929), forearm rotatory exertions and relaxations are ever-present in good piano playing. This is equally true of good guitar playing. The proper management of these pronatory or supinatory stresses is fundamental to every aspect of right-hand technique (and, as discussed in Chapter 3, the left hand's).

The physiomechanics of forearm rotation rely on the primary activity of the two pronators (teres and quadratus) and the supinator. Pronators move the radius over the ulna, making the hand move palm down, and the supinator moves the radius back, making the hand face up. In guitar (plucking hand) or piano playing, of course, there is never opportunity for full supination (palm up), but only refined management of rotation toward one or the other attitude from the intermediate or neutral position (as when the arm lies passively by the body), in support of fingerwork and/or shifting movements.

In the context of stroke type, rotatory stresses are invaluable for achieving smooth, seamless transitions among the positional framing attitudes (free stroke, mixed stroke and rest stroke) that will be the focus of Section 2 of this chapter. In addition, within the same positional frame slight rotation movements, accompanying elbow flexion/ extension and other upper-arm movements, are sometimes indispensable to achieve perfect control of fingerwork, as well as providing the necessary fluidity to the hand's ever-changing positional framing attitudes.

Although for purposes of precise description the present narrative has frequently denuded the processes involved in general digital movement and fingerwork, dissociating them from the upper-limb joint mobility, in actual application great technique is characterized not by static and isolated digitation, but by malleable, always flexible and well-coordinated interaction among all the limb joints, from the shoulder to the last IP joint.

Limb-Supported Strokes

A rich resource available to the player is the use of the whole limb, or segments thereof, as the source of energy for the striking (plucking) of the string, whether in free—or rest stroke mode. This means that digital action, originating at the MCP joint and through the phalanges, is replaced by wrist, elbow or even shoulder movement, while the digital joints are kept stabilized.

The concept, in its traditional empirical application, was for a long time associated with the 'sliding' rest stroke used by Segovia and many of his followers: maintaining a finger fixed on the string, the stroke is executed by forearm rotation toward supination, accompanied by radial wrist abduction (radial deviation). This stroke minimizes the percussive attack on the string and produces warmth in the tone. Exceptionally, it may be done by upper-arm horizontal flexion, accompanied by elbow extension, making the finger slide along the string in a diagonal trajectory that eventually leads to the string being released on the medial side of the nail. This is a 'noisy' approach, even on the unwound strings.

Still with the finger in fixation of all its joints, the stroke can be achieved by flexion of the elbow, carrying the finger across the string (the stroke can be continued through several strings, becoming then a right-hand sliding downward arpeggio.) The reverse action, with the fixed thumb (or a finger resting on the dorsal side of the nail) as agent, is achieved by elbow extension. Both actions can be also executed by upper-arm horizontal extension and flexion, respectively.

The late Uruguayan guitarist and pedagogue Abel Carlevaro (1916 – 2001) systematized this and other limb-supported stroke possibilities (*toques*) through his theory of joint fixation (*fijación*) (Carlevaro 1984), which, simply stated, is the transfer of muscular engagement from smaller to larger muscular groups, providing thus many nuances to sound production on the instrument. A *toque* can in principle be executed by the digit (phalangeal and/or big-knuckle flexion), the whole hand (flexion/deviation at the wrist), the forearm (rotation and/or flexion at the elbow) or the upper arm (transversal extension at the shoulder). Of course, each of these movements requires fixation (stabilization is a better term, since fixation implies a level of static tension that is not really necessary in most cases) of all the joints between the active one and the distal end of the finger.

REVIEW

Summary of the Physiomechanics of Finger Stroke Types

- Succinctly put and in very general terms, one can perceive the (placed) free stroke as either a scratching movement of the finger, led by the IP (long) flexors, or as a pushing-in movement, led by the MCP (intrinsic) flexors, the latter similar, in its initial phase, to the rest stroke, but different in its outcome, given the difference in the initial alignment of the knuckle and middle-finger joints.

- The (placed) rest stroke, through its trajectory, normally feels more like a sweeping or brushing motion across the string, involving, mainly, the two distal segments only (PIP flexion and full DIP extension) or, in speedier playing, all three finger joints. The player may, however, point the finger more towards the nail, thus changing somewhat the brushing sensation into more of a scraping feel.

- In terms of the four phases of either stroke-type, the following sequence may help as a simplistic but useful guide:

For the placed strokes:
1. Finger pointing culminating in string contact (preparation: IP extension, MCP flexion; primary movers: lumbricals);
2. Pressure (finger push; continued MCP flexion with IP's extended; lumbricals and interossei);
3. Scratch or Brush (IP and/or MCP flexion; extrinsic flexors, with more or less interossei support; lumbricals remain inactive but their presence provides necessary 'stiffness' factor to maintain IP joint stability);
4. Curl (MCP extension; passive IP flexion; primary movers: ED, EI; passive pull of long flexors)

For the hovering, continuity strokes:
1. Finger pointing (lumbricals) culminating in contact
2. Pressure phase missing
3. Scratch or brush (extrinsic/interossei)
4. Curl (extensors)

These images may provide proprioceptive models to achieve coordination, in an intuitive way, in the various phases of joint motion along the length of the finger.

- The following table shows the application of different finger joint behaviors to right-hand fingerwork. Digital abduction/adduction is not accounted for, although they always accompany movements of extension/flexion, respectively. Limb-supported strokes are not considered:

Muscular Activity	Resulting Joint Movement	R. H. Fingerwork
'Pure' common extensor	Active MCP extension and passive IP flexion	Recovery (fourth) phase of stroke ('curl')
Combined action of the common extensor with intrinsics	Full-finger active extension.	When intrinsics precede ED, it's the normal finger extension movement, basis of the downward *rasgueado* stroke.
'Pure' hand intrinsics (primarily lumbricals)	Active IP joint extension and passive MCP flexion.	Preparation (first) phase of stroke ('point'). Present but incomplete in non-placed stroke.
'Pure' intrinsics (primarily interossei)	Active MCP flexion with maintained IP extension	Pressure (second) phase of placed stroke. Absent in continuity (non-prepared) stroke.
Combined action of both long flexors with intrinsics (the interossei only, lumbricals are not involved or else the DIP would not flex)	Full-finger active flexion (gripping movement. Has different gradations, from the hook or briefcase grip to the fist or strong grip)	The third phase of the stroke ('scratching' free stroke.) If hovering, it's the 'swinging' stroke.
Combined action of intrinsics (interossei) with FDS	Active flexion at MCP and at PIP, but no flexion at DIP	Third phase of stroke (the 'sweeping' or 'brushing' stroke, with more or less initial MCP and/or PIP flexion - more in free stroke, less in rest stroke.) Basis of upward *rasgueado* stroke.
Combined action of ED and long flexors (FDP mainly)	Active MCP extension, active IP flexion (active 'claw' hand).	Exceptional in the course of normal guitar technique, because of the active antagonist involvement, may be used for special, brittle and 'naily' tone colors

Role of the Thumb

Given its particular anatomy, the relationship between extension/flexion and stroke-type, so clear for the fingers (flexion = free stroke, extension = rest stroke), is much more malleable for the thumb. It can bypass the rest stroke, even when extended, by incorporating more palmar adduction to the regular flexion movement. Nonetheless, past a certain limit, the rest stroke is the natural stroke for the thumb extension as well. This relationship is particularly evident with the thumb's flesh stroke, which is, physiomechanically, the normative behavior of the digit on the strings, as it requires the least amount of adjustments. Artistically, however, the nail stroke is fundamental, since the requirements for a broad palette of dynamic levels and tone colors could not be fulfilled otherwise. The discussion below, therefore, focuses on the use of the thumb nail.

Furthermore, the thumb nail is supposed to be of such length and shape as to allow unimpeded execution of the rest stroke. This is a fairly common problem affecting many players who, because of the way they managed their nail, abandon the use of the thumb rest stroke altogether. It is unwise to condition one's technique to one's nails, rather than the reverse, unless nature determines otherwise.

Since in the resting position, off the strings, the thumb lies naturally abducted in relation to the palm, its flexion from that position would take it across the latter. The rest stroke trajectory is more aligned with the resting position and, hence, requires less or no adduction. In order to approach the radial side of the index, though, assuming a passive index, it needs to adduct as well as flex. This is what happens in the usual thumb free stroke on the guitar.

This becomes more and more necessary as the requirement for speed in its movements increases, since fast recovery from the rest stroke to start a new stroke cycle is, generally speaking, more cumbersome than from the free stroke. This is so because while in the free stroke the flexion/adduction movement moves the thumb dorsally and away from the plane of the strings, thus avoiding a back-stroke on the string during the recovery movement, which is a simple extension, in the rest stroke (flexion movement without adduction) this is not the case and in the recovery the digit would need to adduct before extending, in order not to hit the string with its backside.

Dynamic levels, though, have a determining impact: in *forte* playing, the rest stroke can still be functionally more advisable than the free stroke when the thumb is extended. In these cases, the role of forearm rotational stresses is particularly important. Any good Flamenco player doing thumb *falsetas* will demonstrate this relationship.

Another important consideration is whether the thumb needs to pluck the adjacent string immediately after plucking the previous string, in which case the rest stroke would make things simpler, as it would then be a single 'sliding' stroke through the two strings, rather than two distinct strokes. The sliding stroke requires that the thumb remain abducted throughout the flexion movement, as well as requiring appropriate positional alignment (as discussed in the next section).

In summary, placing of the thumb from a previous rest stroke involves a preliminary movement of palmar adduction (bringing the thumb further out from the plane of the strings, thus avoiding a back-stroke), followed by extension to reach the string and palmar abduction to contact it. The thumb draws an elliptical rather than a circular arc, which may be shallower or more pronounced, depending on whether the thumb is articulating a flesh or a nail stroke.

From a previous free stroke, placing is simpler and would involve only extension and abduction, as the adduction movement needed to clear the backwards trajectory was incorporated in the release phase of the previous stroke.

An important *caveat*: the preceding discussion assumes thumb movement from the CMC joint, that is, movement of the whole digit as a unit articulated from the basal joint. The stroke-type/flexion-extension relationship changes drastically if the thumb stroke is executed by the IP joint flexion alone, with fixed MCP and CMC joints. In this type of stroke the thumb will be able to play a free stroke no matter how separated (extended) it is from the index, but the rest stroke will be more cumbersome to achieve. In this case the placing phase of the stroke will require less initial adduction, therefore less final abduction to contact the string, and the extensors (short and long) will divide labors, EPB acting isometrically, to keep MCP and CPC extended, and EPL isotonically, to actively extend the IP.

A significant issue in the tip-only stroke is the degree of palmar abduction, usually supported with extra wrist flexion, so that the digit is aligned more perpendicularly to the string, improving the leverage of the IP flexion movement. The rest stroke, though possible, becomes cumbersome if the IP flexion is not accompanied by flexion at the proximal joints as well. The pressure phase is primarily an abduction movement led by the basal joint that pushes the string in (toward the soundboard). This can be achieved in both the whole-digit and the tip-joint stroke-types. In the latter, it is important to realize that were the pressure phase to be implemented by continued tip-joint flexion, the movement would risk 'slapping' the string against the fretboard upon release, as it pulls the string out rather than in.

The release phase in the whole-digit approach is a movement combining flexion of the three joints (the level of flexion at the IP is variable) either with an accompanying palmar adduction, to clear the higher strings in free stroke or, if absent the latter, to rest on or slide through the adjacent string. In the tip-joint stroke, the release is a simple flexion movement of the IP, more natural in free stroke, but possible in rest stroke if positional alignment is properly managed.

A.   B.   C.

Photo 2-5 through 2-7. A: Thumb prepared for full-digit rest stroke on 5th string. B: Thumb resting on 4th string after rest stroke. The thumb position would allow for a free stroke with the flesh, but it would need a slight adjustment to engage the nail (at C.). Photos by Wayne Armstrong.

A.   B.   C.

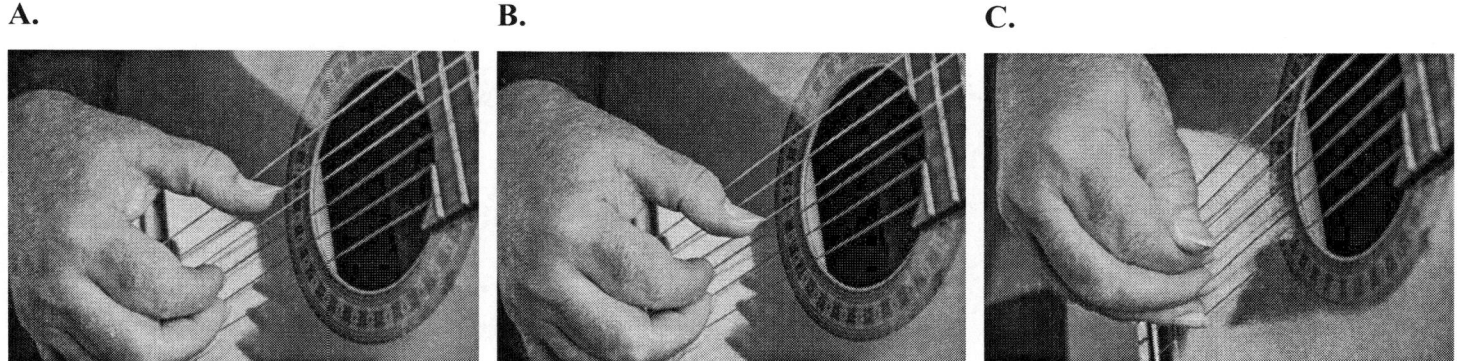

Photo 2-8 through 2-10. A: Thumb prepared for tip-joint rest stroke on 5th string. B: Thumb resting on 4th string after rest stroke. A nail free stroke is feasible without too much adjustment. C: Thumb resting by index after release. Photos by Wayne Armstrong.

In summary:

1. As with the fingers, the thumb stroke may be led by the IP joint (long) flexor (tip-joint stroke), as in a scratching motion, or by the basal joint flexors, primarily the short flexor and the thumb adductor, the 'pinching' muscle (Rybski 2004, 109), as in a sweep (whole-digit stroke). Normally, and within the boundaries established by the hand position, these two approaches would result in a free stroke and a rest stroke, respectively.

2. Other factors, like wrist alignment and the individual variable mobility of the thumb joints, influence the outcome, particularly in the latter instance, where the full-digit sweep can with relative ease produce a free stroke if accompanied by appropriate adjustments in the trajectory of the sweep through the timely application of palmar adduction. If playing a single string, this will cause the thumb to end its stroke by the radial side of the proximal index phalanx (as when making a cross with the index, see photo 2-10 above), rather than on the adjacent string as in the rest stroke. If sweeping through several strings, the thumb can still end the sweep in a free stroke mode if the adduction movement is delayed until the release phase of the stroke on the last string of the sweep-span.

81

3. Needless to say, the tip-joint-led rest stroke is also feasible (see photo 2-8 above), with proper adjustments to the initial thumb demeanor (more extension at the CMC and MCP joints and more flexion at the IP joint than in the full-digit stroke).

Thumb Dampening

A special role of the thumb is as a damper, controlling durational values in the bass strings and stopping undesired sympathetic resonances.

1. The most common approach to the technique is by way of returning the thumb to the string previously plucked at the musically appropriate time, normally immediately after the next bass-note has been plucked. The mechanism of this movement is the same as the placing phase of the normal thumb stroke.

2. A special dampening technique involves the radial side of the thumb and is most frequently, though not exclusively, used in situations where the string to be dampened lies adjacent to the string the thumb needs to pluck next. In this case, the dampening happens slightly ahead of the sounding of the next bass-note. The following description applies to the thumb's nail stroke only. The dampening on the side with a flesh stroke is much less convoluted.

> The thumb extends further than necessary for the simple placing movement (angling the finger more towards a flesh stroke), and there will usually be a slight flexion of the IP joint at the moment of preparatory contact with the string to be plucked, as this raises the distal phalanx and approximates it to the adjacent lower string that needs to be dampened. This will position the distal phalanx on the string to be plucked mostly on the pad, but in such a way that continued IP flexion, as for a tip-joint stroke, would engage the nail toward its midline and carry it along the string before releasing it, thus producing an undesired scraping noise. Therefore, the release of the string needs to be accomplished either through basal joint flexion/adduction, without further flexing the IP, which will produce a flesh stroke, or with a simultaneous passive extension of the IP, caused by the string resistance to the stroke, allowing the engagement of the nail for the stroke. There usually is movement of inward rotation, as well as (palmar) abduction, to favor even further the engagement of the nail on its radial side. The degree of IP flexion for dampening depends on the angle of wrist flexion: more wrist flexion increases the distance between the basal joint of the thumb and the soundboard. Within limits, increased IP flexion will compensate for the greater separation of the thumb and still achieve thumb contact with the lower string, but in some cases the wrist flexion will be such that the only thumb dampening possibility will be returning the thumb to the vibrating string (as described in 1. above).

 Section 2. A Positional Framing Approach to Right-Hand Fingerwork

This section attempts to give name to some of those 'intuitions' and insights mentioned at the beginning of the chapter by considering a topic that, though infrequently discussed in the didactic literature for the guitar, is relevant to every single action executed with the right hand, whether trained intuitively or through years of rigorous academic methodology: the relationship between right-hand positional placement (what is called *framing* in this text), and fingerwork. It proposes a descriptive method for analyzing the latter, based on a positional or mapping schema analogous to that used for the left hand. An example will provide a tangible introduction to the issue and why a theory of positional placement for the right hand might be of benefit:

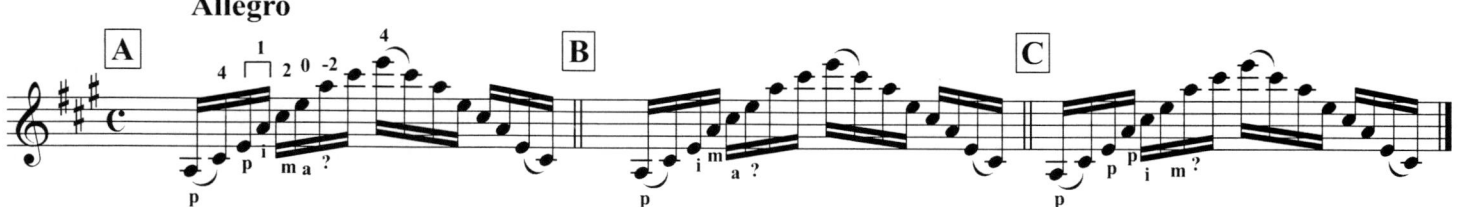

Example 2-1. Heitor Villa-Lobos: Estudo No. 2 (Villa-Lobos 1953)

The example, taken from one of the most demanding etudes in the repertoire, presents three possibilities for right-hand fingering of the first five or six notes, and leaves open the question of how to proceed henceforth. Without getting into an in-depth analysis of the alternatives, premature at this point in our discussion, suffice it to say that any right-hand fingering decision taken by the performer will perforce involve mobility to and fro different right-hand placements on the strings, a demand presented by the heterogeneous nature of the arpeggiated texture.

The question, thus, is how to best group the notes within an arpeggio span so that the transition to the ensuing arpeggio is executed with utmost precision, clarity and flow. Each of the fingering possibilities notated in the example can be seen as presenting a different *positional framing* approach, which determines not only a logical grouping of strings and notes encompassed within the 'frame', but also how the continuation of the ascending arpeggio would best be fingered, and how to achieve logical continuity with subsequent arpeggios. The first obstacle to this type of analysis is the lack of a commonly accepted nomenclature for discussing right-hand positional placements, although a basic vocabulary may be established fairly easily by finding an analogical equivalent to left-hand terminology. A common-sense approach to this issue is attempted in the next section.

The second is the apparent obscurity and density of the physiomechanics and functional anatomy of the right-hand playing apparatus, topics deemed to be of specialized interest only to practitioners of the healing arts. However, as stated in the Preface, this knowledge becomes more and more relevant to teachers and players to increase understanding of the all-important *pre-technical* circumstances that condition the behavior of our hand during playing activity, and how the leverage conditions ensuing from the player's overall approach to arm/hand position affect the muscular involvement during the act of playing. Not only effective but healthy technique depends on the proper understanding of these relationships.

The preceding sections of this book have dealt in detail with these issues. They also introduced the nomenclature of anatomical and technical terms and abbreviations used in the main body of this section and the next chapter. More specific nomenclature and symbology, relevant to the topics under discussion, will be presented as they become necessary.

Theory of Positional Framing

Mapping Territories

All instrumentalists playing on a fingerboard face the challenge of accurately aiming for and landing on specific locations from which an area encompassing a certain number of notes can be clearly determined and accessed. Players of both fretted and un-fretted instruments train themselves to mentally 'see' their fingerboards subdivided into positional 'territories' that help guide their left-hand activity. Despite the different dimensions and planes where movement occurs (and the absence of a fingerboard for the right hand), *both* of the guitarist's hands confront this issue. Guitarists must also train their right hand to 'see' positional subdivisions of the total six-string span of the guitar. Of course, the concept applies as well to 8- and 10-string instruments.

All good players resolve this challenge empirically, but not necessarily with a clear theoretical understanding of what it does and why some things 'fall in place' more easily than others. The consideration of these possibilities can be made more systematic and with more conscious awareness if the player has a theoretical framework within which they can be mapped *positionally* in reference to the string span (and group of notes) covered in each case. A positional theory, in other words, would provide a logical foundation to the performer's thinking about effective and efficient right-hand fingering options. This would be analogous to the way left-hand fingering is approached.

Right-Hand 'Positions'

When addressing left-hand positioning on the guitar, the following is universally understood and agreed upon:

1. A position is defined as the span of four contiguous frets.
2. Positions are numbered according to the fret number where finger 1 (index) is placed, or could be placed. The position is established the moment at least one finger is placed on the fingerboard. Hence, there are as many positions as there are frets on the board, plus 3 theoretical positions falling outside the board if the first fret is played by 2, 3 or 4, unless these are considered contractions of the first position.
3. Derived concepts include extended positions, when the fret-span covered between the 'framing' digits, 1 and 4, is greater than four, and contracted positions, when the span is less than four. The technical concepts of positional extension and contraction are not descriptive, per se, of finger joint behavior and should not be confused with the anatomical concepts of extension and flexion.
4. A shift is the movement from one position to another (Chapter 3 proposes a more ample viewpoint concerning left-hand shifting, not relevant for now).

One can easily map these concepts to the right hand. When playing free strokes, and by analogy with the left hand:

1. A right hand position could be defined as the span of four contiguous strings (the basic arpeggio configuration in free stroke).
2. Positions would be numbered according to the string number where *p* (thumb) is placed, or hovers over. The position is established the moment at least one finger is placed on a string. Hence, there are as many positions as there are strings, plus 3 theoretical positions falling outside the string-span if the sixth string is played by *i*, *m* or *a*, unless these are considered contractions of the sixth position.
3. Derived concepts would include extended positions, when the string-span covered between framing digits *p* and *a* is greater than four strings, and contracted positions, when the span is less than four. Again, these concepts are not descriptors of the physiomechanics of digital behavior.
4. A shift would be defined as the movement from one position to another (the reader may want to take an anticipatory look at Chart 2-1, below, showing normal positions in free- and rest- stroke modes).

The approach proposed here may be easily enhanced to include *c*, the little finger. We limit ourselves, however, to the four-finger span in order to keep within the traditional boundaries of right-hand technique for this first exposition of the positional framing theory. Those readers interested in technical training for *c* should consult Charles Postlewate's books (Postlewate, Five Fingers 2001, Postlewate, Homage 2001) and the author's *Kitharologus* (Iznaola, Kithar. 1997).

Positional Framing and its Relationship to Stroke Type

As stated earlier, and as in the case of the left-hand, positions can be defined as normal, extended or contracted. Also as with the left-hand, extension and contraction may occur from either end of the span: in the left hand, 1 or 4 may cause the extension/contraction (as well as the inner fingers). In the right hand we can, then, identify thumb (*p*)-extended or (*p*)-contracted positions, as well as finger (*i*, *m*, *a*)-extended or (*i*, *m*, *a*)-contracted positions ('fingers' refer to the hand digits other than the thumb.)

For those players that limit themselves to the free stroke mode of playing the theory of positional framing presented here will be straightforward and relatively simple. For those that use both stroke-types, it is more complicated. What follows attempts to provide a clear exposition of how the relationship between positional framing and stroke-type would manifest itself in specific, well-defined positional presentations, or frames, of the right hand on the strings.

 Free-Stroke Framing: Anatomical Framing

The Hand at Rest
Anatomists (O'Rahilly, et al. 2008) describe a 'position of rest' of the hand which can be achieved by relaxing the arm and hand on a surface, without exerting any effort. The hand will lie slightly pronated, all fingers adducted, the tips of middle, ring and little finger aligned, the tip of the index protruding slightly, and the thumb close by or touching the index finger, as when pinching lightly.

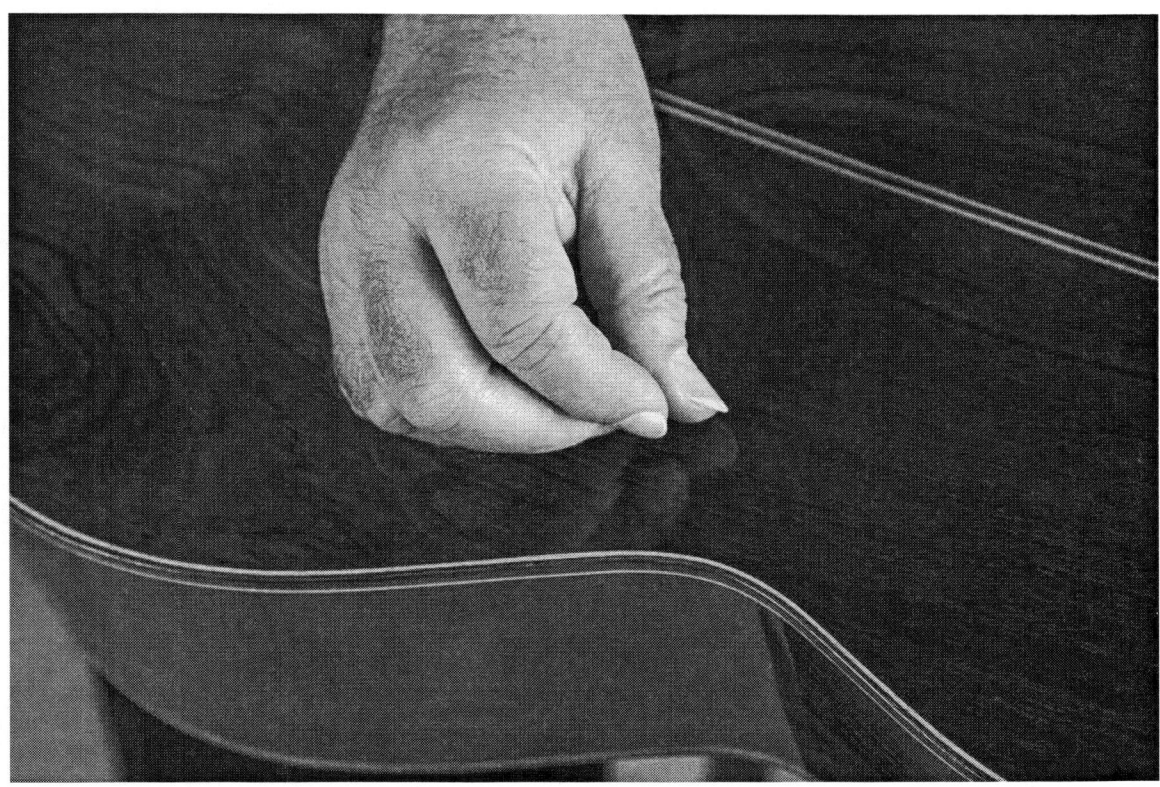

Photo 2-11. Hand-at-rest on back of guitar. Photo by Wayne Armstrong.

We can do this as well on the strings:

Photo 2-12. Hand-at-rest on strings. Photo by Wayne Armstrong.

For some students, an intermediate step may be needed, in which the hand-at-rest on the strings is first achieved with the guitar lying flat on the student's lap, before placing the instrument in playing position, without altering the hand's demeanor.

The hand, when thus positioned passively on the strings, will rest the tips of middle and ring fingers on the same string (that of the index may or may not come to rest on the string, depending on the length of the digit). The thumb and little finger may or may not establish contact with any string, but their tips will also align with the others (the thumb may also fall on the adjacent lower-pitched string). This positional demeanor of the hand is mostly devoid of any muscular effort counteracting the effect of gravity on the hand's digits as they first establish contact with the strings.

Their degree of joint flexion/extension is the result of the anatomical characteristics of each joint, principally through the 'stiffness' factor brought about by the flexor/extensor musculotendonal structure. The resulting hand position is the outcome not of active muscular engagement, but of the functional anatomy of the passive hand.

Pedagogically, it may be a useful tool to introduce students to concepts related to weight release and weight lift, the role of passive (gravitational) vs. active (muscular) resources in guitar playing, the poised limb, etc. In this attitude, though, the digits do not yet encompass a string 'territory' that may serve as a foundational reference for a positional framing approach that would help analyze and differentiate the myriad variations possible to the right-hand's fingerwork.

Keeping the premise of an initial state of passivity as our guiding principle, we can obtain a more applicable approach if, instead of relaxing the hand on a fixed surface, we let it hang freely in the air, with a flexed elbow, from the passively flexed wrist and a pronated forearm.

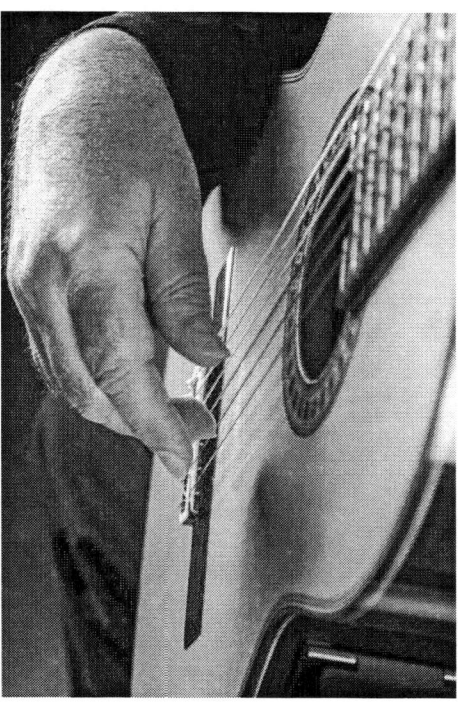

Photo 2-13. Hanging hand (hovering hand-at-rest).

Photo 2-14. Hanging hand establishing initial string contact.
Photos by Wayne Armstrong.

Photo 2-15. From hanging hand on the strings to functional position by weight release through elbow extension.

Photo 2-16. Resulting anatomical frame (on 3rd string).
Photos by Wayne Armstrong.

If positioned without adjustments on the instrument, again we see the tips of middle and ring fingers aligned on the same string, but, most frequently, with the thumb establishing contact two lower strings away. Some players may see the thumb fall three strings away.

The index usually would hover over the same string as its ulnar companions and its MCP joint will be slightly more extended than the other fingers. In some players, it may establish contact with the string.

Without adjustment, the wrist will be excessively flexed and pronated. If we let the weight of the arm 'fall' through elbow extension, making sure the thumb and fingers slide passively on their strings toward the fingerboard, the wrist will passively extend and rotate slightly toward supination, adopting a more functional demeanor, without altering the digits' relationship to their respective strings.

Following Shearer's terminology, in this position the thumb, middle and ring digits are in what he calls their 'optimum position' for joint motion (Shearer, Learning the Classic Guitar 1990, 1:61), and the degree of flexion in their joints is optimal for the free stroke mode.

The index, however, is slightly more extended than would be ideal for a solid, good-sounding free stroke (although it is perfectly situated for a rest stroke). By flexing it slightly it will come to lie on the adjacent string superior to that where middle and ring rest.

This results in what we now identify as the *anatomical or basic positional frame, or, in short, the anatomical frame*, the primary functional demeanor of the right hand on the strings, from which the theory of positional framing develops.

Given the stated possibility for the thumb to align three, rather than two, strings away from the top-most fingers, the anatomical frame can be further described as 'closed' (two strings away) or 'open' (three strings away). This concept, of course, is not related to the open or closed hand positions described elsewhere in the book.

Aaron Shearer, the late eminent American guitar pedagogue, seems to have been the first to identify and incorporate the basic alignment characteristics of the resting hand in guitar methodology, mainly the tip alignment of *m* and *a* on the same string, given the difference in their MCP joint positions on the dorsum of the hand (Shearer 1990, 1:79).

The little finger, *c*, being, normally, the shortest finger and with its knuckle level with or slightly more proximal ('higher', as Shearer describes it) than that of *a*, will hover somewhere in between or over either of the strings where *i* and *m-a* are placed once the basic frame has been achieved, without quite touching either of them. In order to engage *c* in fingerwork, many players (not all) will need to change the wrist alignment through forearm rotation (toward supination) and even slight radial deviation, unless their pinkies are markedly long. We will not deal with these circumstances in this discussion.

It is also useful to see how the anatomical frame may be achieved easily from the previously described hand-at-rest demeanor on the surface of the strings: since the wrist is already in a functional position, all that is needed is to extend the thumb one or two strings away, and flex the index to the adjacent lower string (photos 2-17, 2-18).

However, it is not always easy for students, especially beginners, to learn to relax to the point needed for either of the initial hand-at-rest attitudes to be achieved. The concept of the basic positional frame, nonetheless, can be also taught by guiding the student's hand to place the digits in this configuration, preferably with the instrument lying flat on his or her lap, so that the passive resource of Gravity helps them acquire the appropriate kinesthesia.

After placing the fingers in the anatomical frame position, a very simple but useful 'pre-technical' exercise may be developed by alternately pulling out of the anatomical frame, by 'pushing' on the strings, extending the fingers

Photo 2-17. Thumb extension from hand-at-rest position.

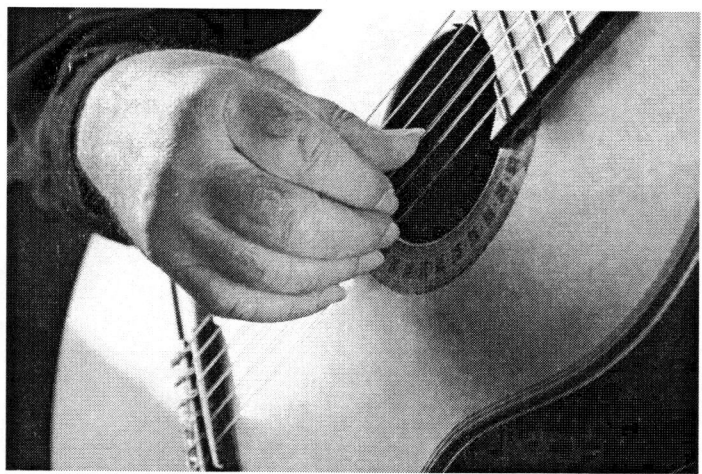

Photo 2-18. Index flexion to adjacent string: the anatomical frame. Photos by Wayne Armstrong

without lifting the tips, and 'squatting' back to it. The thumb, if kept planted, must be allowed to slide on its string, to accommodate the change of hand demeanor. It may, as well, be kept free from contact with any string, lying in a relaxed manner by the index side. This exercise is, in fact, the equivalent of adopting the 'open hand' position discussed earlier, and is a good way for the player to experience and learn to manage the 'lumbrical effect' so important in right-hand technique.

Thus, the player may stop the gradual push of the fingers that 'lift' the hand at any moment and, by fixing the digits' joints and resting the arm weight on the digits, see and feel how various levels of joint flexion and extension work.

In functional terms, the hand goes from a variant of the *hook* or *briefcase* grip, in the anatomical frame, through various gradations of the *precision* or *pinching* grip, when extended.

This silent exercise may help the player enhance her experiential awareness of the relationship between digital flexion/extension and corresponding joint movements in the wrist and arm, of the different sensations of weight release and weight lift, of the relationship between finger flexion/extension and stroke-type, of the relationship between planting and positional placement, and of the role of the thumb and the ring finger as the principal positional 'framing' digits (even in the five-finger technique that incorporates the use of the little finger).

It is also a good experiment to deepen one's understanding of leverage as applied to guitar playing: the behavior of the fingers pushing on the strings, without releasing them, transforms the leverage action to a type 2 form: the axis or fulcrum is now the string, the load or resistance is the weight of the hand, projected at the intermediate IP joint, and the force is the action of the lumbricals, extending this joint, thus the resistance is in between the fulcrum and the force, as in a wheelbarrow. This is what happens, as well, in the traditional push-up or in tiptoeing, one of the few naturally occurring type-2 leverage conditions in the human body.

What Is a 'Positional Frame'?

Given the immense richness of possible combinations and the subtle differences among the positional placements whence digital action emerges, the analysis or mapping of right-hand framing is a complex task. We will attempt to systematize our approach based on the following working conventions. The rather cumbersome system here presented is, hopefully, just the first step toward developing an analytical tool for right-hand technique that could provide valuable insights into the wondrous biomechanical choreography of the well-trained guitarist:

POSITIONAL INDICATOR: THE BRACKETED INTEGER

1. For purposes of analysis of the examples in this section, the technical identification of a position is always given by the thumb placement and is indicated by an integer within vertical brackets that identifies the string where the thumb is placed or over which it hovers: [1], [2], [6], etc. When it is presented without other additional numbers or symbols, it stands for the closed anatomical frame on the string identified by the number.

EXTENSION AND CONTRACTION MARKERS: THE 'PLUS' AND 'MINUS' (+, -) SIGNS

2. 'Plus' and 'minus' symbols to the right of the number in brackets will be used to identify extended and contracted positions, respectively, followed by another integer, in parentheses, denoting the *closed* anatomical frame of *origin* for the position being analyzed. For instance: [5+(4)] would mean *p*-extended frame on 5th string from the anatomical frame on 4th (this is what has been identified as the *open* anatomical frame). [4-(5)]: *p*-contracted frame on 4th string from anatomical frame on 5th; etc. In this case, the first number, with the – or + sign, identifies the position being achieved by extension or contraction of the thumb from the closed anatomical frame, identified by the number in parentheses.

3. Digital contraction and extension are indicated as well by the symbols - and +, respectively, and appear to the right of the fingering letter: **p-**, **i+**, etc. When further detail is deemed to be needed in the analysis, they may become part of the bracketed formula. This is particularly useful to identify mixed and rest stroke frames: [5-(4i+m+a+] would indicate a contracted thumb on 5th string, from the anatomical frame on 4th, and with extensions in the other three digits (which normally would play rest strokes. See below).

REST-STROKE INDICATOR: THE UNDERLINED LETTER

4. Additionally, finger letters will be underlined to indicate a rest stroke: **p**, **a+**, **m-**. For the fingers, but not for the thumb, this indicator is redundant, in principle, when combined with the '+' symbol, but will be used to further clarify the specific finger conditions under analysis, as it is possible for the finger to be engaged in what has been called a 'half-stroke' or the 'recoil' stroke (see examples at the end of the chapter).

PLACING/PLANTING INDICATOR: THE CIRCLED LETTER-NUMBER SET

5. The set of a fingering letter (*p*, *i*, *m*, *a*) accompanied by a string number, both within a circle, indicates a placed or planted finger on that string. The letter may have as well the extension or contraction symbols (- or +) to the right. These symbols may be stacked, so that a full finger plant, for instance, would show a column of three superimposed letter-number sets within circles (see examples, also, in Section 4 below).

HOVERING INDICATOR: THE CIRCLED DASH

6. In contrast, particular moments when no finger is placed on any string and the hand hovers are indicated with a dash within a circle.

POSITIONAL FRAMING SCHEMA: THE OSSIA STAFF

7. Below the main staff of the music being analyzed an *ossia* staff will present a schematic representation of the framing 'choreography' for the passage, indicating the open string frame in play at a given moment by notating with stemless noteheads the open strings where the right hand acts.

8. A notehead in parenthesis above or below a non-parenthesized note indicates where that finger would be sitting (or hovering over) in the anatomical frame of reference for that particular moment.

9. A tie linking two noteheads played by the thumb or any finger shows that the digit has remained aligned with that string (either placed or not) since it first arrived at that position. Occasionally, it is used to show changes of thumb positional alignment accomplished by rest stroke.

10. More detailed analysis of the top fingers' activity may also be notated, as needed, following the same notational protocol described above, but in general the framing schema represented by the stemless noteheads tells the story of what these digits are doing, and where.

11. Finally, horizontal brackets under the small staff play the same role as the positional indicator formulas within vertical brackets under the top staff: they graphically delimit the framing territories in the passage. Both should align vertically.

The fundamental basis for this pragmatic but admittedly rather coarse, incipient notational code is based on the axiomatic principle that, physiomechanically, the position of the arm/hand mechanism is always related to the closed anatomical frame. An example will clarify this:

Example 2-2

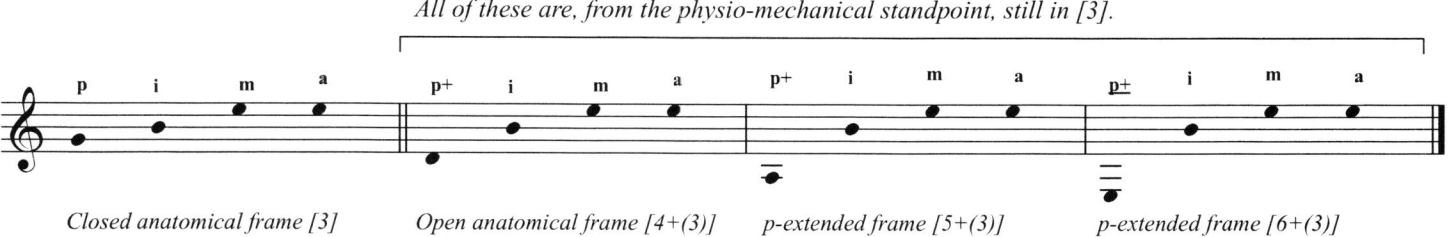

All of these are, from the physio-mechanical standpoint, still in [3].

Closed anatomical frame [3]   *Open anatomical frame [4+(3)]*   *p-extended frame [5+(3)]*   *p-extended frame [6+(3)]*

In the example above, the second measure shows movement of the thumb from its resting position on the 3rd string (as in the first measure) to the 4th, *without an accompanying arm shift.* The resulting position is, thus, indicated as [4+(3)], that is, an *extended* position (accepted, pragmatically but not theoretically, as the 'open' variant of the anatomical frame) that *seems* to be a 4th position but is really the outcome of the thumb's extension from the *real* frame on [3]. Likewise for the last two measures, showing extensions to the 5th and 6th strings respectively. Obviously, it would be a bit baffling to call a hand position that has the thumb on the sixth string as being a 'third position.' Nonetheless, the awareness that it is an extension of the anatomical frame in [3] is indispensable for the proper application of the theory.

Track 2-2   *Free-Stroke Framing: Technical Framing*

From the anatomical frame, the technical frames are achieved by active flexion or extension of the digits. Thus, the frame for *i-m* scales (free stroke) may be achieved either by flexing *m* to rest on the same string as *i* or by extending *i* to reach the string where *m* sits. It is assumed that the arm will NOT move, in either case. However, in the latter case *i* would be jeopardized in producing a clean free stroke, because of the increased extension at its middle joint, which puts the finger at risk of contacting the adjacent lower string by accident. Clearing of the adjacent lower string, in that case, can only be achieved by a 'bicycling' stroke, in which the passive follow-through flexion at the big knuckle (MCP) joint has to be substituted by an active knuckle extension in phase three of the stroke, the plucking phase, occurring simultaneously with flexion of the IP joints. However, we will later describe what could be termed the 'half-stroke' or the 'recoil' stroke (Biberian 2012, 50), in which the bicycling movement is minimized by limiting the range of the plucking action.

The technical frame for tremolo is achieved by flexing *m* and *a* so that their tips fall on the same string as *i*. Were *i* to extend to touch the string where *m* and *a* lie, it would encounter the same difficulties as described in the preceding paragraph. These situations are illustrated in photos 2-19 to 2-21, above.

The Basic Four-Note Arpeggio

A particularly interesting, perhaps even counterintuitive, relationship exists between the anatomical frame and the basic four-note consecutive-string arpeggio (what we will call, from now on, the **basic arpeggio**).

Photo 2-19. Anatomical frame in 4th position [4]

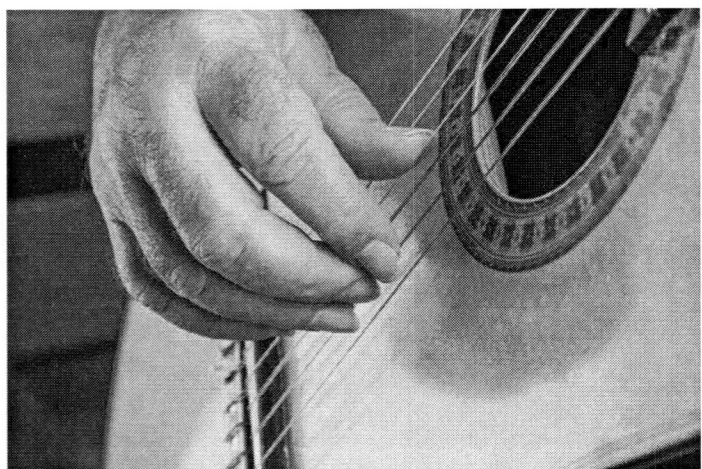

Photo 2-20. Extension of index to 2nd string

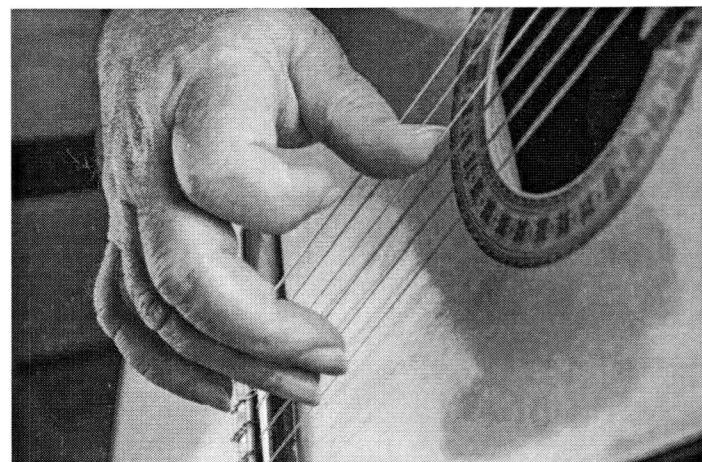

Photo 2-21. 'Bicycling' stroke of index to avoid brushing 3rd string. The tone is thin and metallic. Photos Wayne Armstrong.

From the closed anatomical frame, the basic arpeggio is configured by leaving *a* in its anatomical frame position and moving its companions to their adjacent superior strings (without an accompanying arm movement!). This means that *i* and *m* 'contract' slightly or, as Shearer would put it, they function on 'the flexion side of mid-range,' (Shearer, Learning the Classic Guitar 1990, vol. 1, 55) while the thumb extends to the adjacent lower string (as it does for the open anatomical frame.)

If we left the position in its initial anatomical frame, and reached to the higher string by extending *a*, *a* would feel the same constraints in executing the free stroke as *i* encountered in the two situations described earlier. This extension, however, would allow it to play a rest stroke, thus achieving the mixed stroke framing approach discussed below.

Mixed-Stroke Framing

For players using the free-stroke mode exclusively, a passage requiring finger movement to a higher-pitched string from a given anatomical positional frame will require a positional shift, since finger extension jeopardizes the proper execution of the free stroke.

92

Photo 2-22. Anatomical frame in 4th position [4].

Photo 2-23. Extension of 'p' to 5th string [5+(4)]

Photo 2-24. Flexion of 'i' to 4th string [5+(4)(i-)].

Photo 2-25. Flexion of 'm' to 3rd string: basic arpeggio, 5th position [5+(4)(i-m-a)]. Photos Wayne Armstrong.

For those that also use the rest stroke, a different alternative is possible. Indeed, an intermediate framing mode is achieved when, from the anatomical frame, one or two but not all three of the fingers (*i*, *m*, *a*) extend to reach one or more higher strings. The extended finger(s) will then be able to play rest stroke, while its companion(s) remain in free-stroke mode. The situation described before, concerning *a*, would be resolved by playing rest stroke with this finger (photo 2-26).

Likewise, for *i*, in the preceding scenario (photo 2-20). The frame indicator would be [4(i+)]. This mixed-stroke framing mode is very useful in allowing the right hand to maintain position, if shifting is unadvisable. A case in point would be the aforementioned Estudo No. 2 by Villa-Lobos, where the upper reaches of the beginning arpeggio can be accommodated without shifting right-hand positions by mixing in rest strokes:

Example 2-3. H. Villa-Lobos, Etude no 2 (*Douze Etudes*), bar 1

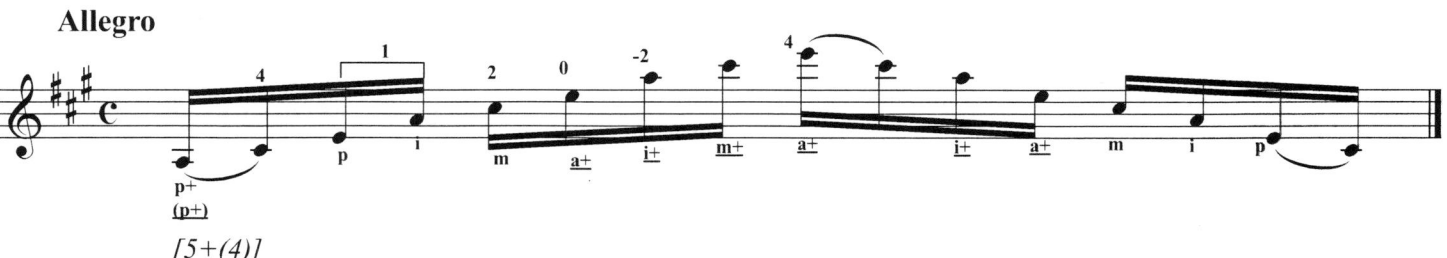

Photo 2-26. Mixed-stroke frame on 4th position through extension of a [4(a+)]. Photo Wayne Armstrong.

Of course, the issue of whether the mixture of stroke-types is artistically desirable or appropriate will, eventually, determine the player's choice. The mixed-stroke framing mode offers innumerable combinations, many of which, though possible, are impractical in actual performance. However, they all possess great pedagogical value, as we shall discuss presently.

Rest-Stroke Framing

Ultimately, and as a logical development of the relationship naturally existing between finger extension and rest stroke, fingers may be so extended that all of them can accommodate rest strokes. From the anatomical frame, a rest-stroke frame is achieved by extending all the fingers so that fingertips come to rest on higher strings, adjacent or even higher, without moving the arm or thumb (the frame number does not change):

Example 2-4

Anatomical frame [6]

As explained earlier, changing to rest stroke on the same strings can also be achieved by re-aligning the PIP joints at least one string lower than they were in the anatomical frame. The fingers pivot on their placed fingertips, extending their IP joints and flexing the MCP. This latter approach, however, cannot really be used in many circumstances involving swift transitions from arpeggiated to scalar textures, therefore, the examples that follow will focus on the more standard procedure of re-aligning the arm.

In either case, the more extended presentation of index, middle and ring fingers impels them all to play rest strokes. In this extended position, free strokes, if attempted, will be jeopardized, and clearing of the adjacent lower string can only be achieved through the 'bicycling' stroke described earlier, if at all.

Framing and Planting

The concept and practice of 'planting' has been dealt with in explicit terms only in modern guitar methodology, although it has always been a part of the actual performance practice of popular (most significantly, Flamenco) and many classical players, and despite the fact that it is intimately related to the foundational concept of 'placing' used in classical harp technique.

Its recognition as a fundamental aspect of right-hand training has happened only in the didactic literature after Pujol, although there are illustrious predecessors that imply this procedure in their writings, but without the modern terminology (Romero 2012, 20-21). Many modern authors have dealt with planting with more or less detail in their publications. Among first-tier players, John Williams has been perhaps the most influential exponent. It is an indispensable element in the theory of positional framing presented here. Its value in providing stability to the right hand as a solid base for independent, accurate and fluent fingerwork is seldom questioned anymore, although for many years the concept itself was vigorously disputed.

Richard Wright, the distinguished English pedagogue, puts it succinctly. In describing one of his exercises for early thumb training, he states:

> With *i*, *m* and *a* planted on the top three strings, the solitary thumb can begin to develop controlled, independent movement from a completely stable platform – itself an essential prerequisite for the eventual independent movement of the fingers (Wright 2001, 82).

Mr. Wright's statement describes one of the fundamental roles of planting: positional support. The others are contact preparation and note-duration control in dampening and articulation. An important factor is the timing of planting. Planting is most easily achieved if it coincides with metrically strong beats or subdivisions, rather than on the off-beats, a psycho-physiological factor of substantial importance, given our instinctive propensity to associate musical tension and release with lifting and falling (or 'up and down': upbeat and downbeat). In this fashion, the weight factor becomes an intrinsic proprioceptive guide to the timing of the planting behavior, which is then felt as a passive release of the fingers on the strings. In fact, this sensation is what distinguishes planted contact from its more active cousin, placing.

This is, of course, only possible generally in support planting and, frequently, in contact preparation planting, but less so in dampening or articulation, where placing (active, rather than passive contact) is more frequent. Within the context of planting proper (passive or weight-released contact), its absence for prolonged periods of playing time may present problems to efficient and effective fingerwork in free stroke mode. Indeed, every free stroke that is articulated from a hovering hand attitude, without a resting digit on a string, has to contend with the issue of limb support, the fact that the weight of the limb needs to be held by the active and isometric engagement of the muscular support-base that keeps those limb joints proximal to the torso (shoulder, elbow, wrist) stabilized.

In this context, the role of the thumb, when not actively involved in playing, is indispensable, as it is the digit most frequently available to support the limb passively during fingerwork, as an anchor-digit in weight-released planting. This diminishes the work load of the support musculature considerably, and increases the accuracy and artistic control in the fingerwork.

However, the degree of separation of the thumb from the fingers is of great importance: because of the need for adequate flexion in the fingers for the proper execution of the free stroke, the player should be aware of the tendency of the hand (particularly in players with a smaller hand-span) to bear towards the thumb when it extends past the boundaries of the open anatomical frame, with the consequent misalignment of the fingers. This, again, would jeopardize the free stroke by putting the interphalangeal joints of the active fingers on the extension side of their mid-range of motion.

Second in importance in planting is the ring finger, which can and should be used for this function as frequently and freely as it is feasible. Thumb and ring finger are the 'framing' fingers of the hand, so to speak. When planting *a*, special attention should be given to avoiding tip-joint (DIP) flexion, as this may create problems with the independent behavior of the middle finger, for reasons detailed in Chapter 1.

Five-finger players may deduce that the little finger could take over these support responsibilities from the ring finger. However, as described elsewhere, individual variability in the tendonal arrangement linking ring and little finger may be a factor impinging on the freedom of movement of the ring finger in some players (as it could be for *c* as well). Therefore, for them, *c* could be used as support when fingerwork is limited to *p*, *i* and *m*, but less so if *a* is involved.

In rest stroke mode, support planting, mainly provided by the thumb, is less significant, since the resting outcome of each rest stroke results, in effect, in an anchored hand (less so in short-arm players). However, it is a tool used frequently in melodic or scale playing to provide better leverage to the fingerwork, as it shortens the load-arm by providing a secondary pivot-point between the point of support of the arm on the instrument and the finger's point of contact with the string, thus allowing the wrist-joint to be stabilized passively, rather than by muscular engagement, as when the thumb is not planted.

It may also provide support in speedy scale playing since the resting phase of the stroke in each finger is minimized as the rate of speed of the finger alternation increases. In these cases, the thumb placement is at least two and, most commonly, three or more strings away from the active fingers, to accommodate the extension in the fingers and to improve the leverage conditions. This has its obvious limit when playing on the bass strings, since the thumb will run out of strings where to rest. Some players (Flamenco players in particular) continue resting on the wood of the soundboard (Romero 2012, 43), others prefer to leave the thumb in the air. A third alternative could be to use a mixed stroke framing approach and use free stroke for these strings (see DVD clip 8). All of these alternatives will be explored in some of the analyzed examples in section V.

Of course, the richest possibilities lie in preparatory and duration-control placing: the string contact preceding and after fingerwork. It is here that the benefits of contact preparation can be fully experienced.

Placing and planting present major pedagogical challenges to both teachers and students, if the latter have not been introduced to these techniques early and well. However, planting should not become a crutch, which it may, given its direct relationship with weight release on the string. This may be an impediment, for instance, with a planted thumb when initially training for rest-stroke finger alternation, since the thumb takes away some of the weight-support function that, in rest-stroke mode, the resting finger should learn to feel after each stroke.

Weight-release, as a technical approach, needs to be understood always from the point of view of the overall readiness for action characteristic of the well-trained, alert demeanor of the poised limb (Iznaola, Rest and Free 1990, 42-43). Therefore, hovering is as much an indispensable part of advanced training as planting is in more elementary levels.

Within the domain covered by this narrative, the direct relationship between planting and solid positional framing is a fundamental awareness. The planted hand makes explicit to the (trained) eye the positional frame being utilized at any given moment.

The non-placed, hovering hand, however, is, likewise, *always* utilizing a specific frame, which, nonetheless, may remain unacknowledged by the player, since it does not show explicitly to the eye, as with the planted hand.

The capability of the player to mentally 'map' the positional frame at any given moment, either with or without planting, is what this text strives to enhance. The reader may allow her right hand to 'discover,' in an intuitive way, the role of planting when trying out the various positional placements and frames in the following charts (which may easily become exercise material with the addition of repeats and proper continuity).

Likewise, by lifting the digits from their respective planted position, without moving the arm, the reader may begin to 'see' positional frames, as well, when the hand hovers over the strings, without contact.

Positional and Framing Charts

The charts below will serve as illustrations and 'experimental labs' for the main concepts discussed so far. Some clarifications are in order:

1. The basic (anatomical) positional chart (2-1, below) precedes the framing charts, and shows the complete normal 'positional territory' for free- and rest-stroke modes. As with the technical framing charts, fingering is presented in the usual *p*, *i*, *m*, *a* sequence. This order is not significant.

2. Because of the reasons presented earlier, the free-stroke frames accept no finger extension. All mixed-stroke and rest-stroke frames are finger-extended variants of the normal free-stroke frames, and all finger-extended frames are either mixed stroke or rest stroke frames. In actual practice, there is more flexibility in how free-stroke and mixed-stroke frames really function in relation to degree of finger extension, as shall be shown in the analysis of examples in section V. However, for now the theory will be defined according to the simplest and, therefore, less malleable premises.

3. The first technical framing chart (2-2) shows *p*-extended and *i*, *m*, *a*-contracted free-stroke frames for the first three positions ([1], [2], [3]), as models that can be applied, fully or partially, to the other positions. This is followed by framing charts for mixed stroke in [4] position and rest stroke for [5] only, since the number of possible combinations increases so much that a full cataloguing becomes impractical. Although not indicated, *p*-extended frames may be tried with both rest and free strokes of *p*.

4. When trying out the framing approaches, it is indispensable to maintain the arm and hand in the anatomical frame of the model position. This is easier said than done: our hand and arm are used to continuous micro-shifting movements that help fingerwork, in particular when the thumb is involved, and it is very easy, especially for less experienced players, to overlook noticing that the position has changed from a previous activity (usually, to favor *p*, as noted before). However, in order to properly feel the subtle but definite differences among the various framing approaches, a totally stable arm position is indispensable (the same applies to wrist/hand alignment). In this context, Richard Wright's concept of a 'stable platform' through planting, quoted above, is a vital tool.

Chart 2-1

Normal Free -Stroke Positions

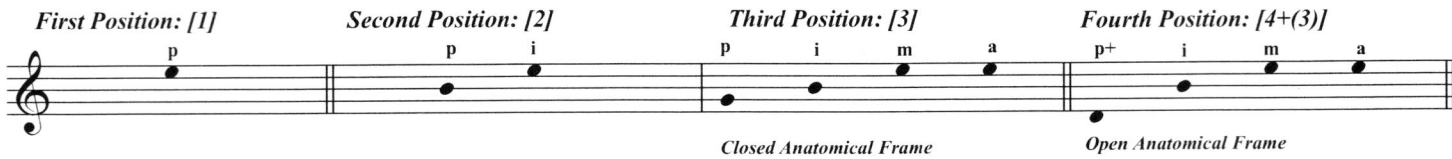

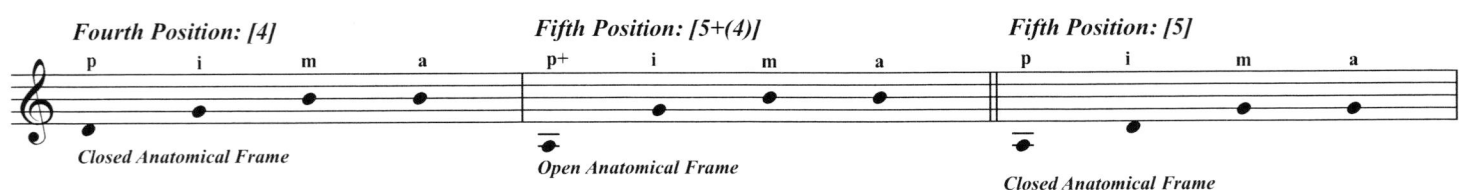

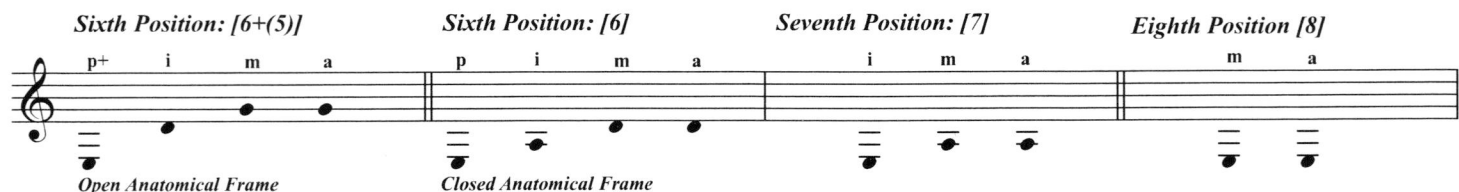

Normal Rest-Stroke Positions

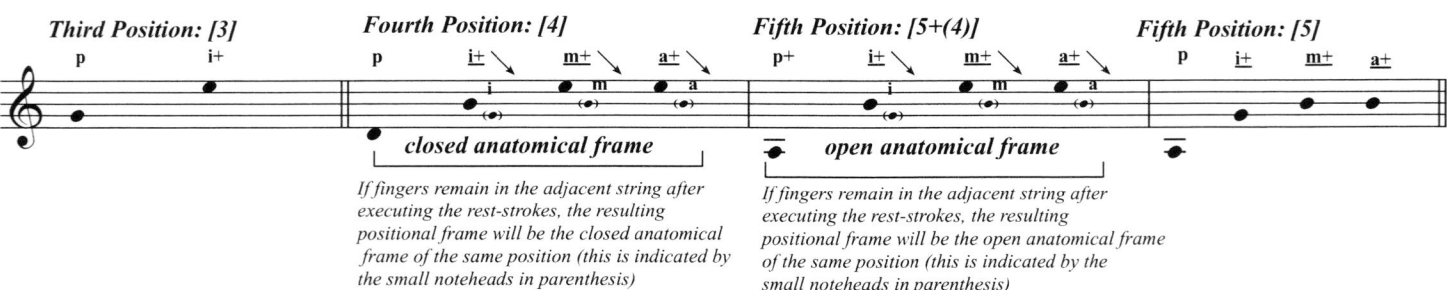

If fingers remain in the adjacent string after executing the rest-strokes, the resulting positional frame will be the closed anatomical frame of the same position (this is indicated by the small noteheads in parenthesis)

If fingers remain in the adjacent string after executing the rest-strokes, the resulting positional frame will be the open anatomical frame of the same position (this is indicated by the small noteheads in parenthesis)

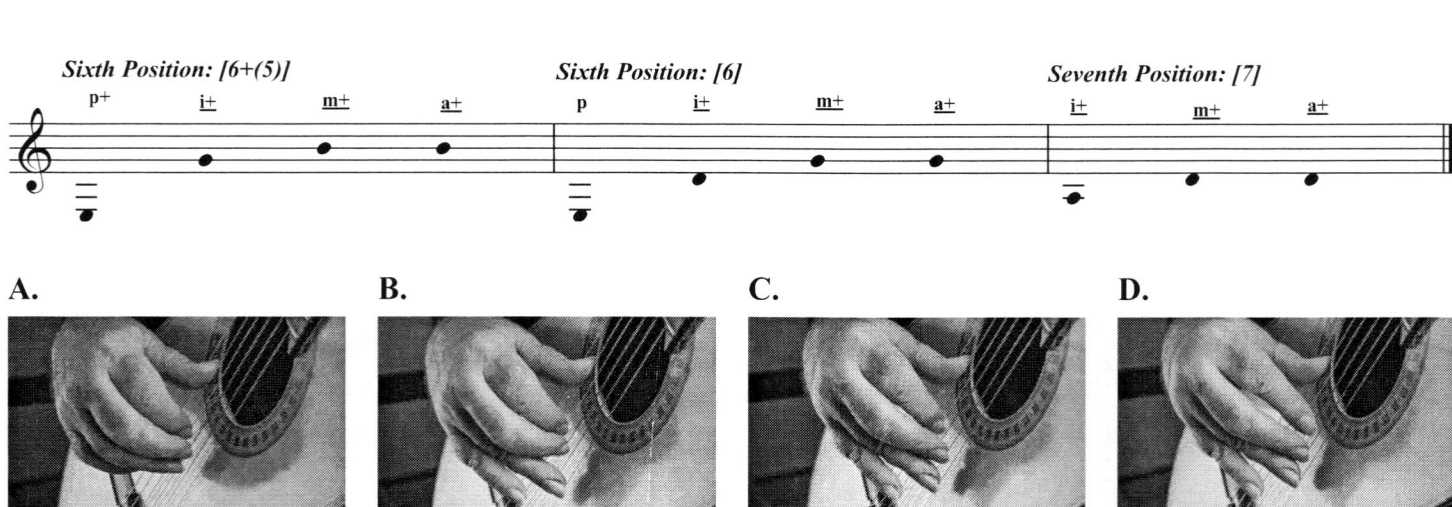

Photos 2-27 to 2-30. From free-stroke frame [5] to its rest-stroke counterpart by double extension of a and single extension of i, m. Photos Wayne Armstrong.

The following charts show possible technical frames using free-, mixed- and rest-stroke modes with numerous combinations of digit extension/contraction, across the positions. The player should find how the various positions expand or limit the number of possible frames, as compared with the models given in these charts.

Chart 2-2

Extended and Contracted Free-Stroke Positional Frames
([1], [2], [3])

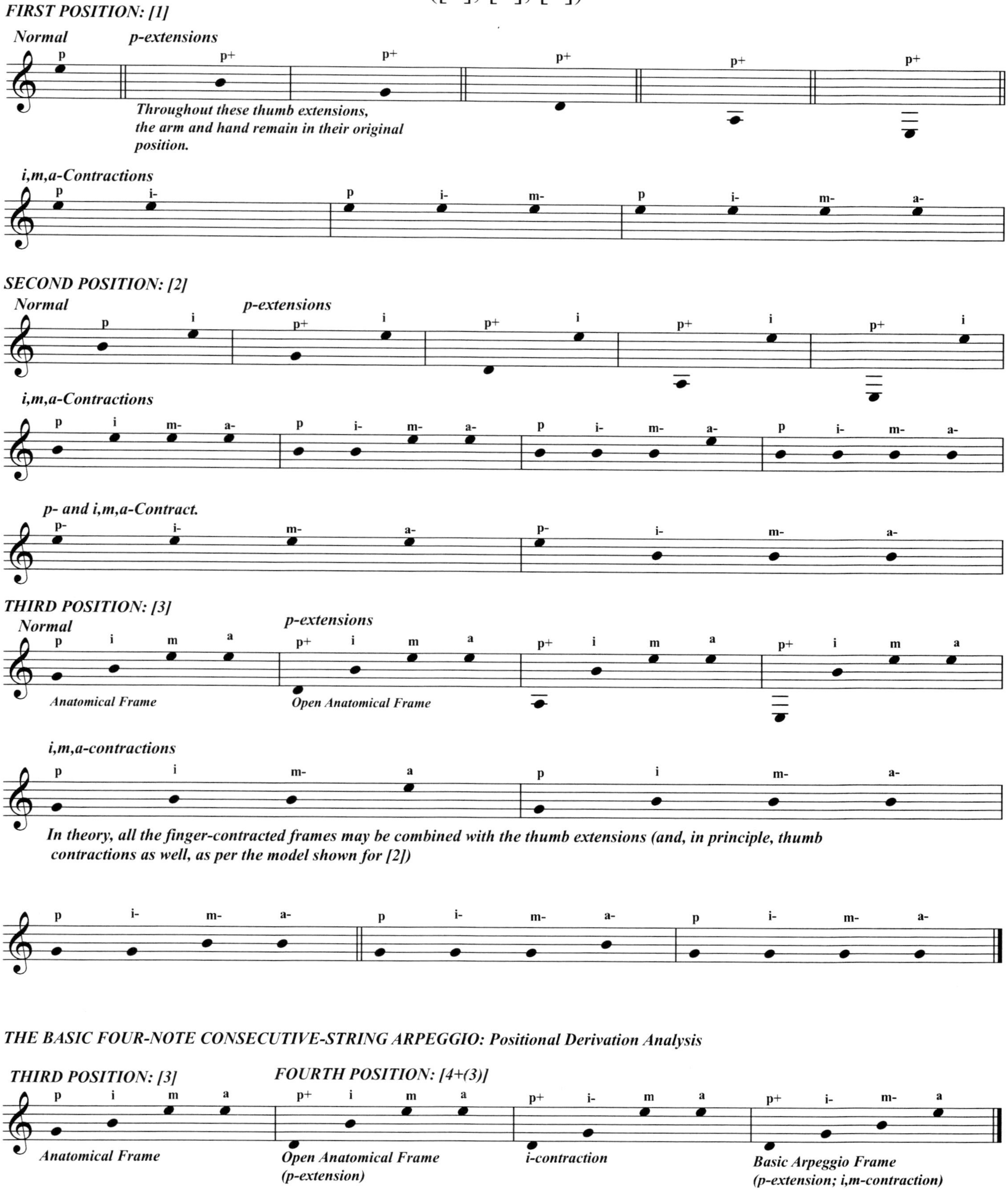

FIRST POSITION: [1]

Throughout these thumb extensions, the arm and hand remain in their original position.

SECOND POSITION: [2]

THIRD POSITION: [3]

Anatomical Frame   *Open Anatomical Frame*

In theory, all the finger-contracted frames may be combined with the thumb extensions (and, in principle, thumb contractions as well, as per the model shown for [2])

THE BASIC FOUR-NOTE CONSECUTIVE-STRING ARPEGGIO: Positional Derivation Analysis

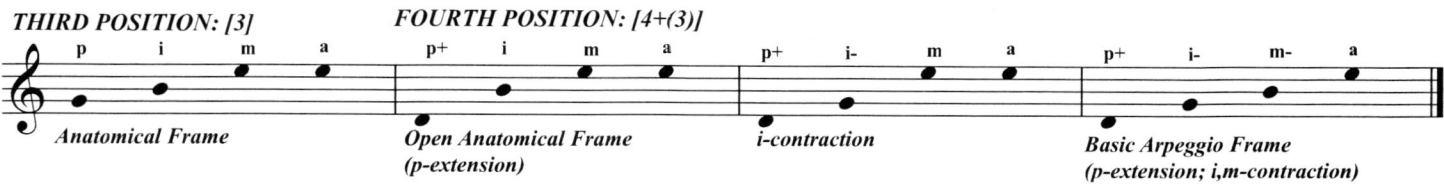

THIRD POSITION: [3]   *FOURTH POSITION: [4+(3)]*

Anatomical Frame   *Open Anatomical Frame (p-extension)*   *i-contraction*   *Basic Arpeggio Frame (p-extension; i,m-contraction)*

The last staff in the chart above shows how the basic arpeggio ([4+(3)]) derives from the anatomical frame position ([3]). Photos 2-22 to 2-25, above, showed a derivation starting on [4].

These framing possibilities, of course, apply to the other positions as well. The chart does not pretend to be exhaustive or exclusive. The following charts provide various examples of mixed- and rest-stroke frames.

Chart 2-3

Mixed-Stroke Frames
[4]

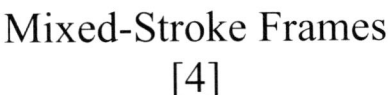

Chart 2-4

Some Rest-Stroke Frames
[5]

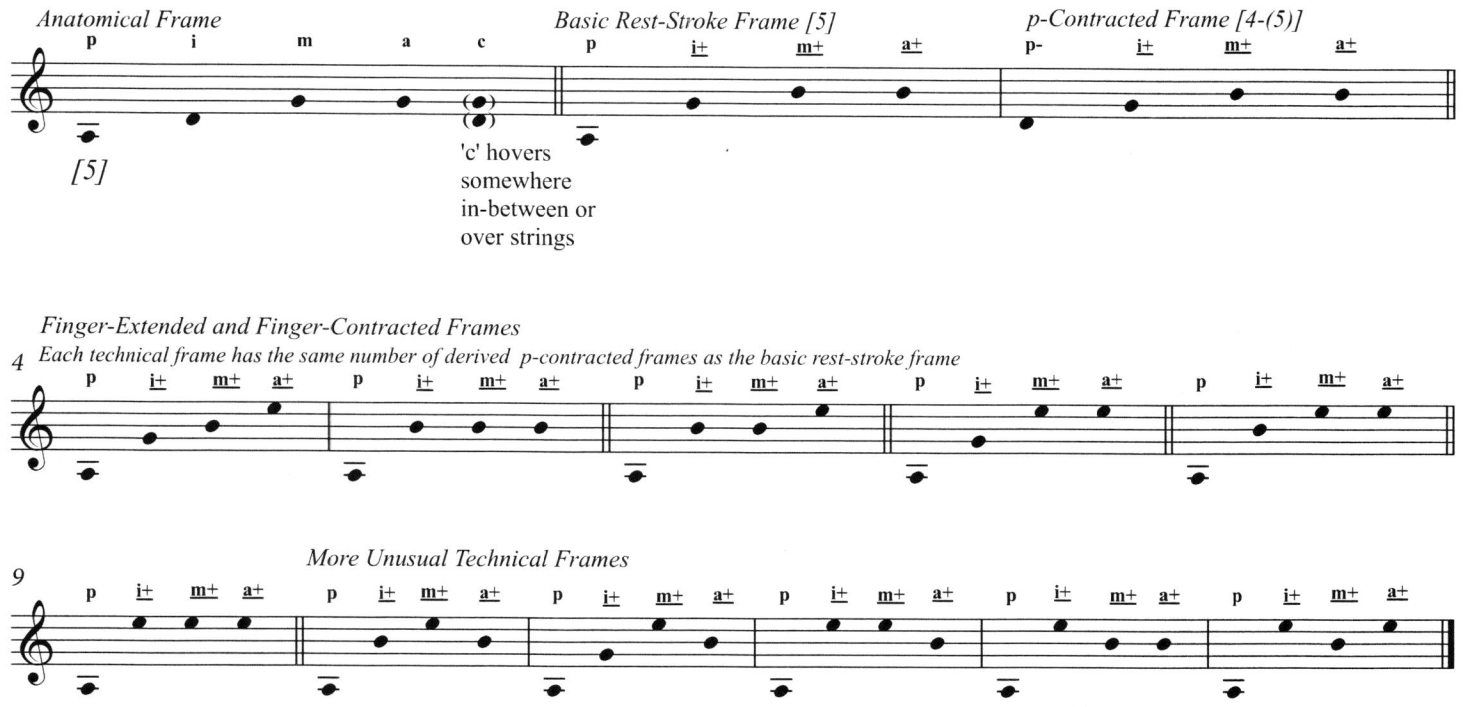

Section 3. Mobility

So far, we have introduced a rather formal and static schema of positional presentations of the right-hand fingers on the strings. The observant reader may have already noticed an important factor derived from the charts above: Positionally speaking, things are not always what they seem to be. A couple of examples will verify this.

Chart 2-5

Positional Analysis: Some Examples

EXAMPLE 1

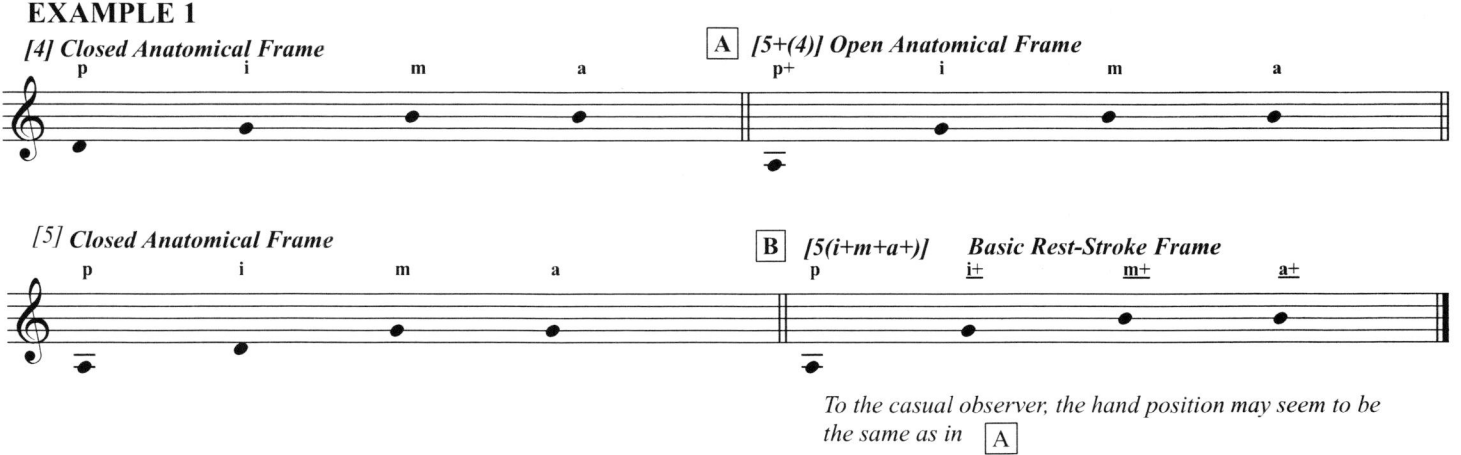

To the casual observer, the hand position may seem to be the same as in A

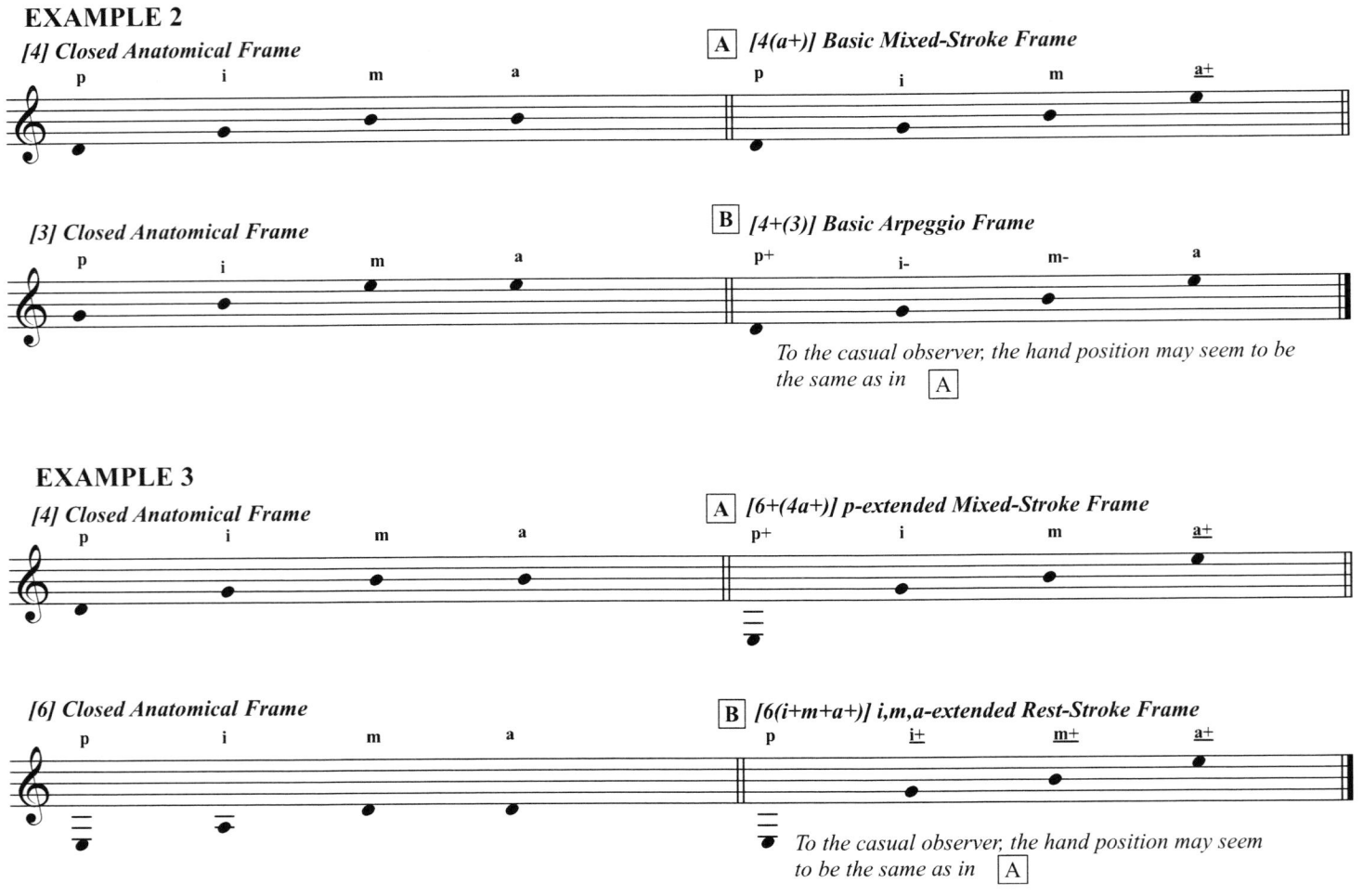

EXAMPLE 2

[4] Closed Anatomical Frame — A *[4(a+)] Basic Mixed-Stroke Frame*

[3] Closed Anatomical Frame — B *[4+(3)] Basic Arpeggio Frame*

To the casual observer, the hand position may seem to be the same as in A

EXAMPLE 3

[4] Closed Anatomical Frame — A *[6+(4a+)] p-extended Mixed-Stroke Frame*

[6] Closed Anatomical Frame — B *[6(i+m+a+)] i,m,a-extended Rest-Stroke Frame*

To the casual observer, the hand position may seem to be the same as in A

Ambiguous as the various frames may appear to be visually (the trained eye of the teacher will, hopefully, disambiguate them), they are distinctly different in terms of the player's proprioceptive sensations, what they 'feel' like. Eventually, this sensory differentiation is what makes the player's intuition develop a positional 'instinct,' so to speak, upon which a more or less functional and flowing technical approach to right-hand fingerwork and mobility is established.

But intuition, though a good student, can be a slow one. It also leans toward one-size-fits- all solutions that limit exploration and experimentation. A theoretical framework, based on verifiable, pre-technical physiomechanical principles, that explains and gives name to (and, eventually, helps refine) the experiential awareness of the player, can be of vital importance from a pedagogical standpoint by enhancing the potential for discovery of the player's intuition while avoiding its traps.

As with the left hand, in actual practice the main issue is mobility: How to get from point *x* to point *y*, accurately, in time and ready for what comes next. For the right hand, this means that the player's hand is always making decisions, with more or less conscious awareness, about the positional placement and the type of frame best fitted to passage *x* and how to effectively and efficiently connect with the positional placement and type of frame best fitted to passage *y*.

Shifting: Arm-Wrist-Finger Interaction
As is the case with the left hand, right-hand shifting technique is infinitely variable and entirely contextual in application. Each case is uniquely particular. Therefore, generalizations concerning the technique run the risk of constraining one's viewpoint to the extreme of impeding a clear and objective study of the specifics of any given

circumstance. Nevertheless, a thorough understanding of the *pre-technical* conditions operating on the playing mechanism from the moment one sits down to play becomes an indispensable prerequisite for any profitable analytical process to take place.

These conditions emerge from the relationships established between the right-arm placement on the instrument and the wrist, and the consequent attitude and demeanor of the digits on the strings. In concise terms, the support point in the forearm (where it rests on the upper arch of the guitar) initially pre-determines the wrist attitude (more or less flexion or extension, more or less radial or ulnar deviation) as well as the level of forearm rotation (towards pronation or towards supination,) with individual variance procured by physiognomy (height and weight, proportions of the body, relative size of the limb and its parts, nails, etc.) This basic set-up provides the foundation for a *preferred*, though not unavoidable, approach to shifting and fingerwork for every fulcrum point chosen by the player. In other words, there is a natural relationship between support point and digital work established by mechanical and physio-anatomical factors that are, in principle, pre-technical in nature.

Thus players who support the instrument on the right thigh, like many Flamenco and other popular players, and hence have, by necessity, a fulcrum very close to the elbow joint (given the full abduction of the upper arm prompted by the displacement of the guitar to the right) will have a very different set-up, in terms of shifting and fingerwork, than a classical player sitting in a 'modern' position, with the guitar held between the legs, and a steep angle of inclination that moves the fulcrum distally towards the wrist. In between these two extremes one can see a progressive evolution in right-hand approaches, from the intuitive to the highly formalized.

Physiomechanics of Arm Shifting: Leverage

Considering the arm-guitar relationship as a leverage system, we can determine the exact type of leverage in effect as the forearm fulcrum point changes.

1. The long-arm approach is a type 3 ('drawbridge') lever: the force, being the action of the elbow flexors, is applied between the fulcrum (point of support on the guitar close to the elbow) and the resistance (the hanging weight of the forearm and hand).

2. With the fulcrum closer to the wrist ('short-arm' approach), the three lever types are continuously interacting in shifting movements.

a. Type 1 ('seesaw'): Fulcrum between force and resistance. It is in effect whenever the player allows the weight of the forearm, at either side of the fulcrum, to 'fall'. In this case, the 'force' is a passive agent (gravity). This can be managed fairly simply, given the elasticity of the skin in the arm, by slightly adjusting the point of support through very subtle, almost imperceptible upper-arm transverse flexion/extension movements. In response to these movements, the wrist will slightly extend or flex further, to accommodate the changing angle between forearm and guitar at the fulcrum.

b. Those occasions when the shifting arm needs fall toward the elbow in a pronounced way (physiologically, adduction and lateral or outward rotation) require the upper arm to be abducted and medially (inwardly) rotated to return to the original position, movements corresponding with a type 2 lever ('wheelbarrow'). In this case, the resistance (the weight of the upper and fore arm behind the fulcrum with the center of gravity at the elbow joint) is located between the force (upper arm abductors/rotators exerting their pull on the proximal humerus) and the fulcrum (point of support on the guitar). The reader may easily visualize these interactions in the latter case by imagining them in the context of an actual centered seesaw in which the weight on one end (in this case, the elbow end) overcomes the weight on the other end (the hand). Absent a third party adding weight on the lighter end (the hand), or moving the positions of the two weights relative to the fulcrum (i.e. changing the length of the lever arms), the only option to achieve balance in the seesaw is to lift the heavier end, a type 2, wheelbarrow-like leverage action.

c. Even with the short-arm approach, lever 3-type movements may be implemented by using elbow flexion and extension, but with a more limited range of motion than in the long-arm approach, given the displaced point of support. The most common use of the type 3 lever in the short-arm approach, however, is at the shoulder joint, in the form of transversal flexion-extension movements. The table below will help clarify these relationships:

Type of Shifting Movement	Joint Involvement	Lever Type
A. Arc-like movement of forearm ('long-arm' approach; fulcrum very close to the elbow joint)	Active elbow flexion, controlled eccentric extension (flexors contracting eccentrically), passive wrist flexion/deviation. When supported by finger planting, passive extension/flexion of fingers.	Type 3 at the elbow (drawbridge)
B. Forward-backward movement of forearm (possible with all placements of fulcrum)	Shoulder transversal flexion/extension, passive elbow extension/flexion. When supported by finger planting, passive finger flexion/extension.	Type 3 at the shoulder
C. Forearm 'fall' on soundboard-side of fulcrum, with fulcrum approximately mid-way between elbow and wrist, managed by slight adjustments in actual positioning of the arm on the guitar	Passive shoulder abduction/inward rotation, passive wrist extension. When supported by finger planting, passive finger flexion.	Type 1 by gravity acting on hand end (seesaw)
D. Forearm 'fall' on backside of fulcrum, with fulcrum approximately mid-way between elbow and wrist, managed by slight adjustments in actual positioning of the arm on the guitar	Passive shoulder adduction/outward rotation, passive wrist flexion. When supported by finger planting, passive finger extension.	Type 1 by gravity acting on elbow end.
E. Forearm 'lift' from backside fall (idem)	Active shoulder abduction/inward rotation, passive wrist extension. When supported by finger planting, passive finger flexion.	Type 2 at the shoulder (wheelbarrow)

Each of these shifting styles, except B., requires adaptations in the behavior of the wrist joint, relative to its initial demeanor, in order to maintain playing attitude across the string span. In A., the wrist needs to deviate to the ulnar side as it is carried toward the bass strings. In C. and E. (these two movements are usually linked), it extends. In D., it flexes. The proper control of these variable attitudes of the wrist as the arm shifting technique changes is one of the most substantial challenges facing the player, which may explain why guitarists usually decide on holding on to one and only one shifting style, except for occasional displacements for special procedures, like tone-color changes or artificial harmonics. Ideally, though, a truly well-developed technique would incorporate all of these possibilities in a flowing technical 'discourse', without solutions of continuity, which is perfectly integrated with the musical narrative and becomes thus choreographed according to the personal interpretive vision of the performer. It is in this light that one wishes to understand right-hand shifting, positional framing and the application of stroke type. As reference, here are normal ranges of motion for the elbow, forearm and wrist joints.

Typical Range of Motion		
Elbow	Extension/Flexion	0/145
Forearm	Pronation/Supination	70/85
Wrist	Extension/Flexion	70/75
	Radial\Ulnar Flexion (deviation)	20/35

Various Approaches to Right-Hand Technique

In the course of this chapter we have assumed almost ideal 'laboratory conditions' concerning the player's right-hand set-up, in accordance with generally accepted ergonomic principles of modern technique involving muscular alignment, joint range of motion, follow-through, etc. But in actual practice there are many variants to these norms, utilized with evident success by many players in different parts of the world. After all, the traditions of playing inherited by successive generations of artists have been conditioned primarily by geographic and socio-cultural circumstances – the degree of relative isolation from or proximity to the great cosmopolitan centers of cultural and educational activity – as well as individual adaptations of those traditions implemented by the top performers and teachers in any given period and locality. It is only in relatively recent times that a more thorough awareness of methodologies and performance practices around the world has been possible for a great number of practitioners, thus 'homogenizing' guitar technique.

There is no denying the fact that there are better ways to play than others and that, from an ergonomic viewpoint, technical approaches that force joints into excessively angular, deviated or static behaviors and attitudes will, over time, create physical (and, hence, psychological) problems for the player. In the context of the topic under study, however, it is necessary to withhold judgment and deal even with these extreme approaches as if they were valid, if more idiosyncratic, alternatives to the established norm. A theory pretending to have universal application has to incorporate those instances where it is put to the test in ways that are unexpected and even in contradiction to accepted wisdom.

Additionally, one must contrast any such theory with personal circumstances that make an individual evolve, through time and experience, in ways that radically change one's initial approach to the art of playing. Does the theory hold, despite these changes? Ultimately, the investigation and elucidation of technical issues in performance is an open-ended endeavor, with each generation (indeed, each individual practitioner) incorporating new insights, discarding the old ways, and reviving forgotten ones, in an ever-recurring cycle of revision and renewal, whose only real enemy is dogmatic adherence to one's preferred practices.

It is, therefore, to be hoped that this introduction to the positional framing theory will prove of use to players of very different backgrounds and approaches, contradictory as they may be among themselves. Only then can the theory claim validity as a factual description of what happens in the course of actual guitar playing.

Angle of Inclination of the Guitar and its Effect on Right-Hand Approach

One can easily trace the evolution of right-hand approaches on the classical guitar, since Tárrega, by matching it to the angle of inclination of the guitar.

Indeed, starting with the original quasi-horizontal alignment of the early Tárrega school (in brief, tuning-head in line with shoulders, as in photos 2-31 and 2-32 below) (Pujol 1956, 1:78), as one lets the guitar's lower bout 'fall' gradually between the legs one can see how the right forearm's fulcrum displaces distally and the wrist extends.

Photo 2-31. Shoulder-level angle with across-lap position using footstool

Photo 2-32. Shoulder-level angle with guitar waist on left thigh (using footstool)

Photo 2-33. The same, at eye-level angle

Photo 2-34. Head-level angle using lap support instead of footstool. Photos Wayne Armstrong.

Revolutionary as it seems at first, the last logical step in this evolution is, of course, Paul Galbraith's approach, with the cello-like set-up and the liberation of the right arm from any supporting role, a far cry from everything we identify with the Tárrega school. Mr. Galbraith's webpage at paul-galbraith.com has good information about his approach and the instrument he helped design, the Brahms guitar.

The XX century saw players coming from other traditions outside the dominant Spanish school, mainly from Central and Northern Europe, enter the international arena with different technical viewpoints, in many cases greatly influenced by lute technique. Also present were highly idiosyncratic variants of the original Tárrega approach, like the one represented best by the phenomenal Ida Presti, whose unique approach to the right hand departed from the general evolution toward a straighter, non-deviated wrist, without apparent dysfunction. American guitarist Alice Artz has produced a series of videos explaining Presti's approach, accessible through YouTube (Artz 2009).

Starting in mid-century, enormous progress in pedagogical thinking for the guitar begins. Great teachers, not all of them prominent players, left their mark on an important group of young performers not through their example (the time-proven method of the old masters) but through their more rigorous, if incipient, application of physiomechanical (and psychological) know-how. Names like Len Williams (first teacher of his son John), Aaron Shearer, Abel Carlevaro (the only great practitioner within the group) introduced and developed new ways of approaching technical training on the guitar that proved to be highly successful, despite their apparently different, even contradictory viewpoints.

The first superior player to emerge from this new wave of pedagogical development was John Williams, in whose approach one finds, perhaps, a brilliant summary of the progression made in our understanding of guitar technique, for both hands, since the times of Tárrega (Winspur and Wynn Parry eds. 1998, 22 ff.).

In general terms, a common feature of newer approaches has been the evolution towards a steeper angle of inclination of the instrument, non-deviated wrist with discreet flexion, and more 'squatted' finger attitude (moderate flexion at the MCP and at the IP.) This translates into a gradual evolution from the rest stroke-driven approach of the early Tárrega school, to the modern prevalence of the free stroke as the normative form of fingerwork in guitar playing, which has prompted even radical viewpoints eliminating any use of the rest stroke (as Carlevaro, at least in theory, proposed, and as implemented, in fact, by numerous contemporary players).

The description provided earlier in this text concerning the anatomical frame follows this general demeanor as its basis, but the theory of positional framing presented here does not discard any stroke possibility, and, in fact, may help players, on either side of the stroke-type divide, discover why one or the other stroke feels cumbersome to their right hand. The theory allows any possibility of arm-wrist-hand alignment that might have practical applications in the course of playing to be incorporated within its reach. The following section deals with these applications.

Section 4. Compendium: The Talented Hand – Positional Framing Analysis

The purpose of these analyses is to describe, in some way, what the intuition of the well-trained right hand might achieve, in terms of mobile adaptability and with more or less conscious awareness, when presented with a variety of technical challenges. They are not meant to be taken as 'how to' instructions.

Carcassi: Etude Op. 60, No. 1. Positional Framing in Scalar Passages

Various approaches to the right hand in the initial phrase of the etude are analyzed. Left-hand fingering is not notated, as the passage is all in first position using open strings whenever possible. The one exception might be for the B in mid-staff, which, following the suggestion in Rey de la Torre's insightful edition of the studies (Carcassi 1996), may be played with 4 on ③, to avoid possible ring-over when the next note events are played. Despite its apparent simplicity, this is a challenging study for less advanced players because of its thumb dampening requirements.

Example 2-5. Mateo Carcassi, Study Op. 60, no. 1.

A.

Thumb dampens at the spots marked with an x

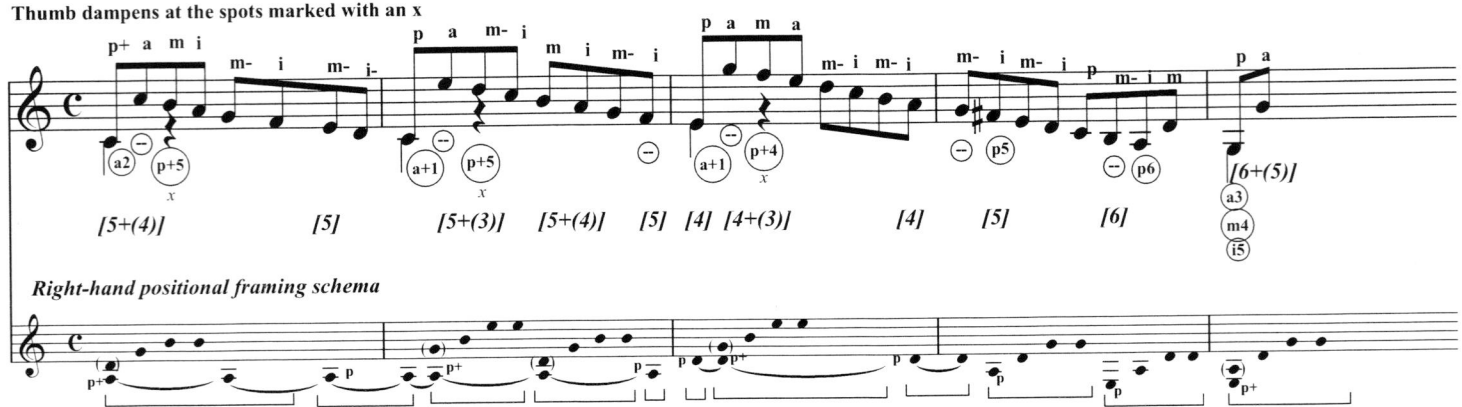

Right-hand positional framing schema

B.

In this version, *p* dampens the string with its radial side as it plants on the adjacent higher string (spots marked with an x).
Although in the example it plays free strokes, its move to the adjacent higher string can be more easily achieved with a rest-stroke.

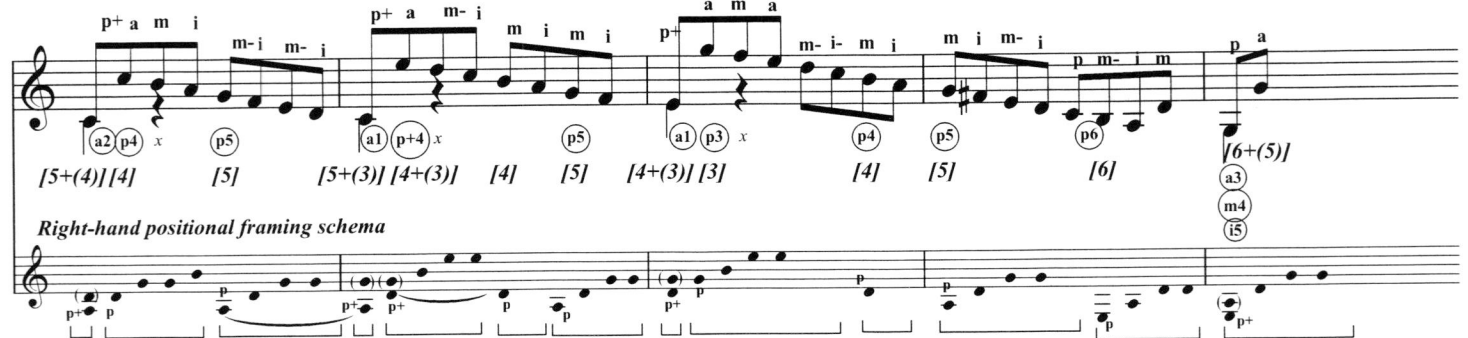

Right-hand positional framing schema

C. In this version as well, *p* dampens the string with its radial side as it plants on the adjacent higher string (spots marked with an x).
Although in the example it plays free strokes, its move to the adjacent higher string can be more easily achieved with a rest-stroke.
In either case, the placing of the thumb, then, serves as a pivot point to change positions.

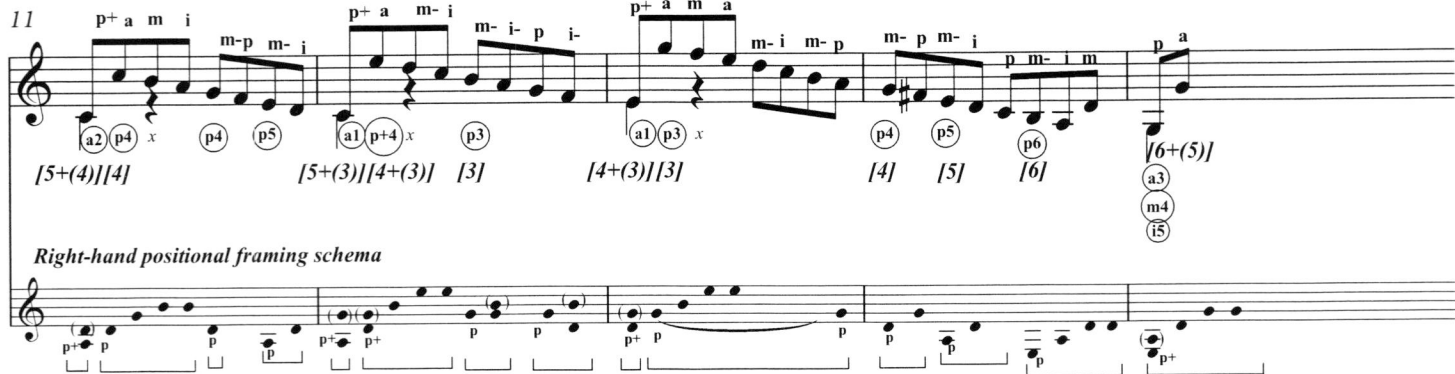

Right-hand positional framing schema

The next example introduces a mixed-stroke frame approach. Right-hand shifting is minimized and *p* is used, as before, as a pivot for position changes when the hand enters free-stroke territory, by using its previous placement as preparation for the next stroke on the same string, although, originally, it was done for dampening purposes.

Example 2-6. Idem, mixed stroke approach with p as positional pivot

Thumb dampens at the spots marked with an x

Right-hand positional framing schema

Track 2-4 **Arpeggio to Scales**

A mixed-stroke approach is used to transition between an arpeggio texture and a scalar passage. Two framing options are shown.

Example 2-7. Arpeggio to scale, mixed stroke framing.

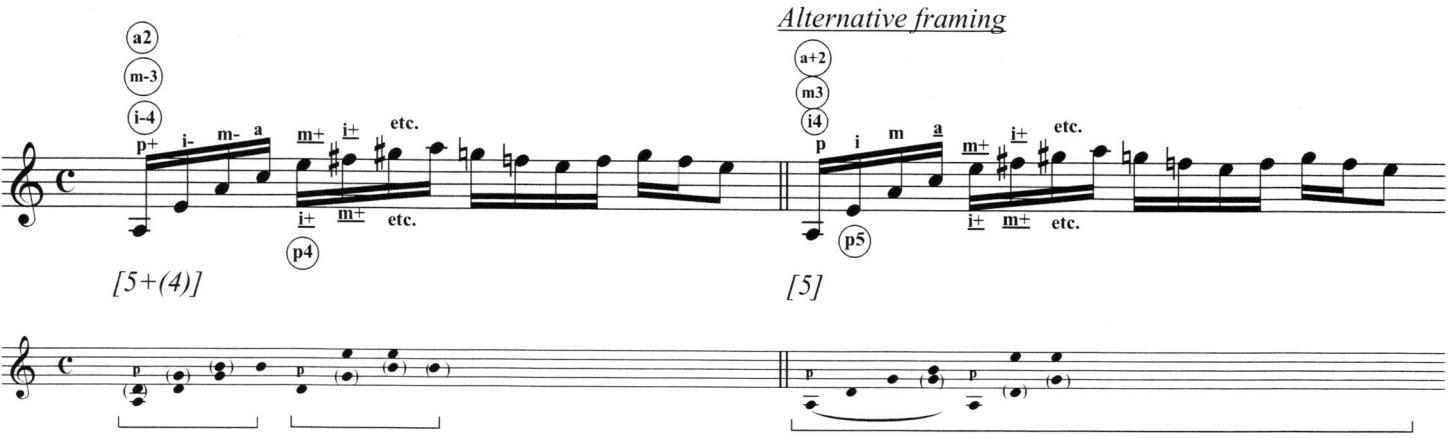

The first measure shows a positional shift from [5] to [4], in the second the alignment remains in [5] throughout. There are subtle differences in sensation that are assimilated instinctively in the well-trained, experienced hand, since these types of situations arise frequently in the course of playing.

Another instance of this same technique, using consecutive (sliding) rest strokes of the thumb, is shown in the companion DVD (clip 9).

A well-known, virtuosic example follows, showing one of many possible fingering options (for both hands. The left-hand issues of this passage will be discussed in chapter 3):

Example 2-7a. H. Villa-Lobos, Etude No. 2, bar 10-12

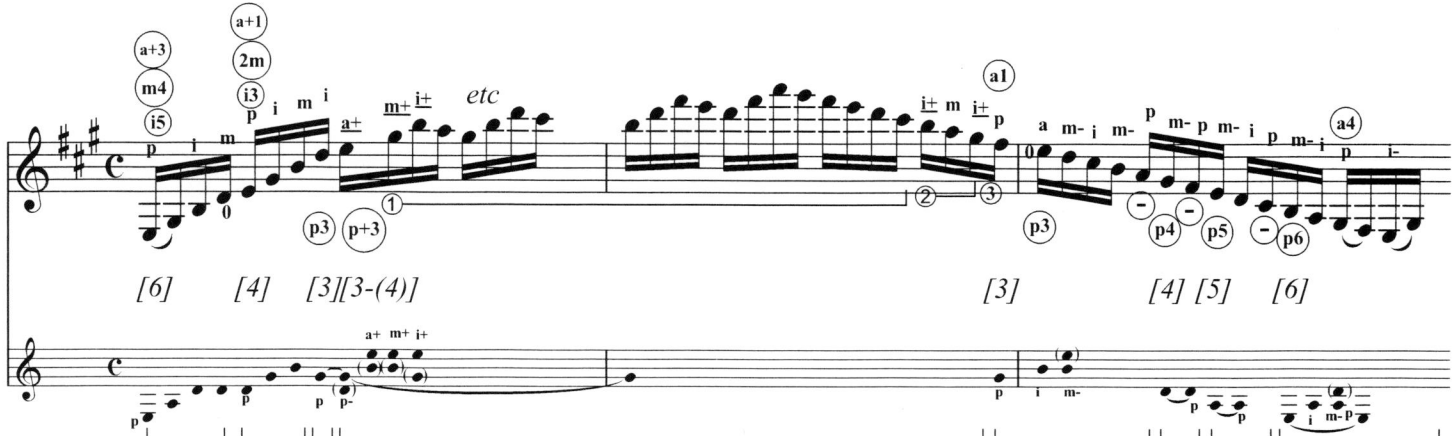

The chosen fingering is particularly interesting because it utilizes a contracted frame [3-(4)] as an anchor for the rest-stroke ascending scale, permitting the hand to use the placed thumb as pivot for the shifts in the free-stroke scalar descent of this brilliant passage. Notice, as well, the full-finger plant at the start and additional placings of both the thumb and the ring finger. Finally, at the end, if the last slur (E to G#) is not done, the hand would shift to [7] to pluck those two notes.

It is worth repeating that there are many other ways of fingering this fragment, using both free-stroke and mixed-stroke approaches, and placing the thumb closer or more distant to the fingers.

Arpeggio to Repeated Notes

Carcassi's 2nd study provides an opportunity to explore different ways of dealing with this very common design.

Example 2-8. M. Carcassi, Study op. 60, No. 2 (beginning)

A. With the indicated fingering, from the anatomical [3] (since 'a' plays free-stroke in its natural attitude), rest strokes of both 'p', which is doubly extended, and 'i' (one extension to the 1st. string) are feasible. The functional frame for the passage is the basic arpeggio [4+(3)].

B. In order for all fingers to play free stroke, a slight shift to [2] needs to occur so as to put 'i' in its proper free-stroke level of flexion. Placing 'p' on the second string could help the framing, but will challenge the hand later on when dampening of ringing basses begins to be a factor (not shown).

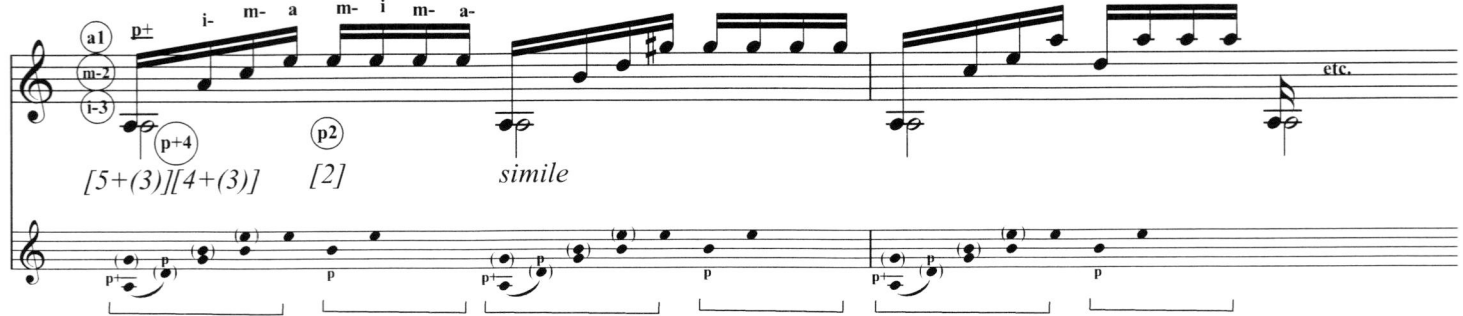

C. A more radical approach, not truly practical (nor very musical) but perhaps good for training and awareness, would position the hand on [5], which would allow the three top fingers to play rest strokes.

In all cases, the formula 'pimamima' used in these examples can be substituted with 'pimamama', good for training and the simplest to analyze positionally.

Interpositional Arpeggios

Villa-Lobos: Etude No. 2 (beginning). Free-Stroke Frame
Earlier, a mixed-stroke framing approach was presented for the beginning of the study (example 2-3). Now, a free-stroke framing approach is offered, with rest stroke in *p*, given its extension. In order for the finger free strokes to flow unimpeded the initial framing needs to be lower ([4+(3)]) than is perhaps assumed.

Example 2-9.

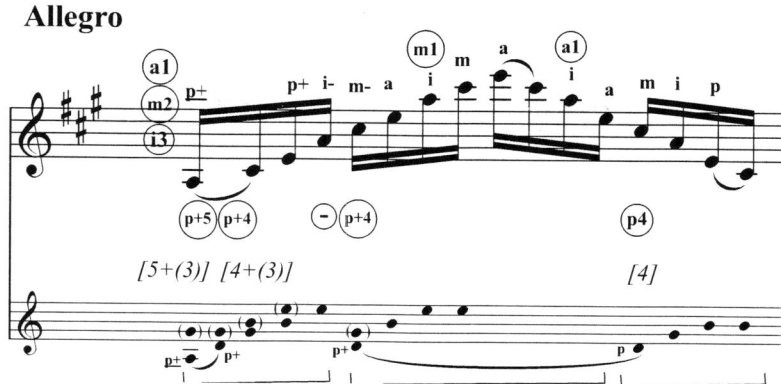

Well-known Arpeggio Formulas

This section closes with a couple of brief arpeggio examples drawn from well-known didactic works that will help summarize some of the most important features of right-hand positioning and mobility, as well as show slightly more challenging analytical situations. Since the focus is right-hand fingerwork, the examples have been simplified, notationally, by using only open strings and eighth notes. This, by the way, is a very effective way to practice right-hand technique in general, in isolation and devoid of concerns for the left hand.

Formulas from Dionisio Aguado: G major study (Method, 3rd part, no 8)

The fingering presented here is a bit easier than Aguado's, which is, on the other hand, great for digital training. The main difference is that in his approach the only note played by the thumb is the initial bass-note of the formula, making *i, m, a* (instead of *p, i, m,* as in the example) responsible for the positional shift.

This approach is not a substitute for Aguado's well-thought out design, but an alternative viewpoint that utilizes all placing (and planting!) opportunities, providing stable anchoring points from which a flowing, unimpeded sense of freedom in the arm's mobility may arise.

Example 2-10.

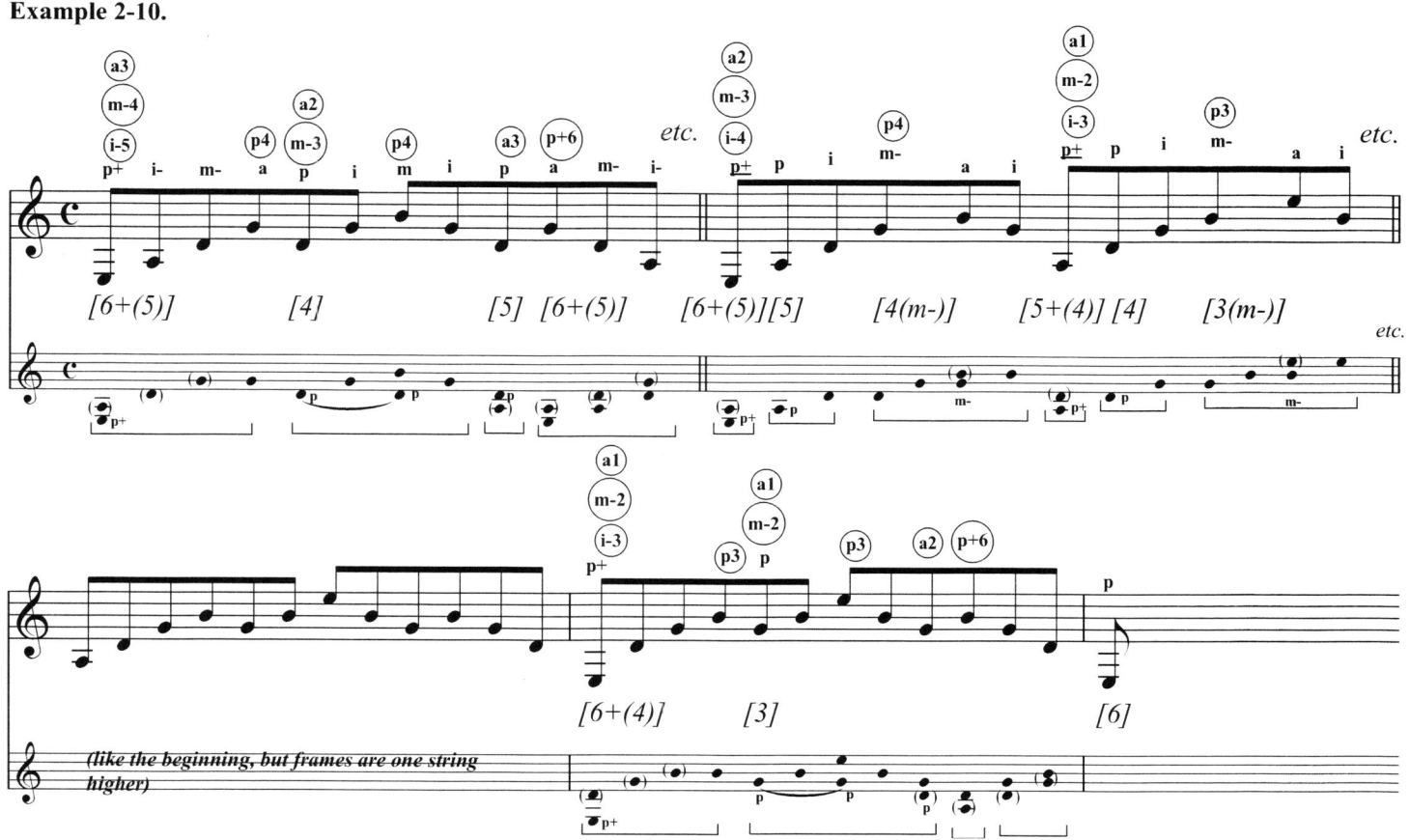

Another interesting approach is the one the author studied under Sainz de la Maza in Madrid during the '70's: a mixed-stroke approach using rest stroke on *a* only.

Physiomechanically, it helps, in any case, to keep the finger tips quite close together and even overlapping as the initial full plant is executed. This will lead to fingerwork driven by the middle joint, thus FDS, rather than the tip joint, because in order to overlap the tips the middle and ring fingers extend a little more than otherwise necessary. Of course, this cannot be maintained on the descending arpeggio, but the kinesthesia provided by the initial engagement in the full-plant moment will help free the hand of tensions that could arise with a more flexed, that is, FDP-driven, approach.

Formula from H. Villa-Lobos: Etude No. 1
The celebrated study allows ample opportunity to dig deep into positional and mobility issues in the right hand. The first example shows the traditional fingering associated with the work, which, again, is open to many different right-hand fingerings.

Example 2-11.

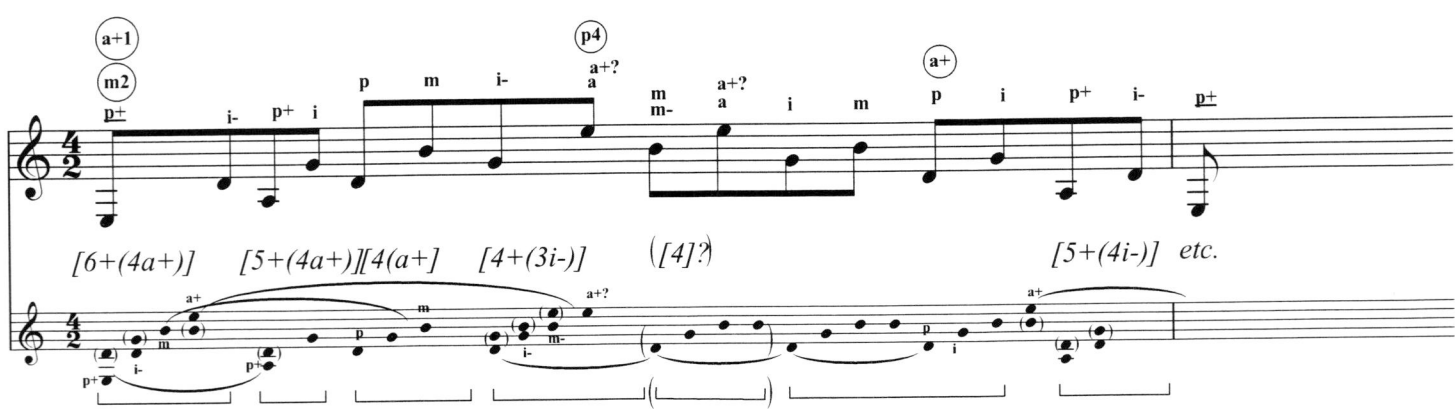

In this study one can perhaps find an instance of the 'half stroke' or the 'recoil' stroke. Indeed, in order to maintain a dynamic attitude upon arriving at the top part of the arpeggio, the positional frame would benefit from beginning to change from [4+(3)] to [4] while *a* plucks ①, thus providing a choreographic momentum to the change of direction in the arpeggio and the positional transitions. Otherwise *p* might find additional difficulties in managing the already cumbersome double stroke on ④ and ⑤. The question marks, double fingerings and parenthetical markings attempt to visually represent these conditions.

This is a good reminder of the wise advice provided by Pepe Romero in his method book: "do not exaggerate the follow-through" (Romero 2012). The tendency to do so is enhanced when positional frames are maintained in a static, unmoving fashion. The rotational support given by the forearm, and the unconstrained flexibility of the wrist, cannot be overly emphasized in dealing with the demands for great nimbleness and speed presented in Villa-Lobos' landmark study.

In the following treatment of the same arpeggio the fingering strives to achieve an arm-oriented rather than a digitally-oriented approach. The difficulty encountered in the original fingering as the arpeggio changes direction in its second half is ameliorated by having allowed p to lead the hand all the way to [2], thus following the natural, gravity-driven impulse of the fingering towards the high-pitched strings, and by the all-important planting of a as p plucks the B on ② and the D (E in the actual score) on ④, which provides the hand with a pivotal anchor

112

upon which to 'bounce' towards the low-pitched strings. The question mark in parentheses muses as to what pitch would the string where *a* would rest, following the natural configuration of the anatomical frame [2], produce.

Example 2-11a.

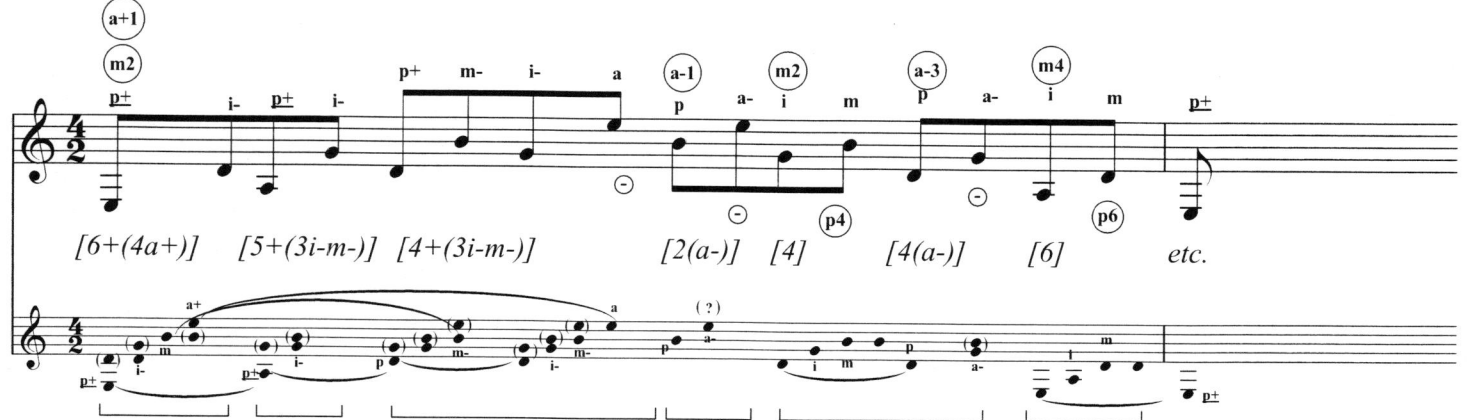

The descending fingering p-a-i-m could be used for the ascending arpeggio as well.

Chapter 3

This hand has occasioned me to make many more reflections than the right.

Fernando Sor

(Sor n/d, 12)

LIMITS TO THE POSSIBLE

Section 1. Physiomechanical Aspects of Left-Hand Technique

The chapter heading pays a modest tribute to the great visionary writer and futurist Arthur C. Clarke (1917 - 2008), by evoking the title of his book, *Profiles of the Future – An Inquiry into the Limits of the Possible* (Clarke 1976). In contrast to his book's bold insights, proven uncannily accurate more than thirty years since, this section attempts no such futuristic speculation but rather an exploration of how the past may condition one's vision of the possible in terms of left-hand technique, by exploring some biomechanical aspects of left-limb mobility on the guitar.

In fact, despite its limitations, Sor's method, quoted above, was a pioneering attempt at developing a scientific approach to guitar playing, probably the first founded on physiomechanical principles. Indeed, it remains one of the few that deal with the theoretical aspects of technique taking into consideration the functional anatomy of the limbs. Much knowledge has been gathered since Sor's gallant effort, and we are the wiser thanks to the legacy left by the curiosity of pedagogues and researchers of yore, like Matthay, Ortmann, Steinhausen, Capra, Polnauer and Marks, Szende and Nemessuri, and others who, since the beginning of the XX century, investigated the biomechanical nature of performance on the violin and piano.

This body of knowledge has gradually made its impact on modern guitar pedagogy and we have begun to see the results in the works of various scholars around the world in the last few decades. As in any discipline enriched with 'new' knowledge, there is little unanimity as to which approach represents the cutting edge, the new-found truth, but, *in toto*, our collective endeavors have changed the nature of the guitar's methodological discourse, forcing teachers and players to recognize the importance of more functional approaches to technique and to become aware of the dangers, both musical and physical, of technical approaches based on force and unmindful imitation.

Notwithstanding this fresh awareness, there are still areas of technique obscured by long-standing procedural approaches that, rather than falling into desuetude, have gained the authority of age, their obduracy made stronger by the apparent success of practitioners of the art who have attained prominence in the field while indulging in such practices. This chapter will engage in a study of left-hand technique from the perspective of the role that *movement* (that is, shifting) plays in the development of masterful control of the fingerboard, and how this viewpoint contrasts with conventional wisdom regarding left-hand position and behavior.

As has been described previously, even the apparently static situation of holding the guitar is an example of **dynamic equilibrium**, of counteracting and balancing forces that provide stability within a context of continuous, though controlled, motility. When studying the issue of the hands' position on the guitar, the same concept should be used, because playing the guitar is a dynamic process that cannot be properly understood (or taught) through approaches that are based on static positional norms.

Cases in point are the traditional descriptions of what constitutes a 'correct' left-hand position on the guitar, still found in many guitar methods. These descriptions emphasize where the thumb should be placed, how the fingers should be positioned so that their tips end up at the proper angle of attack on the frets, the degree of separation between fingers, etc. In other words, these are descriptions that would perhaps be good to sculpt a hand-model made of clay (or wood), but certainly they are not the best tools to teach the proper kinesthetic processes that will lead to efficient and fluid action on the fingerboard.

The important features of the traditional positioning of the left hand are: arm hanging loosely from the shoulder, not too far from the body (older versions of this required the arm to be as close to the body as possible), hand-knuckles parallel to the neck, fingers striking the strings perpendicularly and on the tips, and thumb exerting an opposing pressure on the back of the neck approximately behind the middle finger and with its tip not any higher than the mid-line of the neck.

When one tries to apply this description to the 1st. position (1st. string), the following will happen (assuming the guitar is in well-balanced support): since the upper arm has to keep hanging loosely from the shoulder (i.e., it should not abduct), it has to outwardly rotate to bring the forearm and the hand into position. The hand ends up at a slight angle to the neck (pronated), so the forearm has to be supinated to make the line of the knuckles parallel to the line of the neck.

Even then, the fingers will not fall perpendicularly on their tips, unless the wrist is flexed and the fingers abduct. The thumb has to be brought in behind the middle finger by retraction (i.e., simultaneous flexion, abduction and rotation at the wrist joint, with extension of the two phalanges). At this point, the upper arm is no longer "hanging loosely" from its socket, but has to be kept in position isometrically by the arm adductors, resisting the myriad opposing static tensions acting on the other joints of the arm and fingers. Fortunately, in the course of actual playing one does not stay long in this or any other position.

The simple fact is that there is no one 'correct position' of the left hand that will serve all purposes, and that its presentations on the face of the instrument will change radically from moment to moment if one is guided by the functional principles of effectiveness and ease. Playing an instrument is not a 'photographic' process, but a 'cinematographic' one.

In cases like the hypothetical one above, where one had to keep statically in position for a while, the working principle should be the elimination of *active* approaches and their substitution by *passive* ones. This can best be achieved by allowing Gravity to work for us and by a redistribution of effort that engages more powerful muscles that can help in improving the joint alignment by expanding the overall range of motion of the limb.

For instance, in the case of a 1st. position presentation, the holding in position of the rotated humerus requires more effort from smaller muscles than if a slight abduction were added to maintain the position. The abduction needed is well within the mid-range of the shoulder-joint's motion capabilities and therefore represents but a small effort for the powerful deltoid. But, more importantly, it reduces the amount of rotation necessary by approximating the elbow to the line of alignment of the first position. Thus, the load for the smaller muscles is decreased and, hence, the sensation of effort is diminished.

But this adjustment won't work if one abides by the other instructions concerning thumb attitude and finger presentation. The retracted thumb of the traditional position demands antagonistic efforts of its musculature to take effect simultaneously. Since some of these muscular efforts begin with thumb muscles in the forearm, the wrist joint is also affected and 'freezes' into position (flexed, to present the finger-tips properly on the fretboard). Furthermore, the forearm supination, coupled with the wrist flexion, will compress and weaken the muscles of the hypothenar eminence that control the little finger (thus making even more problematic the training of this digit). And since the fingers have to abduct, in order to keep knuckles parallel and tips separated enough to reach perpendicularly their respective frets, the fingers are placed in a dysfunctional tension state by having to extend their respective base joints markedly while the other joints flex.

The real cause of the problems created by the traditional position described above is that it pre-ordains a formalistic approach on the playing mechanism, disregarding functional effectiveness and ease. If we allow a more natural alignment, we'll see that the fingers will tend to fall slightly diagonally, with the knuckle of the first finger lying closest and the fourth-finger knuckle lying farthest from the neck (Shearer, Learning the Classic Guitar 1990, 1:45). Only a minor adjustment will be needed if the fourth finger is unusually short or inwardly curved .

This alignment diminishes the amount of rotation needed in the forearm, liberates the thumb from its retracted position and straightens and frees up the wrist. Finger abduction is no longer as necessary, since the extension span of the fingers opens up, spiral-like, from first to fourth finger. And yet, the finger action on the frets is more effective and easier than in the prescribed approach. The 'form' of their presentation on the fingerboard is the result of a better understanding of limb design and function and not forced on them as an absolute, dogmatic precondition.

Later in the chapter the all-important issue of the angle of inclination of the guitar, first addressed in Chapter 2, will be revisited in the context of left-hand technique, as it is a fundamental determinant of the hand's presentation on the fingerboard.

The Poised Limb
The concept of *poise* has been extensively used in the technical literature of piano and string pedagogy since the times of Matthay (Matthay 1947 (rev 1997), 27-28), as well as by somatic training practitioners dealing with musicians (Fishbein Adams 1995). It stands for the idea of a weightless, floating limb, ready for movement in any direction, through the perfect balance between the pull of Gravity and the necessary muscular effort needed just to overcome it. In physiological terms, a poised or floating left arm is achieved by slight contraction of the arm abductors working on the support given by the scapular muscles (primarily trapezius and rhomboids).

This, however, should never become a stiff, unmoving attitude, for there is always a certain vibrancy to good poise that gives the limb a springiness and alertness which is exactly the opposite of stiffness and immobility. Poise is the physiological reference from which we depart to states requiring more effort or release. We can think of poise as the mid-point in a range of tension levels that go from total relaxation (collapse) to maximum tension (rigidity). In good playing, one is continuously going in and out of poise, towards intensification or release of effort.

We may think of it as the guitarist's equivalent of what is known in sports science as the *posture of readiness*, characteristic for each sports activity, which prepares the body for immediate responsiveness (Adrian and Cooper 1995). The poised, floating arm takes very little effort to be set in motion. Once the sensations related to the poised limb are well-assimilated, one will see how shifting, even for small distances, can be achieved with great economy of effort, fluidity and precision through arm abduction/adduction.

With the arm abducted, in inward shifts (lower to higher positions), the initiation of movement happens through the *release* of the antigravitational effort of the muscles that are keeping the arm poised. These same muscles then control the ballistic-like, free-fall of the arm through eccentric contractions that manage the arrival of the limb at its destination. In the same shift, the outwardly rotated, non-poised arm would require an initial muscular impulse of the antagonistic rotator muscles previous relaxation of the agonists, since the passive weight factor alone will not provide enough propulsion to the arm. At the point of arrival, the latter have to contract again, this time eccentrically, to counteract the momentum of the arm. In arm rotation the linear speed of the hand, when the elbow is flexed, is quite considerable and so is the muscular effort needed to stop it. This muscular involvement will result in jerky, less co-ordinated movements.

Another way of thinking about the poised limb is as an inverted crane: the joint at the shoulder is the base of the crane, whose 'arms' (the upper- and forearm) carry back and forth the hand in its perambulations along the fingerboard. A major problem with the traditional instruction to 'relax the arm' in guitar left-hand training is that it reverses the support function of arm and hand: the latter needs to continuously hold on to the neck in order to avoid giving in to the dead weight of the 'relaxed' arm. What we need is a relaxed hand and a poised arm to support it.

 Fingerboard Slant and Weight-Release

The fact that the guitar is at an incline to the horizontal plane and, therefore, has dynamic characteristics produced by the action of Gravity that are transmitted to any object positioned in its surface, becomes an important resource in the search for an ergonomically based technique. What this means in the context of our discussion is that fingerwork on the fretboard can be minimized substantially if one learns to utilize this passive resource offered by the slant of the neck. By proper alignment of arm and hand, by properly presenting the fingers on the frets, one can save a great deal of effort in the activities of the left hand.

Concretely, the finger's perpendicular attack on the string can be made more diagonal, thus allowing the finger to feel almost as if leaning against the metal fret, rather than exerting a squeezing pressure through the thickness of the neck. For this to occur, the fingers must learn to avoid all static fixation of its joints so that they can 'cushion' themselves, through flexion, in the direction of the lean against the fret.

The skill to relax while keeping contact with the strings is based on the fact that, once the action of coming to the fret is accomplished, the muscular coordination needed for that movement changes to one of maintenance of the position, requiring less exertion. After the action is completed, the passive effort of staying in position should feel like a release of tension, when properly executed. A clear example of this may be felt if one closes the hand into a tight fist and, then, without opening the hand, one gradually loosens the grip. The sensation of muscular release will be quite marked but, nonetheless, the hand will remain closed.

This 'leaning' sensation in the actions of the left hand is the counterpart and complement of the floating, 'skating' feel it experiences at other times, in more active moments when the 'crane' of the arm carries it, free of all impediment or localized tension. In neither case will there be a need for the 'squeeze' sensation produced when arm/hand alignment and coordination are not properly applied.

Redefining 'Shifting'

As a technical category, shifting has been traditionally defined in relation to displacements of the left hand along the fingerboard, as when changing fret positions. Most methods disregard, or mention only in passing, motions across the strings, or motions of the limb in stretches and contractions. This limited view has produced the rather static approach to left-hand position described above, and hence its general technique, that finds its clearest, classic exposition in the following description by Emilio Pujol:

> The left arm parallel to the body; the forearm extended from the upper arm; the wrist, arched, and the hand, placed on the exterior face of the neck, so that, closing naturally the fingers, the thumb will come to be placed in the lower half of the neck, and the other fingers, curved over the fret board, will exert pressure on the strings with the tip of their last phalanx.

And later,

> The wide part of the hand, given the inequality in finger lengths, must remain parallel to the neck. The freedom in the movements of each finger demands that free space is present between the edge of the neck and the hand… One must avoid the hand coming close to the neck on the side of the index. This defect, besides making more difficult the action of the fourth finger, would make it impossible for the index to sustain correctly the 'ceja' [barré] over all the strings…The left hand moves diagonally to the body and in parallel to the neck and strings. It must never alter this position nor do useless efforts or contractions that would impede its elasticity… (Pujol 1956, 1:85).

Pujol does mention movements across the strings, in the vertical axis, but, as in the preceding excerpts, keeps referring to movements of 'the hand' or of 'the fingers,' not once mentioning the role of the arm in such movements. His main concern, as was the case with most methods, was the maintenance of a finger attitude that would guarantee perfect perpendicularity of attack to the fret, by keeping the hand parallel at all times to the strings with the thumb placed toward the lower half of the neck, offering support and counteracting the efforts of the fingers on the strings. As he states explicitly, this attitude was recommended to keep that hand always ready for barring.

This approach proved to be very successful. It produced some of the greatest players of the XX century (Tárrega and his students, and, to some extent, Andrés Segovia and some of his students, still active in Europe and the Americas; and other less prominent but no less distinguished artists in many countries). The rigors of this hand presentation require a disciplined digital training that, when certain anthropometrical conditions are met (a large hand size and/or stretching capability), produces accurate, solid, even brilliant playing of a good amount of the traditional repertoire. It is an approach that favors positional fingerings, finger stretches and contractions, and avoids shifting whenever possible. The shifts that unavoidably have to occur are executed with minimum upper arm abduction, using instead upper arm rotation complemented with forearm flexion/extension and rotation.

It demands a visually homogeneous attitude of the hand on the board at all times, purposefully minimizing arm and finger movements. Evaluating the approach from an ergonomic viewpoint, however, we can perceive a couple of drawbacks. Firstly, it is comparatively inefficient, in terms of the expenditure of energy required to accomplish effectively the tasks of the left hand. Secondly, in less physically gifted players, the stresses affecting the limb under this method may, over time, cause permanent injury or, at best, produce stilted, mannered interpretations as performers try to accommodate the music to the limitations of their technique. This is particularly noticeable in the approach to *legato* playing across positions.

The problem originates with the basic dogma of the school: keeping the arm close and parallel to the body. So constrained, the displacements of the hand over the surface of the fret board rely primarily on the swift but physically demanding rotation of the humerus which, additionally, creates alignment problems to the hand in the first positions. To overcome the latter, the forearm is required to extend and supinate and the wrist to flex in order to maintain a parallel trajectory to the neck and to allow a perpendicular presentation of the fingers on the strings. In so doing, the thumb will, indeed, fall towards 'the lower half of the neck,' a position that is, then, taken as visual cue to evaluate the correctness of the hand's demeanor. The additional prescription to leave space between the fingers and the neck, while sound for the upper strings, produces substantial amounts of stress when playing in the lower strings, since the hand has to be kept away by increasing the wrist flexion.

Form and Function

In short, this traditional position, still advocated even by authors who, otherwise, have contributed excellently to modern guitar pedagogy, in its well-intentioned search for an effective protocol for technical development in the left hand, prescribes a 'form' that disregards certain elements of the limb's structure, and, as a consequence, defaults on the fundamental principle of organic design, whether in architecture or ergonomics: *form follows function* (Sullivan 1980). By restricting the range of motions in the joints of the left limb it imposes artificial and unnecessary limits to the technical possibilities of the guitarist's left hand.

In order to keep the arm close to the body, the Tárrega school approach, as described by Pujol and others, demanded that the slant of the neck, relative to the ground, be no higher than that which would keep the tuning head level with the shoulder-line:

> The neck must be so inclined as to allow the fingers to be placed parallel to the frets.
> This inclination is about 20 to 25^0, that is to say, one that keeps the head of the guitar
> level with the shoulders (Aguado, Método de Guitarra 1943, n/p). [Author's translation].

This position limits the need for upper-arm abduction while relying, for shifts, on upper-arm rotation and forearm flexion/extension and rotation.

The principle of maintaining the arm close to the body can be made to work more organically by making the angle of inclination of the guitar quite steep. In this fashion, movements of shoulder flexion (when the upper arm moves forward from the body), a less strenuous endeavor, can substitute movements of upper-arm rotation necessary to reach the first positions when the guitar is held at shoulder level. The most successful, and extreme, example of this approach can be seen in the brilliant innovations of guitarist Paul Galbraith, who, taking the change to its logical outcome, has redesigned the instrument so that it be played in a semi-vertical position, allowing him a shifting technique in which not only movements of upper-arm abduction, but also rotation, are minimized.

Though admirable, Mr. Galbraith's solution to the problem of left-hand mobility presented by the traditional approach is akin to Alexander the Great's handling of the Gordian knot. It does not offer practical guidance to those not yet ready to follow his visionary path. The problem may be better understood by posing a series of simple questions: Why should the arm be kept close to the body? Why should the thumb be kept on the lower half of the neck? Why should the hand remain parallel to the neck? Why should the fingers play perpendicularly to the frets? Why should there always be a space between the edge of the neck and the hand?

As anyone who has carefully observed the great guitar players in action will agree, none of them, including avowed proponents of the traditional positional approach, play in this way all the time. In fact, the greater the player, the more versatile and 'functional' his or her left hand-and-arm movements are. It is just physically impossible to achieve virtuosic speed and accuracy by submitting the left limb continuously to the "myriad opposing static tensions" caused by this approach.

Liberating the upper arm (the shoulder joint), allowing full range of mobility towards the tuning head (abduction) and towards the sound box (adduction) becomes, de facto, a pre-condition for attaining the freedom of movement in the other limb joints needed for virtuoso-level mastery of the fingerboard. Liberating the thumb from the dictum of maintaining its position in the lower half of the neck is the next major advance, for this will allow it to move higher on the neck, freeing up the wrist from its excessive flexion.

For these adjustments to work, however, the angle of inclination of the neck has to be increased to about 35 to 40°, placing the tuning head at least at eye-level rather than shoulder level. These three factors will allow the upper arm to align with the hand closer to the position in which the fingers are acting, thus reducing the need for forearm supination. In so doing, the wide of the hand will come closer to the lower edge of the neck, with a slight diagonal presentation that approximates the index knuckle more than the little finger's... Another broken taboo!

On the treble strings, the fingers' presentation on the board becomes more spiral-like, with gradually diminishing levels of finger flexion from the first to the fourth digit. The spatial relations thus created between neck, thumb and index finger configures the hand into what kinesiologists term a **dynamic posture** that has some similarities with the hand attitude described by Kató Havas in her New Approach to Violin Playing (Havas 1978).

Dynamic posture and **attitude of readiness** are concepts from kinesiology that define the body attitudes when actively engaged in an athletic or sports activity, and when readying for such, respectively. Each sport has its characteristic attitude of readiness, for instance the starting position of racers and swimmers, the guard stance of a boxer, or of the tennis player receiving serve, etc. By its very nature, it cannot be maintained indefinitely, as it becomes evident in athletic competition when the starting gun is delayed more than participants expect. The dynamic postures that the body or one of its segments adopts in the course of an activity have the function of bringing the center of gravity of the body, or body segments, closer to the goal of the motion. In contrast, a *static posture* maintains the body stable by keeping the center of gravity aligned with the vertical axis of the body.

Differences apart, caused principally by the different dimensions and orientations of the neck of the guitar and the neck of the violin, both left-hand dynamic postures free the hand from any responsibility of support for the instrument, or any sensation of 'grabbing' to stay in place.

On the guitar, as the hand moves to the lower strings, its position squares off more and more, aided by the adduction movements of the upper arm, until, by the time it reaches the sixth string, it looks quite similar to the ideal of the traditional rule, except that there will be contact between the edge of the neck and the base of the finger knuckles, unless the music requires notes on the open first string, in which case the attitude of the hand and arm will resemble even more the traditional ideal.

Shearer, again, gives good advice:

> Your hand, wrist, and arm must never hinder the freedom and ease of your fingers – any reduction of freedom and ease will cause counterproductive tension. *In left-hand positioning, your hand, wrist, and arm should always yield to the pull of your fingers as they execute movements on the fingerboard.* I refer to this as *left-hand mobility* (emphasis in the original) (Shearer, Left-Hand 1991, 26).

In short, the freedom of movements throughout the limb joints permits a functional match between the *form* of a particular presentation and its *goal*. The best 'forms' are those that combine maximum effectiveness with maximum efficiency. Effectiveness is evaluated by how the procedure *sounds*; efficiency, by how it *feels*. This becomes a great pedagogical challenge, whether we are teaching others or ourselves. Until the appropriate kinesthesia is assimilated, it is difficult to differentiate between more or less efficient movement forms. The visual appearance can help identify dysfunctional approaches, but 'looks' can be deceiving too.

In this new context, the concept of *shifting* becomes the fundamental technical category for the left hand, for, as we shall see, a flowing, unimpeded technique requires continuous co-ordination of fingerwork and arm movement: every left-hand technical procedure used in performance, from extensions to vibrato, has a shifting component.

Section 2. Towards a Typology of Shifting

As a working tool, we will define a shift as **any arm movement that produces a change in the presentation of the fingers over the fingerboard**. Functionally speaking, the hand's work consists of activity along the fingerboard (position changes and horizontal extensions/contractions) and across the fingerboard (across-the-strings changes within a given position). We can, therefore, distinguish three major sub-categories, or types, of shifts:

Interpositional shifts: when the hand moves from one fret position to another, in parallel to the strings.
Intrapositional shifts: when the hand changes attitudes within a given fret position, transversally across the strings.
Compound shifts: when both types are combined.

With these concepts in mind, we can now attempt a description of shifting procedures through which each type can be understood according to its physiological mechanics.

 Interpositional Shift

It is important to reiterate how intimate a connection exists among the limb joints, and how a certain attitude at one joint will either favor or impede the proper involvement of other arm joints. For instance, when playing a descending scale pattern on one string only, the basic joint movements occurring at the shoulder joint are abduction and outward rotation.

However, the degree to which the upper arm will be able to abduct depends to a great extent on the attitude of the thumb behind the neck, since, if it be kept low on the back of the neck (as recommended by tradition), it will demand a degree of forearm supination that will hinder the range of upper arm abduction in the upper arm.

Thus, in this situation, shifting towards the first positions will primarily rely on upper arm rotation, as described earlier, and forearm extension. Freeing up the thumb will allow a more natural attitude of the forearm that will, in turn, allow the full range of abduction at the shoulder. In any case, and precisely because of this relationship, interpositional shifts on the lower strings rely more heavily on upper-arm rotation than do shifts in the higher strings, since the thumb lies, by necessity, lower on the neck to accommodate the 'squaring off' of the hand position.

The co-ordination of these movements becomes the key technical issue, since a whole range of timing possibilities exists, depending on the musical circumstances within which the shifting occurs. Modern methods that have transcended the formalism of the traditional position now recommend that in interpositional shifts "the elbow leads," meaning that the initial stage of the shift is energized by movement at the shoulder joint.

However, not much attention has been given to the timing sequence that co-ordinates the abduction or adduction phase of the movement with the rotation, a fundamental aspect of the technique.

 Upbeats

The rotation movement of the humerus imparts a much greater linear velocity to the hand than its abduction/

adduction, but its range of motion is more limited. (Rigorously speaking, 'linear velocity' is, in fact, a misnomer for the speed of a movement of a limb or limb segment. Since the trajectory of such a movement is always along an arc of a circle, it is more appropriate to speak of *tangential velocity*, which is directly related to the length of the limb from its axis of rotation (the radius of the circle) and the angular velocity, which is the speed of rotation at the joint. The formula relating both is: $v_t = r\omega$, where v_t stands for tangential velocity, r for the length of the radius, and ω for the angular velocity. In the case of upper arm rotation, the speed of the hand's movement is the result of multiplying the speed of rotation or angular velocity of the humerus at the shoulder by the length of the forearm from the elbow to the fingertips, which explains the swiftness of the hand's trajectory.)

Hence, in longer shifts, it becomes necessary to *anticipate* the upper arm's abduction/adduction in a rhythmic relationship to the beginning of the rotation movement that will complete the displacement of the hand to its new position: the abduction/adduction aligns the limb closer to the arrival position, making the concluding rotation more functionally effective. The timing of these two phases of the shifting process runs the gamut from being an almost imperceptibly overlapping sequence, to becoming two clearly delimited, separate movements.

What is inalterable is the need to feel and execute the anticipated abduction/adduction as an *upbeat* to the moment when the change of position occurs. Depending on tempo, and the character of the music, the value of this upbeat will be shorter or longer. Legato phrasing will require, in general, shorter anticipations that dove-tail smoothly with the final rotation, so as to avoid the 'jerkiness' that, unavoidably, accompanies the latter: the faster the movement, the more momentum has to be controlled upon arrival, demanding a substantial amount of energy in the contractions of the opposing antagonist musculature that stops the motion, hence the relative violence of the activity.

However, more disjointed, angular music, containing big registral displacements along the fingerboard, will benefit from a more staggered approach, through which the anticipated arm movement presents the limb in its new position well before the hand is finally taken there by the energetic rotation. Care should be taken, however, not to abuse this last approach, for it imposes a considerably greater amount of stress on the musculature controlling the shoulder joint (the *rotator cuff*).

Pivots

As per the discussion above, a well-executed interpositional shift begins with an arm motion that precedes the hand's. This means that fingers must remain in their frets while the arm moves, momentarily acting as pivots for the arm motion, lest note values are cut short and all musical continuity is destroyed. This is a fundamental insight that opens the door to an investigation of the role of the wrist and the finger joints in shifting.

Indeed, it is at the wrist that many problems related to shifting originate, either because of dysfunctional tension or flabbiness. The wrist must respond to the shifting motions initiated by the arm, by "yielding," as Shearer puts it, in the direction of movement. In general, this means that it will extend in upward and flex in downward shifts. Once again, the degree of wrist involvement will vary according to the strings where the shifting occurs, being greater in the higher than in the lower strings, and the distance to be traversed: bigger shifts will result in more wrist motion than smaller ones. However, it must be emphasized that these wrist movements occur as *passive responses to the shifting actions of the arm*, not as the result of contractions in the wrist's own musculature. Of course, this is a pragmatic simplification of a process that always involves very sophisticated, but intuitive, controlling involvement of the musculature that manages the apparent passivity of the wrist to allow the hand to achieve its goals of accuracy and speed. The degree of relative fixation (as in a straight wrist) or flexibility is managed by the well-trained player's refined sensitivity to the musical and technical context at the moment.

In other words, it is the relative absence of excess tension at the wrist, its flexibility, that allows the proper co-ordination of movements between arm and fingers in many shifting contexts. The same principle applies to the finger joints, particularly the MCP joints: they must be freed from any tension that would impede their passive response to the arm-wrist movements, thus allowing the fingers to hold their respective notes while they extend or flex in the direction of shifting as the arm initiates the move. This particular application of the pivot-finger principle, though related, is of a different nature than the more usual understanding of the concept, which we shall discuss when we study intrapositional shifting technique.

 **Intrapositional Shifts**

Any movement of the hand across the strings and within a given position will benefit from appropriate arm-wrist-hand co-ordination, to avoid dysfunctional tension in the fingerwork. The most common application of this shifting type is when playing a chord sequence within the same fret position, but it occurs also in any form of positional scale playing, slurring, changes from barré to non-barré presentations, extended and contracted fingerings, etc. From a physiomechanical standpoint, these shifts combine upper arm abduction/adduction with *forearm* rotation, instead of the *upper arm* rotation needed for interpositional shifts. Equally important are flexion and extension, both at the shoulder and at the elbow joint. As in interpositional shifts, the wrist plays a vital role in this technique, generally flexing when the upper arm flexes and/or abducts and extending when it extends/adducts. Furthermore, all the considerations discussed above concerning timing factors, i.e., upbeat moments through which the arm movement anticipates the new hand presentation, also apply.

Vertical Extensions

To better understand the mechanism of these movements, the following diagram of the fingerboard seen frontally, representing the two axes of alignment of the hand on a normal, 4-fret position, may prove useful (the schematic diagrams are, obviously, only approximations):

Diagram 3-1

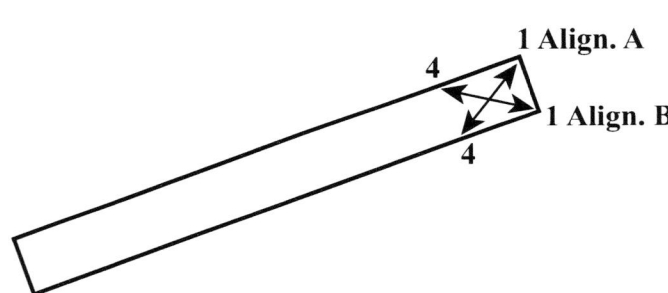

The numbers stand for fingers 1 and 4, and for frets 1 and 4 as well. The diagram summarizes the alignment possibilities of the hand within a position, thus:

Alignment A. Higher-numbered finger is placed on a lower-numbered string than the lower-numbered fingers (in the diagram, 1 plays F on ⑥ and finger 4 plays A♭ on ①).

Alignment B. Lower-numbered finger is placed on a lower-numbered string than the higher-numbered fingers (in the diagram, 1 plays F on ① and finger 4 plays A♭ on ⑥).

Alignment A requires upper arm abduction/extension, forearm pronation and, in the lower positions, wrist flexion; alignment B, upper arm adduction/flexion, forearm supination and wrist extension. In theory, the hand and forearm will align perpendicularly to the imaginary axis line that could be drawn linking the lowest to the highest placed finger. This is generally true in Alignment B, but in Alignment A it applies only to positions higher than the third or fourth, approximately: in lower positions, the perpendicular alignment of the forearm is made less pronounced by wrist flexion, without which the upper arm abduction would have to reach extreme, therefore dysfunctional, levels. Even in higher positions the player may use more wrist flexion than might be needed, because of particular contextual circumstance. However, the dorsum of the hand should keep perpendicular to the imaginary axis. Between these two extremes lie all possible gradations of these joint movements and angles of presentation:

Diagram 3-2: Alignment type A, showing alignment of *hand* with axis.

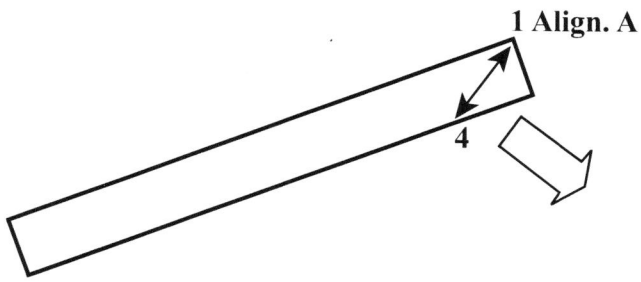

Diagram 3-3: Alignment type B showing alignment of *hand and forearm* with axis

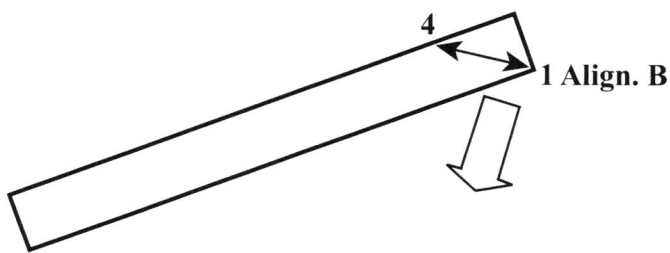

It is important to note that as the fret positions move higher on the fingerboard and the width of the neck increases, the capability of the fourth finger to reach the lowest strings, in forms of the type B alignment, is diminished, until it is no longer possible for this finger to reach across, at which point the player will use the third or even the second finger. The general alignment principles defined earlier, though, do not change.

Photo 3-1. Alignment A   **Photo 3-2. Alignment B**

Photos Wayne Armstrong

Movements from one form of alignment to the other are very frequent in guitar playing and are most easily executed through the use of a pivot finger upon which the arm's movements occur. This is the most common understanding of the pivot-finger principle, and is the foundation for the technique of the so-called 'squeeze shift,' discussed later.

125

The concept at work in these across-the-strings movements is that of *vertical extension*: for purposes of our analysis, vertical extension is determined to be present when the fingers play on strings separated from each other by a number greater than the difference between the finger numbers (for instance, finger 2 playing one string lower or higher than finger 1 would be normal position. Playing two strings or more away would be a vertical extension). The movement characteristics required for each type of alignment, as per the diagram, are exacerbated the more extreme the vertical extension becomes, that is to say, as the respective alignment forms get closer to being parallel to the frets. This alignment (F on ⑥ with finger 1 and A♭ on ① with finger 4).

Diagram 3-4

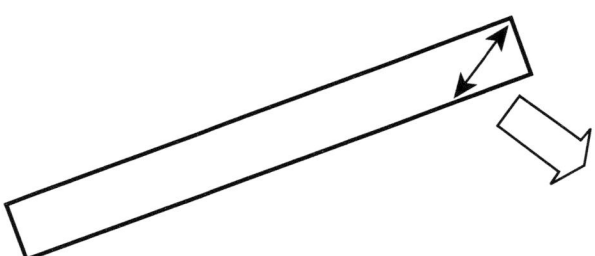

will require less upper arm abduction, forearm pronation and wrist flexion than this (F on ⑥ with finger 1 and F♯ on ① with finger 4),

Diagram 3-5

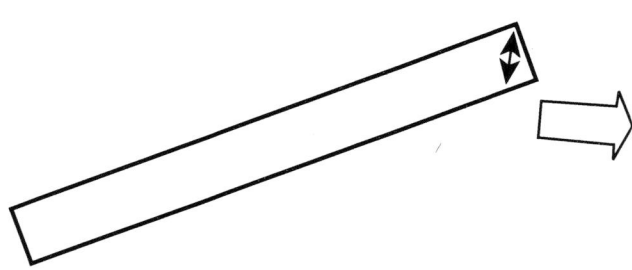

By the same token, as the fingers move closer together, vertically, the arm alignment characteristics of each alignment type, while still applying, become less pronounced.

Diagram 3-6. 1 stops the F on ⑥ while 4 plays F# on ④

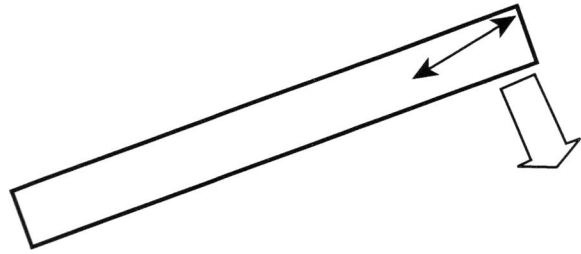

It should be noted, however, that these relationships hold primarily for presentations involving fingers 1, 2 and 3 and 1, 2 and 4. Presentations involving fingers 3 and 4 allow for arm movements that, under certain circumstances, contradict the general principles described above.

This is so because of the location of the little finger's knuckle joint, which, in most hands, lies level with or more proximal than that of the ring finger. This peculiarity permits this finger to "stack" under the 3rd finger, so to speak, and, thus, to allow for arm attitudes that resemble alignment type B more than the type A that, in theory, would prevail when 4 lies on a higher string than 3.

As was discussed previously, the variation in arm-hand co-ordination also depends on which strings are being used: lower strings (musically speaking; the higher-numbered ones) require more upper arm adduction, forearm supination and wrist flexion, than higher (lower-numbered) strings.

A most interesting issue surfaces when *horizontal* extensions and contractions are considered, for they require radical changes to the norms that apply within the normal positional finger span.

Horizontal Stretches/Squeezes

Whenever the left-hand fingers separate (abduct) further than their standard contiguous-fret presentation, one is horizontally 'stretching' or 'extending'. Whenever the fingers come closer than this standard separation (adduct), one is horizontally 'contracting' or 'squeezing'. Technically, a so-called 'stretch' or extension, in the horizontal plane, is any hand position demanding a finger separation bigger than the normal 4-fret span.

Considered physiologically, it is a partial or total finger extension, combined with greater or lesser degrees of finger abduction. This distinction is an important one to keep in mind when dealing with passages where, though the position is, technically, 'normal,' the hand is, physiologically, stretched. This happens in the first and second positions and, depending on the size of the instrument relative to the player, even the third and fourth. Incidentally, this is a major argument against initiating young students into left-hand training on the first positions of the fingerboard: the complexities of the arm-hand-fingers co-ordination in the early positions are considerably greater than in positions from the fifth fret onwards. The use of a capo, though presenting other types of problems, might be a good solution.

The role of intrapositional shifting in handling these situations is often overlooked, causing greater digital effort than would be needed if appropriate arm involvement were allowed. Physiologically, extensions and contractions happen through the complex interaction of the intrinsic muscles of the hand with the longer finger extensor/flexor muscles located in the forearm.

As described in Chapter 1, the common extensor has as its main function the extension of the knuckle joints. Extension at the phalanges occur when the intrinsics act synergistically with the extensor in avoiding the passive pull of the flexors, which would, if unopposed, flex the tip and middle joints, resulting in a claw–like finger demeanor.

In technical contractions (squeezes), the intrinsics act in collaboration with the finger flexors, while the extensor relaxes (although not totally, given its additional role as stabilizer of the MCP joint (Caillet 1994)). This allows for the knuckle flexion without which finger adduction becomes harder. Although the finger adductors may bring the fingers together even if the knuckles remain extended, this action would set the flexor mechanism to work at odd purposes with the extensor, thus creating dysfunctional levels of tension. Adduction occurs more naturally if the knuckle joints flex.

Vertical extension always involves more flexion in one finger than in the other, with some degree of abduction if the position remains normal or extended in the horizontal plane. Frequently, vertical extension is combined with horizontal contraction, as in the so-called *inverted fingerings*, where a higher-numbered finger is placed on the same fret as a lower-numbered finger, but on a higher-numbered string than the latter. These require finger adduction (even hyper-adduction), forearm supination and upper arm adduction/flexion. These techniques are among the most challenging facing the guitarist, and require careful scrutiny lest we force the playing mechanism to excessive states of tension.

Intrapositional Shifting and its Role in Extension/Contraction Techniques

The proper alignment of the arm with the hand and fingers is the most important issue in mastering these techniques. This means that the arm must follow the direction of motion of the extension or contraction movement and not stay statically in place. In this manner, the degree of purely digital muscular effort (i.e., the effort of the intrinsic muscles) will be diminished by the help of arm movements that will favor a better alignment of the elbow and wrist in relation with the extending or contracting finger(s).

This collaboration of the arm will also increase the range of extension possible. Although the infinite variety of contexts in which these procedures may occur does not allow for generalizations about procedural approaches, the following guidelines should be kept in mind when analyzing extension/contraction situations:

1. Horizontal extensions on the lower strings are simpler than in the higher strings because wrist flexion happens while the thumb still keeps good contact with the neck. The higher the hand moves across the strings, the more unstable the thumb support will be and the more effort will be needed to flex the wrist. This flexion of the wrist is needed in many instances of extension because otherwise the knuckles of the fingers cannot be kept extended, a necessary precondition for their separation (abduction) to be possible. Normally, the wrist's movements co-ordinate in opposition to the fingers' (i.e., wrist flexion favors finger extension/abduction while wrist extension favors finger flexion/adduction) (Shearer, Learning the Classic Guitar 1990, vol. 1, 34).

2. As the hand moves to the higher strings and, especially, if its alignment is of the B type described above, a more effective stretch is sometimes achieved if the fingers avoid abduction by approaching the fret board more diagonally. The forearm pronates rather than supinates and the wrist hyper-extends as it slightly deviates radially. The upper arm helps through marked adduction/flexion.

3. In some extreme cases, even the shoulder has to be depressed somewhat (scapular rotation) or the torso flexed laterally to achieve the reach. These are the only instances where these shoulder or torso movements would be needed in guitar playing.

4. Given the structure of the hand, with its tendinous attachments linking the three last digits and limiting the mobility of the ring finger, but with a very independent index extensor mechanism, stretches towards the index from a higher-numbered finger are easier than the opposite. For the same reason, extensions from either finger 2 or 4 to finger 3 are more difficult than extensions departing from finger 3. This condition has important implications when deciding how to finger certain passages involving placement of fingers 2, 3 and 4.

5. Simultaneous finger abduction in opposite directions should be avoided whenever possible, as it requires a great deal of static tension in the whole arm and hand mechanism to serve as support for the opposition of effort. Extensions should ideally always happen from a point of passive support, a pivot (i.e., finger contact with the fingerboard).

6. Adduction (contraction) is, generally, a more passive digital movement than abduction (extension). Again, a pivot-point origin to the adduction makes it even easier. This is what happens in squeeze-shifts, through which a change of fret position is achieved by first contracting the fingering in a scalar passage.

7. The degree of fluidity of the extension/contraction movement is directly related to the arm's cooperation in making the procedure as passive as possible from the standpoint of finger effort. A properly executed intrapositional shift at the right moment will allow the finger extension/contraction to become a relatively passive gesture.

8. The nature of the arm-wrist-hand co-ordination in extensions is similar to that of barré positions. Therefore, the latter should be studied as a sub-category of extension procedures. As a matter of fact, Pujol's warning against

approximating the index knuckle to the neck, lest it becomes "impossible for the index to sustain correctly the 'ceja' [barré] over all the strings…" gives an important clue as to the rationale for the relative immobility of the orthodox position: though recommended to keep the hand ready, at all times, for six-string barrés, it also readied the hand permanently for finger abduction, i.e., for "stretches," without involving the arm. However, as we noted earlier, finger abduction alone will not allow the reach possible when intrapositional arm movement supports the stretch at the appropriate moment.

Track 3-4 *Barrés*

In a barré, finger 1 (occasionally, another finger) simultaneously presses down on two or more contiguous strings by extending one or more phalanges across the strings. The traditional technical concept of the barré has been enriched in modern guitar playing to a level not imaginable a generation ago. Aside from the traditional categories of **full** and **partial** barrés, Frank Koonce, in his article series for *Soundboard* (Koonce, Tricks 1992), identifies **hinge**, **cross-fret**, and **inner-strings** barrés, as well as barrés with fingers other than the index.

Barrés are traditionally defined according to the number of strings covered. Thus a full barré is one covering all six strings, while all others would be considered partial. However, it becomes convenient to approach the definition of these procedures in relation to the finger's attitude, rather than the span covered, given the similarities and differences that, from a physiomechanical standpoint, group various forms into well-defined sub-categories. In what follows, the physiomechanics of the principal types will be attempted, beginning with those executed by the index finger.

Full Barré: Six-string, Hanging and Hinge
Physiologically, a barré is full when the MCP joint flexes and the two IP joints extend (i.e., keeping the finger straight from the bent knuckle). This barré may be used to cover any number of contiguous strings, from three to six, but is not used to cover just a few intermediate strings. A particularly exceptional form is the so-called cross-fret or split barré, in which the index's distal phalanx lies one fret higher than its proximal phalanx. It may well be considered an arch barré (discussed later) rather than a full barré, since the intermediate strings between first and six are hard, if not impossible, to make sound clearly.

We may call *hanging* the barré that, though full, covers only the three, four or five higher strings. A hanging barré, though possible, would not be practical when only the two upper trebles need to be covered, since this will not allow effective fingerwork of the other digits.

Photos 3-3 to 3-6. Full and hanging barrés. Photos Wayne Armstrong.

A particularly useful kind of full barré is the so-called *hinge barré*, in which the finger, though extended at the phalanxes, contacts only the first string by diminishing the degree of base-joint and wrist flexions, typically in preparation of a full six-string barré.

It is important to note that the extension in the distal phalanges during a hinge barré is not necessarily as pronounced as it is for a full barré, since only the base of the proximal phalanx is in contact with any string. Excess tension, in this context, will make the hinge feel more difficult to achieve than it really is.

Photo 3-7. Hinge barré. Photo Wayne Armstrong.

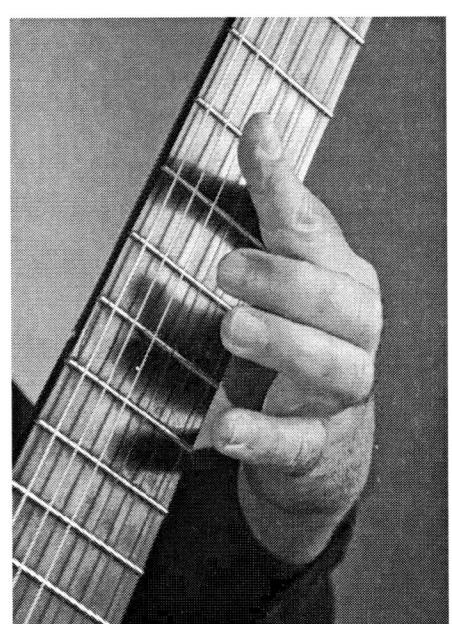

Another common use of the hinge barré concept is when a note sustained by the first finger in one of the lower strings serves as a pivot point for the index to subsequently extend itself across the remaining higher strings in either a full, hanging or partial barré.

Physiomechanics of the Full Barré
It seems safe to speculate that the primary muscular effort in the full barré is that of the intrinsic hand muscles acting on the index: the index finger lumbrical maintains IP joint extension while the index interossei (dorsal and palmar) forcefully flex the finger's MCP joint. The extrinsic flexors and extensors do not seem to be involved.

However, this presentation may be assisted by appropriate flexion in the wrist, to provide better support to the work of the intrinsics. If the wrist is kept straight, the muscles' angle of pull will be too shallow to provide enough power for the flexion to overcome the strings' resistance. The full barré will not be strong enough to produce clear, clean notes, and, in fact, the proximal IP joint will flex unavoidably as the wrist straightens.

By flexing the wrist, while the intrinsics maintain the first finger's attitude, the force against the string resistance is applied in part by the pull of the more powerful wrist flexors, bigger muscles that also act at a much more advantageous angle of pull.

Aside from the problems presented by the action of placing the barré, it is the independence of motion of the other fingers that needs special attention. As discussed in Chapter 1, forceful intrinsic activity in one finger tends to produce parallel 'slave' responses in neighboring digits.

To achieve its independence, the middle finger needs to overcome this reflex response by extending its base (MCP) joint as it abducts to the ulnar side, and the other fingers should also extend their base joint in order to allow for whatever finger activity might be required. Were they to follow the index' attitude of MCP flexion, they

130

would be incapable of abducting enough to manage whatever fingerwork might be required, since MCP flexion forces adduction of the fingers. It is precisely this complex coordination of muscular efforts that makes the barré such an arduous task for beginning (and even more advanced) players.

However, the circumstances that made intrapositional shifting an integral part of finger extension technique are also in effect when doing barrés. For instance, appropriately timed arm abduction/adduction movements are helpful in accommodating 2, 3 and 4 in the various strings, while the barré sustains its position.

The static effort of holding the barré, combined with the muscle work required for the arm movements, superimposed upon which are the individual finger movements, creates one of the most physically demanding tasks in guitar playing.

The scales in the beginning section of Villa-Lobos' *Estudo No. 7*, if played in barré positions, are a classic example of this situation, as is the second section of his *Estudo No. 2* (measures 14 through 20), with its intrapositional arpeggios (Villa-Lobos 1953).

The latter is a particularly challenging application of the pivot-finger principle (i.e., intrapositional arm motions around a fixed point of finger contact with the fingerboard, in this case, the barré).

An important element in finding an appropriate solution to this passage is the hand's capability to change its attitude from full to hinge-type barré, as the arpeggio moves to the top string. The hinge releases momentarily the accumulated tension of holding the full barré, thus refreshing the muscular apparatus of the hand and improving the hand's endurance.

This move is easily achieved if the arm is left free to abduct/adduct as the arpeggio evolves, but becomes quite arduous if opposed by excessive tension in the hand (as tends to happen with less experienced players).

The arm's alignment in barrés becomes more cumbersome in the lower positions. The tendency to tilt the barré towards its outer side (that is, rotating the forearm towards supination) increases, especially in weaker hands or if the instrument is too big for the player. The middle finger then tends to help the index by abducting towards it instead of ulnarly and, as a consequence, the other fingers become extremely limited in their independent motility.

It is for these reasons that it might be advisable to introduce barré technique in higher positions first. Despite the fact that string tension is slightly higher in these positions, the problem of arm alignment will not be such a detrimental factor as it is in the lower positions.

Physiomechanics of Partial Barrés
Partial barrés are of different kinds, but all have in common the fact that the finger's middle joint is flexed while the tip joint extends. This implies a primary engagement of FDS and no activity of FDP. The MCP joint may be more or less extended: in full extension, the ED must be fully engaged, with no activity of any intrinsic musculature, while greater MCP flexion might indicate some interossei involvement (the lumbricals remain inactive, unless the proximal IP joint begins to extend).

Generally, partial barrés are used when no more than four contiguous strings are to be covered. However, depending on hand size relative to the instrument, in the first five, six or even seven positions, five strings may still be covered with the middle joint somewhat flexed. The uses of partial barrés are numerous and applicable in a great variety of contexts. Although it would be futile to attempt a comprehensive survey of their different types, a few general elements common to the technique at large may be identified:

1. Equivalent levels of flexion or extension in the wrist match the level of flexion or extension in the base joint of the index.

   Based on this, we can identify two major types of partial barrés, which we may call *nested* and *unnested*. In the former, the knuckle joint and the wrist extend, bringing the palm closer to the neck and making the angle of presentation of the fingers more diagonal thanks to the unavoidable forearm pronation. This favors access of fingers 2 and 3 (but not 4) to some of the lower strings. (In general, in barré situations, full six-string barrés are better than partial barrés for allowing freedom of action of the other fingers in the lower strings.)

   In the unnested type, the base joint and the wrist may adopt various degrees of flexion or extension, but the alignment of the fingers is more perpendicular, and the hand is supinated. In fact, the unnested partial barré could be considered as an intermediate state between the hanging barré and the nested partial. This attitude favors action of the other fingers in the trebles (as does the hanging full barré) and helps somewhat with access of the 4th finger to the fingerboard.

   Choosing one or another approach, however, is mostly conditioned by the context of movement within which the situation occurs, i.e., where is the hand coming from and where is it going.

Photo 3-8. Unnested partial barré

Photo 3-9. Nested partial barré

2. The capability of the tip joint to slightly hyperextend, given the slackness in the FDP tendon, is an advantage for achieving partial barrés, particularly on the lower or intermediate strings (inner-string barrés).

Photo 3-10. Inner-string barré. It may also function as a hinge barré , from which the index may extend more or less fully to engage the remaining higher strings. Photos Wayne Armstrong.

132

3. In situations when only the two top strings need to be covered, a nested barré, with the finger bent at the middle joint, will give much better leverage than a full hanging or even an unnested partial barré because it allows the thumb to establish more perpendicular contact with the neck.

4. For situations in which three upper strings are covered, the context of what the other fingers have to do will tell whether a hanging or a partial barré (of either type) is better.

5. For barrés that cover four or five contiguous upper strings, the length of the finger will decide if a partial, bent barré is enough, or if a full hanging one is preferable.

   For shorter fingers, the flexion at the mid-joint might not be strong enough to overcome the resistance of the four strings, since the primary agonist is the FDS, acting at a rather disadvantageous angle of pull, and the added support of increased wrist flexion, possible only when the finger has its IP joints extended, will be a valuable asset.

6. Some scholars suggest the capability of the index to cover the first five strings at the fifth fret with the finger bent at the middle joint as an anthropometrical marker of appropriate instrument size (Duncan, The Art of Classical Guitar Playing 1980, 18).

As mentioned earlier, perhaps the most decisive factor determining whether to use a full or a partial barré is the alignment conditions at the moment of coming into the barré situation.

Traditionally, it is common practice to barré only from the lowest-pitched string used in the passage. However, this approach disregards the all-important issue of arm-hand alignment in the ever-changing dynamic attitudes of the fingers on the fingerboard. This topic will be dealt with in greater detail when we discuss compound shifting.

Barrés With Other Fingers

Although fairly common in the electric guitar, barrés with fingers other than 1 are used exceptionally in the classic guitar. These will, by necessity, be partial and need the support of considerable upper arm involvement, to align the hand in appropriate ways for the proper execution of the barré. The alignment approach for these barrés should be considered as more extreme variants of the type A alignment described above.

Photos 3-11 to 3-13. Partial barrés with fingers 2, 3 and 4 (the last two in combination with a full barré).
Photos Wayne Armstrong.

Nowadays even using the thumb over the fingerboard, in similar fashion to the cellist's *capotasto*, is not unusual, but the technique falls beyond the scope of this survey.

Intrapositional Scales, Arpeggios and Chords

Arm-hand alignment issues figure prominently in intrapositional passages of a scalar, chordal or arpeggiated nature. The didactic literature of the Classico-Romantic era is plentiful in examples of these procedures but, unfortunately, the technical instruction provided by the authors is, at best, broad and conventional or, at its worst, constraining and static. Nonetheless, these materials can be as useful today as they were when first introduced, if a more functional understanding of left-hand technique is applied. A few examples, drawn from XIX century sources as well as more modern materials, will provide valuable insights into the intricacies of intrapositional shifting procedures.

Intrapositional scales

The beginning of Carcassi's Study Op. 60, No. 1 is a classic example of an intrapositional scalar passage in which the arm's alignment is key to properly resolve its technical challenges:

Example 3-1

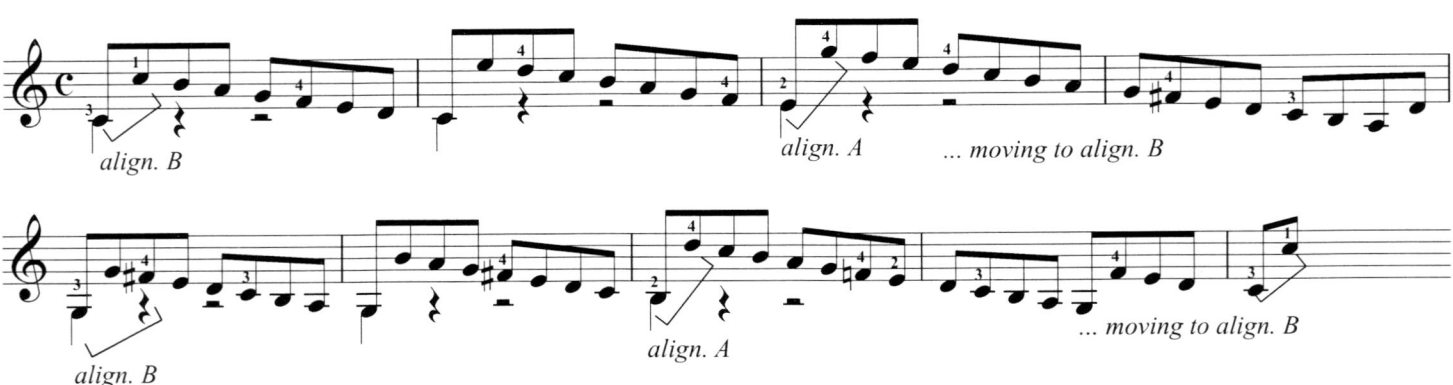

Although it might appear, at first sight, that the whole passage may be resolved without any arm involvement (and, indeed, it is possible to perform it in this fashion), a richer approach, incorporating appropriately timed intrapositional shifting movements, will prove to be more productive and illuminating.

1. The initial type B alignment becomes a type A alignment at the 3ʳᵈ measure, when 2 reaches E on ④ and 4 plays G on ①, immediately to rotate back to type B as the scale continues through the F on ① with 1.
2. The same occurs at measure 7, as B and D are played. Additional intrapositional adjustment will also favor the small stretch needed to reach the 4ᵗʰ fret for the F♯ on ④ at measures 4, 5 and 6.

> This mobility can be so well timed and flowing as to become inconspicuous to the casual observer. In fact, if these movements become noticeable, the player is probably over-exerting and, hence, defeating the whole purpose of this choreographed, rotationally free, liberating arm-hand coordination.

Intrapositional Chordal and Arpeggio Passages

Intrapositional arm-hand alignment issues become more complex when three or four left-hand fingers work simultaneously, as in chordal passages, or in relatively rapid succession, as in a chordally based arpeggiated sequence. The example below, drawn from the author's Miniature No. 1 (Iznaola, Two Miniatures 1993), shows a three-voice chordal texture within the confines of the first position.

Example 3-2. Ricardo Iznaola. Miniature no. 1, beginning.

A common problem, frequently found in the classical didactic literature, is presented here: vertical displacements of a finger (in this case, 1) to a higher or lower string, within a position.

An orthodox approach would read the passage as an exercise in fingerwork, with minimum arm involvement. In the context of our discussion, however, the role of intrapositional adjustments in the arm/hand alignment becomes the fundamental technical issue: how can properly timed and executed limb motions help finger 1 in its displacements, so as to provide the required legato articulation to the texture.

Upper arm abduction (when 1 moves to ③) and adduction (when it moves back to ①), combined with appropriate wrist flexion (in the former case) and extension (in the latter), provide the solution (some forearm rotation is also present, although so minimal as to be inconspicuous).

Sor's Study in Bb Major, Op. 29, No. 13, is a lovely example of chordally based arpeggios, where intrapositional and compound shifting technique can be thoroughly explored (Sor, Complete Works 1977, Sor, Twenty Studies for the Guitar 1945).

Example 3-3. Fernando Sor, Studio in Bb, op. 29 no 13, bars 1-4

Not infrequently, a problem when dealing with these textures arises by the natural tendency in many players to anticipate the chords upon which the arpeggio texture is based, thus placing left-hand fingers ahead of the moment when their particular notes are executed by the right hand.

At times defended by some teachers and even prominent players, who argue that the anticipation of the chord frame adds security to the execution, this is, in fact, one of the most common causes of tension build-up in the left hand and, hence, a real obstacle to left-hand mobility and virtuosity. This is a misunderstanding of the nature of security in technique.

True security in instrumental playing comes from well-coordinated movement, not from static, forceful approaches that fix the hand in position disregarding the rhythmic flow of the musical discourse. Well-coordinated movement when both hands play is defined by the simultaneity of action between the hands, a timing factor ignored whenever these anticipations of left-hand finger placements take effect.

From the standpoint of synchronized bilateral activity, these movements are not well coordinated and are, therefore, tension-inducing. Sometimes it is argued that these anticipations are similar to the finger preparation procedures of the right hand. In fact, they are not, since the left-hand finger's stroke, except in pull-out slurs, occurs at the moment of contact with the string, while in the right-hand finger it is the action of plucking posterior to string contact.

These two actions (left-finger arrival at the note and right-finger plucking action) must coincide in time in order for the effectiveness and feel of a well-coordinated movement to be sensed. This is particularly important in arpeggio playing: *both* hands must play the arpeggio, not just the right hand.

This type of coordination, however, needs to be trained well, since the right-hand fingers (and thumb) have a natural tendency to pluck a note in anticipation of the arrival of the left-hand finger to its fret. In cases where this happens, a good remedial training approach is the so-called 'stop-place-pluck' sequence, in which the left-hand stopping of the note(s) briefly anticipates the placement of the right-hand finger(s) prior to their plucking activity.

Apart from this training protocol, there are also some exceptional circumstances when the anticipated placement of left-hand fingers is justified. These are those moments where unique finger presentations impose cumbersome attitudes to the 3rd (ring) finger: because of its tendinous constraints, it at times needs to be placed in advance of the rest of the arpeggio configuration, or simultaneously with the middle finger, as shown in Example 3-12b.

Coordination issues pertaining to certain right-hand patterns may also impose constraints to the left-hand's capabilities for individualized finger placements (see Compendium, below). Nonetheless, in Sor's example above, the staggered placement of each left-hand finger is a major factor in resolving its technical demands successfully. This requires, again, a keen sense of how appropriate arm movements 'take' the fingers to their respective frets smoothly, seamlessly and with minimal stretching/contracting efforts. Specific details worth mentioning are:

1. Ms. 1: The beginning arpeggio does not need to begin with the barré on fret 1: through the evolution of the arpeggio the arm will bring each subsequent finger to its fret by gradual adduction movements pivoting on the low B♭, until the arm aligns finger 1 with the first fret in a way that allows it to rest on the F on ① in what could be called (somewhat paradoxically) an 'arched barré.' This approach will considerably diminish the strain of sustaining a straight barré from the beginning of the arpeggio, unless desired for particular training purposes. This barré type can be used frequently throughout the study.

Photo 3-14. Arch barré. Photo Wayne Armstrong.

2. Ms. 2: Finger 2, playing F on ④, may seem to be an ideal pivot finger to execute the change to the V⁶ᐟ⁵ arpeggio. In fact, if kept as such, it will impose a vertical stretch on finger 3 which can be eliminated if the whole hand is released at the time the low A is played. The freed limb will, then, be able to execute the upper arm adduction, forearm supination, wrist extension required to bring 3 to the E♭ and, subsequently and sequentially, fingers 4, 2 and 1, to their respective frets. The extension between fingers 3 and 2 will be much less demanding than the one between 2 and 3 required if the 2 is used as pivot, for reasons explained earlier in this article.

3. Ms. 3: The return to the B♭ arpeggio requires a well-anticipated arm abduction, to help 1 in its trajectory across the strings. This is accompanied by forearm pronation and wrist flexion. The barré is, as in measure 1, arched.

4. Ms. 3, second half: The release of the barré should occur a moment after 3 plays the low G and not at the same time. This will allow for a much easier, gradual coordination of movements that use 3 as a pivot to distribute the fingers in the II$^{4/3}$ arpeggio.

5. Ms. 4: Perhaps the most demanding movement of this passage occurs here, as 1 moves from the C on ② to F on ⑥. The upper arm flexes while slightly abducting, the forearm extends, the wrist flexes while 1 extends. The precise timing of the "upbeat" moment when these movements begin is of the utmost importance.

This study is a marvelous "laboratory" to study in detail shifting technique, of all types, in an arpeggio texture. We will return to it when we discuss compound shifting.

Slurs

It would seem that a discussion of slurring technique within the confines of a study on shifting might be unjustifiable, since slurs are the most "digital" of left-hand procedures and, hence, the most static from the standpoint of arm mobility. Indeed, it is through slurring that a great deal of left-hand strength and finger independence is achieved.

Nevertheless, there are subtle but very real and useful ways of coordinating upper and/or forearm movements and attitudes in the execution of slurs and trills without which, once again, the true technical possibilities of the left hand will remain untapped.

In order to clarify the relationship between arm attitude and fingerwork, it is valuable to remember the importance that the 'discovery' of forearm rotation had in the development of modern piano technique.

The principle of rotational freedom in the forearm became one of the foundations of modern technique, particularly after the teachings of Tobias Matthay (1858-1945), the British pedagogue, who spent a good amount of energy struggling to communicate his concept to a not always welcoming or understanding community of peers.

In his *The Visible and Invisible in Pianoforte Technique*, first published in 1932, Matthay calls the forearm-rotation element "perhaps the most important of all pianistically, physiologically and pedagogically" (Matthay 1947 (rev 1997), 49). Matthay clearly differentiates his approach from the already well-established technique of applying rotational movements in tremolando passages and similar, adopted decades before. His concept is an all-encompassing one, defined by internal processes in the arm that are, mostly, "unaccompanied by any movement whatsoever." (Matthay, 50).

> …my discoveries on this point do not refer merely to the actual rotatory *movements…* but, on the contrary, deal particularly with those *invisible* changes of state rotationally (momentary reversals or repetitions of stress and relaxation rotationally) which, although *unseen,* are needed for every note we play, whether we know of them or not, and ever have been needed, and ever will be – so long as keyboards are used. (Matthay, ibid.)

In the case of guitar playing the concept of rotational freedom is equally important, but, in contrast with piano playing, its application involves "rotational stresses and relaxations" not only of the forearm but also the upper arm. In fact, all of the preceding discussions on the various applications of shifting attitudes in left-hand procedures depend on this rotational freedom, which is the basis of Shearer's concept of left-hand mobility, quoted earlier.

Slurring technique is, nonetheless, the most directly dependent on the refined application of this principle. The perpendicular alignment of the traditional, orthodox position produces an angle of flexion in the fingers that improves the mechanical advantage of the lever system by shortening the distance between the knuckle joint and the tip of each finger. In this approach, hammer-ons and pull-outs can be articulated clearly and strongly by all digits, even by the apparently weaker little finger.

The price paid by the hand, in exchange, is a considerable amount of static tension throughout the limb and a corresponding constraint in left-hand mobility. Muscular fatigue is prone to occur more rapidly, unless the mechanism is trained to increase endurance by a fairly substantial amount of repetitive exercises during a relatively long period of time.

The level of stress in the hand joints and the musculotendinous apparatus is substantial and, unless the hand is well endowed in terms of size and stamina, may over time lead to dysfunction and injury. In this position, the principle of forearm rotational freedom cannot be applied. It is, already, in a state of extreme supination and, although the upper arm's range of rotation is not affected, it would be useless, since any rotation at the shoulder joint would displace the hand to another fret position, but would not be helpful in making the fingerwork any easier *within* the position.

As described earlier, allowing the forearm to pronate (by freeing up the thumb and the upper arm) will diagonalize the finger presentation, will 'nest' the hand. In the higher strings, each finger will fall at a slightly different angle of flexion on the fingerboard, greater at the index, lesser at the little finger, particularly in the first positions.

The newfound freedom in the arm will permit slight 'rotational stresses' (towards supination in the ascending and pronation in the descending slurs), so minute as to become quasi invisible, that will help the articulation of ascending and descending slurs with minimal finger effort.

However, the less sensitive player may impede these rotational adjustments by holding in place the position, by not yielding in the direction of finger movement, in which case slurs with the 4th finger, in particular, will feel extremely tense, as the finger is, in fact, in an attitude of stretch or extension. Said player will probably decide to go back to the tried-and-true orthodoxy, which at least provides an effective, albeit inefficient, protocol.

An important factor to consider is the influence that adopting one or the other approach may have in the behavior of each finger in its slurring action. Arm movements or attitudes aside, the flexion movement that brings the fingertip in contact with the string in a hammer-on may be of two types: the first type allows all finger joints to flex together. This requires a previous extension of all the phalanges.

A second type of finger stroke flexes the base (knuckle) joint while the middle and tip joints extend. This requires a previous finger attitude of extension at the knuckle and flexion of the two other joints. In the first type of motion the fingertip draws an arc of a circle in getting to the string, while in the second type the tip follows a straight-line trajectory.

Although the first type has a mechanical disadvantage in terms of leverage, because its approach to the fingerboard is not as straight as in the second type, it has more power because it is produced by the bigger finger flexors, located in the forearm, and it imparts more linear speed to the tip. The second type has better leverage because the tip moves straight against the resistance. It is, however, a weaker muscular coordination because it depends on the action of the intrinsic hand muscles. The linear speed of the tip, also, is considerably less, given the shorter trajectory of its movement.

In a pull-out slur the finger, after having established contact with the string, has to flex even further at its middle and distal joints to 'pluck' the string and produce the note, after which movement it has to be drawn out through extension of the base joint. This extension, however, cannot be accompanied by extension at the IP joints, for the finger would strike the contiguous lower-pitched string upon extending. Therefore, the movement of recovery becomes similar to that phase in the second type of stroke described above, producing the kinesthetic sensations corresponding to this approach and, hence, creating the tendency to approach the string, in a hammer-on, through the complementary, though opposite, small muscle action: flexion of the knuckle, extension at the other joints (the 'lumbrical effect').

This is one of the problems affecting beginners when learning pull-out technique. They must learn to extend the phalanges *after* extending the base joint and before the next action of approaching the string occurs.

Of course, a more fundamental problem affecting students working on pull-out technique is maintaining in place the support finger upon which the pull-out occurs and counteracting the action of the slurring finger in producing the desired note. This is a coordination that requires precise specialization of muscular function, since the same mechanism that is keeping the support finger statically is the one that has to act dynamically on the slurring finger to create the slur. It is at this point that a refined sense of weight release applied to left-hand action can be of great usefulness.

But the traditional positioning of the left hand does not allow for the sensation of weight leaning in the direction of the slanted fingerboard to be felt and, thus, the possibilities for developing a flowing, easy and effective left-hand slurring technique become (again) limited.

In summary, pull-out technique may be summarized in the following sequence::

a. **Approach to the string**, through an arch trajectory (unified flexion movement in all finger joints).

b. **Slurring action**, through flexion of the phalangeal joints. The aftermath of slurring, normally, is a resting moment on the string beneath the slurred one, from which the next phase of motion begins. Other approaches will be discussed later.

c. **Separation from string**, through extension of the knuckle joint, while phalanges keep flexed.

d. **Extension of phalanges**, through continued extensor contraction and assistance from intrinsic muscles in hand. This movement frees up the flexors, allowing them a release phase before the next exertion. It is the absence of this phase in the sequence that creates a cycle of accumulating tension which may hinder the execution of subsequent pull-outs. If the phalanges do not extend prior to their next effort, a summation process begins in which new tension is added to the previous one, until muscular fatigue begins.

Hammer-ons are simpler, mechanically and physiologically, than pull outs. They can be described as a process that starts with phase "d" above (extension of phalanges), combined with "c" as well (extension of base joint,) and continues with "a" (contact with string, in this case percussively enough to produce a note, that is to say, by using the more powerful arch-trajectory flexion of all the finger joints). "B", of course, does not exist.

The problem with the hammer-on begins when the player tries to execute it with the IP joints still flexed. The hammer-on will be weakened to the point that no clear note will be produced. To compensate, the player may then try to use excessive forearm rotation (supination) or wrist flexion to give added impulse to the slurring finger, now immobilized in its retracted attitude. A liberating movement of extension at the phalangeal joints is the only remedy needed for this problem.

In general, however, the traditional positioning will favor the straight-line, small hand muscle-based slurring technique, while the more diagonal (nested) presentation, with the freed upper arm and thumb, will favor the arch-trajectory, big-muscle approach. The latter, as previously indicated, will also allow a degree of rotational support not possible in the former: freedom in one part of the limb stimulates freedom in all parts of the limb.

Other Slurring Approaches

Resting on the contiguous string after a pull-out is not always an option, since another note executed on that string may have to be sustained throughout the slur duration. In these cases, two alternatives are possible:

a. Phases "b" and "c" above are combined in one continuous movement (like a bicycling-out motion) or,
b. Phase "b" is achieved by an arm movement that flexes the wrist, while the finger keeps its level of flexion, in fact 'hooking' the string and setting it in motion through the energy of the arm motion. This motion is a combination of upper arm flexion and abduction, forearm extension and wrist flexion. Abel Carlevaro calls this type of slur "slurs by exception" (Carlevaro 1984, 115).

Occasionally, slurs need to be executed without a previously plucked note serving as its base. When prolonged for a while in a passage of music, the indication 'left hand alone' (or its equivalents in various languages) will be marked on the score. The physiomechanics of the slurring techniques involved (whether pull-out or hammer-on) does not change.

More frequently isolated hammer-ons across strings happen (see Example 3-14, below, for an instance extracted from the beginning of Estudo No. 2 by Villa-Lobos). Commonly called 'indirect slurs', they are but an isolated instance of the 'left hand alone' procedure. In isolation, pull-outs are less common.

Ascending and descending slurs may also happen with one or more notes interspersed between the plucked note and the slurred one. Known as 'delayed slurs', they produce a charming effect but, again, their physiomechanical execution is unaltered except for the added challenge of interpolating one or more plucked events in between the two slurred notes. The sixth book of lessons by Julio Sagreras provides ample material for the study of this technique (Sagreras 1956). In particular, nos. 1, 3, 20, 30 are worthy of detailed attention.

Finally, double or triple slurs procedures, also possible, demand very special coordination of arm and finger movements, a detailed description of which would fall outside the scope of this book. Again, Sagreras' *Lecciones* provide abundant and good training materials.

Trills

The rapid sequence of ascending and descending slurs poses problems of endurance and control to the finger extension/flexion mechanism. Although the fundamental physiomechanics do not change, the need for increased static support in the limb, added to the speed of the repetitive phasic movements, demand careful preparation based on keen awareness of the kinesthetic sensations.

Of special importance is the release of tension that occurs after the pull-out and before the hammer-on, with the extension of the finger phalanges. However, this releasing movement is limited by the demands for speed, which requires that the lever never be too long lest the effort needed to bring the tip to the string be excessive and dysfunctional. It is in cases like these where the rotational support of the arm (both upper and forearm) becomes vital to the successful execution of many trills.

In prolonged trill passages, in fact, the gradually increasing involvement of arm rotation may be the only possible way of maintaining both the speed and volume of the trill, while avoiding muscular fatigue of the digital mechanism. The procedure gradually transforms the initial digital alternation, requiring minimal rotation support, to one requiring a totally unimpeded, coordinated upper and forearm rotational movement very similar to that needed for a moderately fast arm vibrato. This is frequently combined with the use of a third finger that alternates with the first slurring finger in trilling with the base finger (1-2-1-3-1-2-1-3-, etc.).

However, this alternation can also be achieved without much arm involvement, by appropriate angling of the hand and arm, and finger adduction of the third finger, so that both the second and third finger can fit within the same fret space (Carlevaro 1984, 117-118).

Again, the presentation of the hand on the fingerboard pre-determines if these possibilities are available to the player. In quite a number of instances, certain passages in the literature that are obviously designed to be performed with left-hand slurs are changed, even by major performers, to be plucked by the right hand. As an example we might cite the written-out *grupetti* in the second movement of Joaquín Rodrigo's *Concierto de Aranjuez*, one measure after rehearsal number 5, and again at one measure before 6.

 Vibrato

The complex physiomechanics of this most expressive of technical procedures demands a high degree of refinement in proprioceptive sensitivity. This complexity makes it one of the most difficult techniques to teach, if the student does not have great imitative or imaginative powers, because descriptions of muscular function and movement type will not be of too much help until the appropriate kinesthesia is in place.

In general terms, two types of vibrato are used in guitar playing: a **finger vibrato** and an arm vibrato. A third type, much used by violinists and violists, is the wrist vibrato. However, the alignment of the neck of the guitar, roughly parallel to the body's coronal plane, impedes the degree of forearm supination required for its proper execution, but works excellently in the antero-lateral plane of the violin or viola neck.

The finger vibrato relies on rapid alternation of flexion and extension movements of the finger phalanges, with little dynamic involvement of the more proximal limb joints which are kept statically fixed to provide support to the finger action. Because of the relatively high intensity of muscular work required of the finger flexors and extensors, this type of vibrato is best utilized for shorter note-values, where a quick vibrato will give a touch of color and emphasis to the note.

If the finger action is slowed down, the alterations of pitch will become more individualized and marked, sounding more like a 'bend' than a true vibrato. This vibrato alters the pitch through string displacements that add tension to the string, raising its pitch in the finger flexion and returning to pitch in the extension. The thumb keeps in contact with the neck throughout.

The arm vibrato relies on the great speed of the upper arm's rotation movements. The fingertip is set to pivot from side to side about its point of contact with the string, in line with the string length, by swift and short forearm 'shifts' caused by alternating lateral and medial rotation of the upper arm.

However, the player should not try to approach the vibrato by controlling this upper arm movement, which in fact happens as an oscillatory, vibration-like reaction to the pendular motion of the forearm initiated by the opposition of the upper arm rotation effort against the effort to maintain finger pressure on the string. Once started, the momentum of this motion can be easily maintained with minimal muscular exertion.

As with a pendulum, a force (the rotation of the upper arm) gives impulse to an object that is fixed to a pivot point (the forearm aligned with the hand all the way through to the fingertip, from which it 'hangs'). As the rotation moves the forearm one way, its attachment to the fret board pulls in the opposite direction. At the end of the rotation in that direction (determined by the range of rotary motion at the shoulder joint), the counteracting force towards the pivot point initiates the change of direction in the rotation, which is then given new momentum by a new, though minimal, muscular response of the opposing rotators. The behavior resembles the way a 'tumbler' doll, with its lead weight at its base, swings from side to side without falling.

It should be obvious that, since the finger remains fixed to a point of contact on the fret board, minute flexion/ extension and even rotary movements of the finger take place in response to the vibrato movement. These are all passive movements.

Less pronounced are rotation movements of the forearm, although the 'rotational freedom' advocated by Matthay is a fundamental state of the arm to produce an effective arm vibrato. When absent, the wrist will stiffen, and so will the hand, producing the familiar 'pseudo-vibrato hand' with splayed fingers and hyper-extended wrist, so common in less experienced, but 'expressive,' players.

In contrast with the finger vibrato, the arm vibrato alters the pitch by changing the string length as it pivots in line with it. This means that the pitch fluctuates on *both* sides of the note pitch and not only towards sharpening it, as is the case in the finger vibrato (Duncan, The Art of Classical Guitar Playing 1980, 90 ff.).

 Compound Shifting

The concept of compound shifting helps clarify technical left-hand situations where complex patterns of movement take place. They are, by far, the most common form of movement patterns in the concert repertoire, as well as the more advanced didactic literature.

Characteristically, compound shifts require the use of all arm, forearm and wrist movements, to a greater or lesser degree, in a particular sequence that varies with each context. As a consequence, the thumb will change its position both along and across the neck.

Given that compound shifts, by definition, combine inter- and intrapositional shifting movements, it follows that the most important consideration is determining when and how the transition from one movement form to the other occurs in a passage. This determination can be achieved only through a clear understanding of the alignment conditions within which the limb acts at any given moment.

Multi-string scales along the neck, positional changes into and out of barré positions and in and out of extensions, shifts arriving on chords, arpeggiations along the fingerboard, all are instances of compound shifting technique.

Alignment Issues
For the fingers to move along and across the fingerboard with virtuosic effectiveness and efficiency, the arm must be continuously adapting to the ever-changing patterns imposed on them by the musical content.

This is, fundamentally, a choreographic endeavor, that is to say, a well-designed, artistic sequence of steps that allows the performer to move his/her body, or parts thereof, from one point in space to another. This sequence is what the fingering indicators on the score seem to communicate. (The concept of the *choreography of the hands* or *keyboard choreography* has been incorporated into instrumental pedagogy, principally for the piano, by figures like Dorothy Taubman and Seymour Bernstein).

Rather, it is what lies beyond the fingering, its *subtext*, that we are after, for it is at this deeper, hidden level that the arm/hand/finger interaction wields its beneficial or deleterious influence.

Foremost among the components of this choreographic process is alignment: how does the hand's presentation at the point of departure relate, spatially, to its configuration at arrival, and how this, in turn, is conditioned by the next move, etc. The photos below may help clarify alignment issues in compound shifting:

Photo 3-15. Alignment A at the 4th fret.   **Photo 3-16. Alignment B at the 1st fret.**

Photos Wayne Armstrong

In the first photo, 1 plays ⑥ on the 4ᵗʰ fret (G♯) while 4 plays ① on the 7ᵗʰ (B); the second photo shows 1 playing F on ① while 4 plays G♯ on ⑥.

In both cases the elbow aligns (approximately) with the finger playing the low G♯, as shown by the photos.

Of course, this is a simplification of the many variables that might affect the real alignment conditions of the arm, most importantly the level of flexion in the wrist (in alignment-type A, conditioned both by the fret position and the string separation), but it shows a basic principle that will be helpful in the analysis and solution of compound shifting situations involving changes in vertical alignment: the fret position indicated by the placement of finger 1 coincides, approximately, with the arm's alignment, as indicated by the position of the elbow, in alignments of type A only. In alignments of type B, the elbow aligns with the higher numbered finger. Attention should be paid to the fact that, as the hand moves up positionally and the neck widens, the capability of the fourth finger to reach the lower strings diminishes, and stretch fingerings with 3 or even 2 will work better. This factor does not change the alignment principle discussed.

In addition to the relationship between vertical alignment and interpositional movement, the issue of alignment may also be studied through the perspective of understanding the problem of changing the hand's gripping attitude.

There are two major categories of handgrip function: grabbing (or power grip: the fist) and pinching (or opposition: pointing) although, in terms of functional anatomy, four basic forms are differentiated: pinch grip, hook or key grip, handle grip, and power grip. The hook or key grip (used, for instance, when one carries a piece of luggage by its handle, or when using a key to open a door) and the handle grip (when using a tool like a screwdriver or a pair of scissors) are intermediate variants of the two major categories, pinch and power grips.

In terms of guitar playing, the aforementioned 'nestling' of the hand, with a slightly diagonal finger presentation, abducted upper-arm and less flexed wrist, approximates its demeanor to that of a loose fist, while the traditional perpendicular position, with the adducted upper arm, supinated forearm and greater wrist flexion, resembles the pointing or pinching attitude (used for the full barré) or the hook grip (similar to how the hand behaves in partial barrés and certain stretches).

Determining when and where one or the other gripping demeanor is needed, and realizing that there is an inalterable relationship between the hand's grip mode and the arm's attitude, will allow for a better understanding of the arm movements needed to successfully play the passage. There are relationships among the various movement types of the limb joints that feel more natural and organic than others, and will produce easier-feeling results than their alternatives.

Barrés and Compound Shifting

For instance, the common situation of having to move from a normal position at fret *x* to a barré position on fret *y*, can be analyzed, in terms of alignment, as being a case in which the hand gripping attitude goes from nested (fist-like) to perpendicular (pinching or hook grip-like).

If the shift is from a lower to a higher position, then the abduction-pronation-wrist-extension attitude of the former resolves itself quite naturally during the shift into the barré position through upper arm adduction, forearm supination, wrist flexion, by allowing the gravitational pull to act on the limb (the thumb must not offer any resistance or else this controlled fall will not be effective). The transition from the inter- to the intrapositional phases of the compound shift is seamless, and the sensation of effort is distributed quite evenly through the limb. The first two measures of Example 3-4, below, show an instance of this situation:

Example 3-4. Compound shifts.

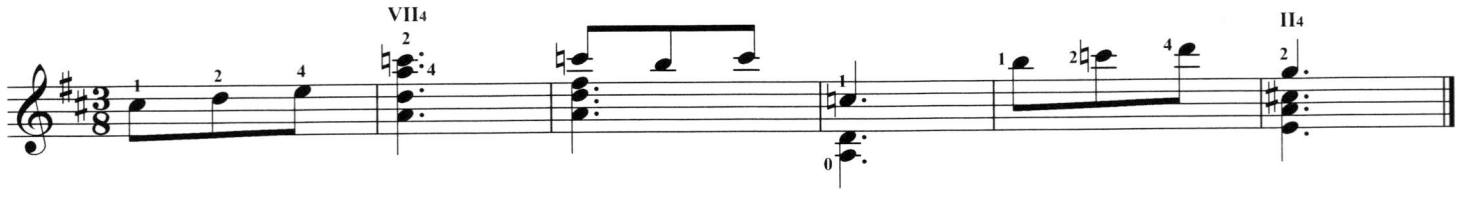

In the case of movement in the opposite direction, shown in the third and fourth measures of the same example, but with the alignment conditions also reversed, the trajectory feels quite natural as well, despite the fact that a greater muscular involvement is needed, initially, since the arm moves against gravity: the perpendicular position of the barré transforms into the nested attitude at the arrival point by the natural tendency of the forearm to pronate as the upper arm abducts.

Finally, in the last two measures the same alignment conditions as in the first two (nested to perpendicular) apply, but the shift is reversed, therefore the movement relationships are not as natural as in the preceding measures and special approaches must be taken.

Two alternatives exist:

1. The forearm supinates as finger 4 plays the D (an intrapositional shift) and then the upper arm outwardly rotates and flexes slightly, without abducting, bringing the hand to the barré position already aligned perpendicularly (interpositional shift),

2. The upper arm abducts as 4 plays the D, without changing the 'nested' alignment (interpositional shift) and the forearm rotates (towards supination) upon arrival at the new position (intrapositional shift). In this case, the upper arm abduction is complemented by outward rotation to complete the interpositional phase of the shift. The final supination of the forearm also is accompanied by a release of the abduction effort of the upper arm, a sensation that makes the whole movement feel as if the arm 'bounced back' into position after its trajectory.

Which approach to choose is, of course, a matter of contextual convenience. Matthay's principle of rotational freedom becomes a vital ingredient in the successful implementation of these technical procedures, for the least amount of effort exerted in opposition to the direction of motion will result in inaccuracies and a feeling of struggle and difficulty.

It is clear from these examples that the *upbeat* phase of these shifting situations is as important in compound shifts as it is in simpler inter- or intrapositional ones.

Shifts through Extensions and Contractions

Similar principles are at play in compound shifting situations involving stretches and squeezes. The so-called 'squeeze shift,' favored by many modern players, is a relatively simple example of compound shifting, in which a finger (most commonly, 1 or 4) acts as a pivot upon which the forearm extends (the upper arm also flexes somewhat), thus allowing flexion of the finger knuckles that make the adduction of the two fingers involved in the squeeze easier. This is the intrapositional phase of the shift. Smoothly, abduction/rotation of the upper arm completes the change of fret position. This is the interpositional phase.

Example 3-5. Squeeze shifts.

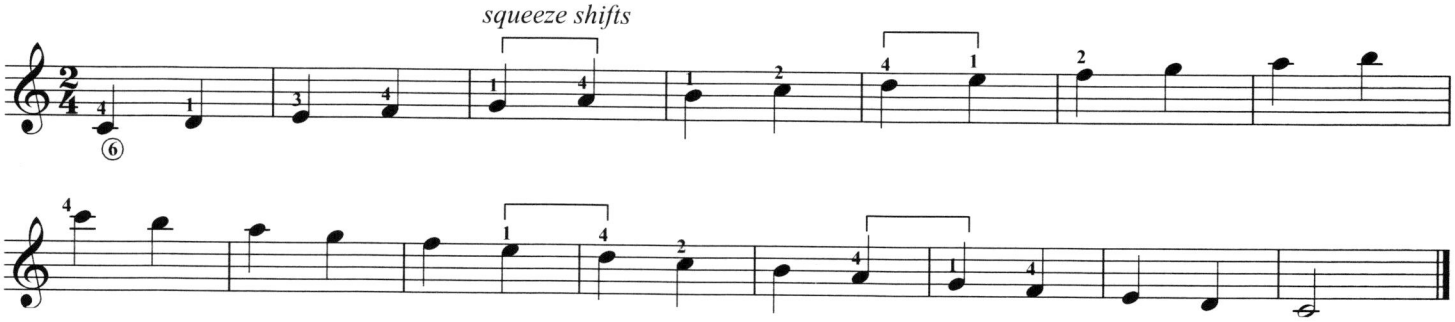

Obviously, the more the fingers have to adduct, the more pronounced the intrapositional movement becomes, even demanding more motion of the upper arm (abduction/adduction):

Example 3-6. More extreme squeeze shifts.

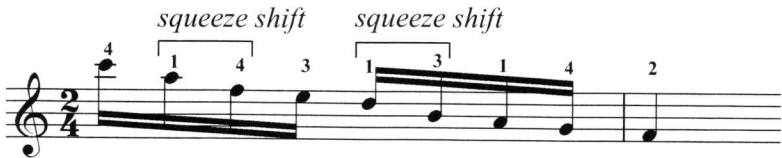

Less common is the shift by extension, used most frequently by the stretching of the normal fret distance between fingers 1 and 2, but also possible between other fingers. The timing of the intrapositional and interpositional phases of the shift varies with the fingering selected:

Example 3-7. Extension shifts.

In Example 3-7, the easier stretch between 1 and 2 notwithstanding, the subtle difference in timing of the arm/hand movement when using 2 instead of 3, or vice versa, will also be a factor to consider in deciding which fingering to choose.

It must be noted that these procedures, though convenient in many instances (e.g. certain scalar patterns, like the whole-tone scale, are cumbersome to finger except through the use of extension/contraction), are particularly demanding of the intrinsic finger adduction/abduction mechanism.

Whenever possible, the distribution of effort in the limb should be such that the major workload is allocated to the bigger muscles of the arm, rather than the relatively weaker hand muscles. Many passages which, at first sight, might seem to require squeeze or extension shifting procedures can be resolved through simpler movement types if the arm is properly poised and aligned (Iznaola, Rest and Free 1990, Matthay 1947 (rev 1997)). The arm, by becoming more mobile, will allow less 'labor-intensive' fingerwork:

Example 3-8. Squeeze vs. guide-finger shifts.

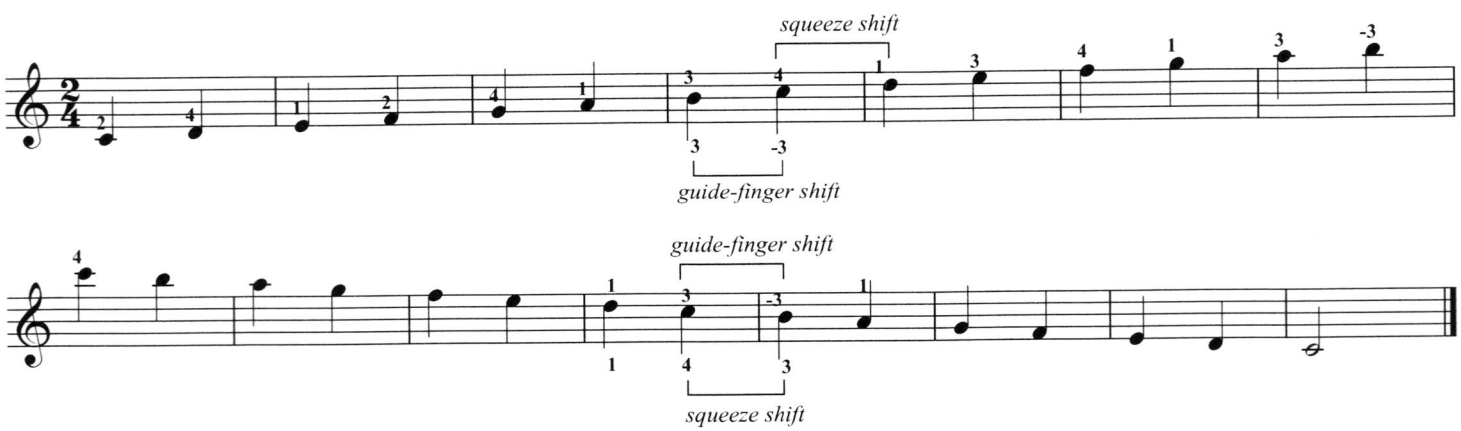

However, tempo is an important factor in deciding what procedure best fits the passage. Example 3-8, performed at a slow to moderate tempo, will feel more comfortable with the use of squeeze shifts, while, at a faster tempo, it will benefit from interpositional shifting through guide finger. This is so because every squeeze shift is compound, while the guide-finger shift is the physiologically simpler Interpositional.

If the tempo is so slow that the ratio of movement per unit of time falls below a certain point, the arm cannot utilize dynamic postures to assist in its movement trajectory. In these cases, the attitude of readiness of the arm is less poised, weighing down more than if the tempo were brisker. This is one reason why players who favor the traditional position find more comfortable shifting through contraction (i.e., the squeeze shift) than by guide finger, even at faster tempi: as they maintain their arm close to the body, the particular sensations associated with the poised limb are not present and, naturally, they will favor an approach where "the fingers do the walking," so to speak.

146

Shifts To and From Extended Positions

These movements partake of some of the same characteristics that apply to movements to and from barré positions: if the rotation of the forearm matches the abduction/adduction of the upper arm, the movement will feel easier and more natural than if they contradict each other, that is to say, forearm supination, needed to accomplish the extension, is easier when the upper arm adducts, and forearm pronation, which returns the hand to a more nested attitude, is more natural with upper arm abduction.

What this means is that, as far as arm movement is concerned, upward shifts to extensions are easier than downward shifts to extensions. So far, this is exactly the same relationship that prevails in shifts involving barrés.

What makes shifting passages involving extensions particularly demanding is that the finger separation, or abduction, needed in the extension works, physiologically, at odd purposes with the arm movements: extensions *from* the index finger are more demanding than extensions *to* the index, which means that, from the digital standpoint, an upward shift to an extended position is more demanding than a downward shift.

These contradictory factors demand a careful scrutiny of fingering alternatives in passages involving shifts and extensions. Relying on the strength and stamina of the hand to resolve these technical problems, in an unthinking way, will eventually result in slovenly execution or, worst, physical injury. The following example, excerpted from Antonio Lauro's beloved Venezuelan valse *Natalia* (Lauro 1963), is a well-known instance of a shift *cum* extension problem:

Example 3-9. Antonio Lauro, *Natalia*, bars 19-20

The conventional fingering (above the staff), though possible, requires a rather aggressive 'bounce back' movement involving upper arm adduction and forearm supination (aside from the unavoidable wrist flexion) after the abduction of the upper arm has reached the low G. The extension to the high C, initiated from 1, is arduous on the hand.

A smoother transition may be achieved by substituting finger 4 at the high D♯ (alternative fingering under the staff), while the barré lifts (1 acts as a pivot for the initial movement of abduction of the upper arm). Finger 4, then, acts as a guide finger for the change of position, which is accomplished by upper arm flexion and outward rotation, forearm extension and supination, and wrist flexion. The extension *towards* 1, from the already-placed 4, feels easier on the hand.

This example also reveals interesting relationships in alignment between extended and contracted positions. The alternative fingering suggested places fingers 1 and 4 in an acute contraction, properly resolved through intrapositional upper-arm abduction.

If one observes carefully the new alignment of the elbow at this point it will become apparent that it is aligned with fret 8, which is the fret where 1 would be in the normal positional frame that would have finger 4 on the 11th fret.

The subsequent extension between 4 and 1 requires that the upper arm's vertical alignment be maintained at this position (that is, aligned at the 8th fret with the 4th finger), while the upper arm and forearm help the extension of 1 through their respective movements of rotation.

In other words, the vertical alignment of the arm in the extended position is similar to that of alignment type B, discussed previously: the arm aligns with the higher placed finger, not with 1. This insight, obvious to anyone who has accumulated experiences in playing through passages of this nature, is invaluable in defining a workable 'choreography' in many instances where the issue of left-hand mobility is prominent.

Agility Issues

Alignment elements in shifting situations need to be studied under the premise that the simpler the movement, the more effective (and efficient) it will be. In actuality, this means that fingerings that put excessive demands on digital work will prove to be more strenuous and cumbersome than others relying on a better distribution of effort throughout the limb, no matter how well the player understands, and applies, the alignment procedures in the passage.

Situations like this occur frequently in music of a contrapuntal nature, given its multi-layered rhythmic structure and its textural richness. Counterpoint requires much more independent fingerwork than most other music and this, in turn, means that intrapositional adjustments, extensions and contractions, will occur with considerable frequency in any piece of this type of some complexity.

Given the additional demands posed by these efforts on the relatively weaker muscular apparatus of the limb, there is a marked diminution in the levels of agile mobility possible to the limb. Though in many cases there might not be any alternative, careful analysis of other situations may provide more flowing, dynamic solutions that will give a new-found freedom and direction to the passage.

Various examples, drawn from the Fugue in J. S. Bach's Lute Suite BWV 997, may illustrate some of these options.

Example 3-10. Johann Sebastian Bach, Fugue BWV 997/ii, bars 1-3

The fingering on top of the staff shows a change of position (from 2nd to 3rd) by means of a squeeze shift between the C and D. Once arrived at 3rd position, the extension of 4 to reach the E on ⑤ is primarily finger abduction with some intrapositional shifting support from the supination of the forearm.

Delaying the squeeze shift, as shown in the alternative fingering below the staff, allows for the movement of the arm during the arrival of 1 at the F to link with the rotation of the forearm to assist the extension of finger 4: the fingerwork is incorporated into a choreographic arm-movement pattern that reduces somewhat the sensation of effort.

The following examples offer a more radical viewpoint:

Example 3-11a. Idem, bars 55-6

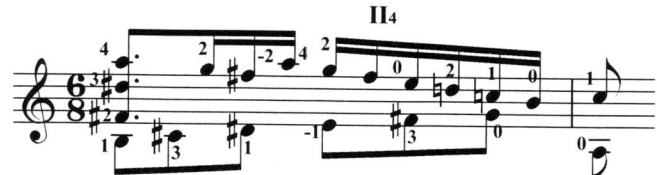

Example 3-11a is a fairly standard fingering for this passage, proposed by Frank Koonce in his admirable edition of Bach's lute works (Bach 1989). It requires a good amount of finger acrobatics supported with appropriate intrapositional movements of the arm. Compare with example 3-11b:

Example 3-11b. Idem.

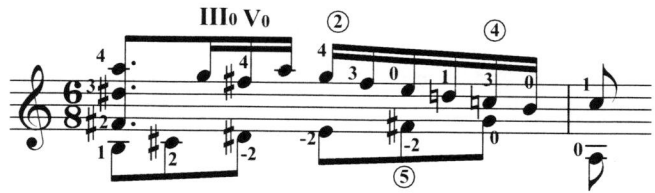

Here the major responsibility for the passage has been allocated to the interpositional displacements of the upper arm while the fingers fall into place without big efforts of extension. Note the use of hinge barrés to maintain evenly the overall alignment and direction of the arm/hand coordination throughout the fragment, thus avoiding 'compound shifting' movements. The nested attitude of the hand can be kept throughout and the 'backward' stretch (abduction) of 1 at the end of the passage is readily resolved by the overall diagonal presentation.

Of course, the example disregards any consideration of the aesthetic consequences derived from the adoption of one or the other fingering, which, when all is said and done, should be the *sine qua non* of all technical decision-making processes in musical performance. Example 3-11a, if well played, sounds better than 3-11b. Besides, the latter is not ideal given the complexities it presents to the right hand towards the end of the passage. A more viable alternative is the following:

Example 3-11c. Idem.

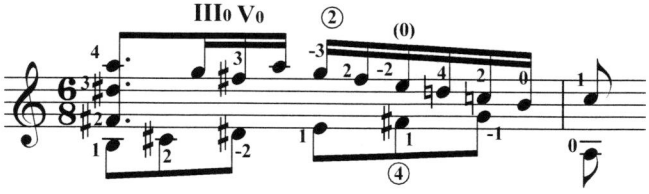

The hinge barrés in 3-11c are a little more perpendicular than at 3-11b because of the use of 3 on②, a vertical extension. Example 3-11d, below, does away with that issue but adds a slightly more complicated move of finger 2 from ⑤ to④:

Example 3-11d. Idem.

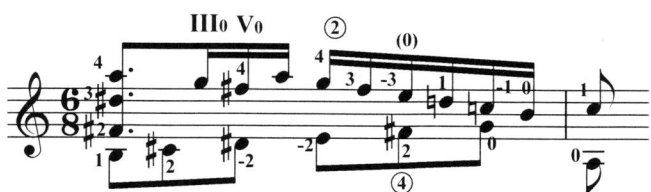

The last two examples offer a better tonal quality to the fragment, not as bright as in Example 10, but clear and homogeneous nonetheless.

As mentioned earlier, the staggered left-hand finger placement principle for arpeggios has exceptions in certain situations where finger 3 is involved. An interesting instance occurs in the following passage, drawn from Dionisio Aguado's Lesson in E Major, from the first part of his method (Aguado, Método de Guitarra 1943):

Example 3-12a. Dionisio Aguado, Lesson in E, bars 4-5.

The C♯ minor arpeggio in the second measure requires a rather extreme spread between fingers 4 and 3, which, depending on the anatomy of the hand of the player, may become impossible to achieve if finger 4 is placed on the low C♯ ahead of the placement of 3.

Although the most practical fingering, for performance, would be to substitute 2 for 3 (bringing 2 from the E in ④), an interesting training alternative, not very practical for performance, is to anticipate the placement of 3. It is slightly easier if 2 is placed simultaneously on its note.

Example 3-12b. Idem.

This requires a rather energetic upper arm abduction movement (interpositional shift from second to first position) that 'bounces back' to place 2 and 3, and helps the stretch of 4 afterwards, an easier movement given the comparatively freer extension mechanism of 4. This would be the intrapositional component of the compound shift.

The upbeat moment when the upper arm movement occurs has to be timed to perfection in order for the musical continuity to survive unaffected.

Interesting as this exploration might be, in this and other similar cases involving extreme stretches between fingers 4 and 3, or 2 and 3, the physical characteristics of the player's hand should be objectively evaluated to avoid training procedures that might be injurious or, at best, frustrating and ineffectual.

The following example, drawn from Sor's B♭ Study, previously quoted, shows an interesting sequence of movements:

Example 3-13. Fernando Sor, Studio in B♭, op. 29, no 13, bars 68-72

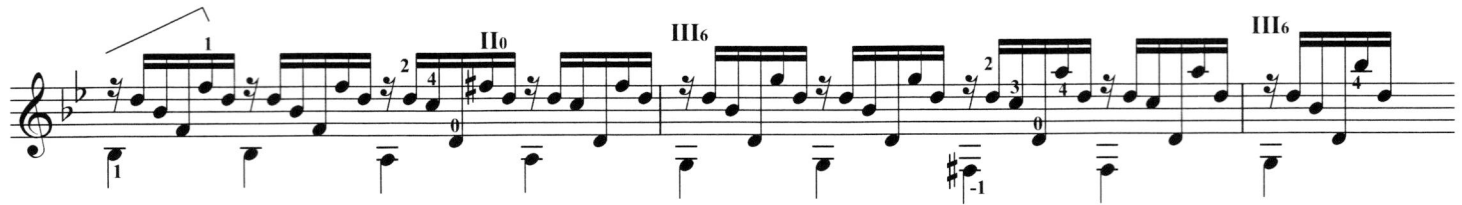

(In this book, the following left-hand fingering conventions for barrés have been followed: a Roman numeral marks the fret where the barré, either full or hanging, is placed, followed by a subscript number indicating how many strings are covered by the barré. A '0' following the Roman numeral indicates a full hinge. For partial barrés, nested or not, inner, arched and across-frets barrés, a bracket is used).

The left-hand finger-by-finger placement of each arpeggio is, as noted earlier, a fundamental element of the passage. The bracket indicates the hinging movement of the arm, taking the first finger from the low Bb to the high F and ending in the arched barré described earlier. The hinge barré at measure 2 makes the transition to the third-fret barré in the next measure smoother and easier. The interpositional movement to the low F# is the beginning of a trajectory through which the upper arm abduction gradually increases (as does the wrist flexion) to assist the stretch between 2 and 3, and the placement of 4 on the A on ①. The return to the third-fret barré is better executed through arm movement after the low G played by 1 has been reached. Finger 1 then acts as pivot-finger for the upper-arm adduction, combined with forearm supination, needed to complete the barré.

Interpositional arpeggios are particularly demanding of compound shifting procedures, as the following example, extracted from Villa-Lobos' Estudo No. 2, which was a major protagonist in chapter 2 as well, shows:

Example 3-14. Heitor Villa-Lobos, Etude No. 2 (from *Douze Etudes*), bar 1

alt. fingering: IX_0
or better: IX_4

The brackets indicate inner-string barrés. The fingering, as written on top of the staff, uses 2 as a guide finger, but forces a rather uncomfortable trajectory to finger 1, whose displacement to the first string C# from the inner barré, and back, may be better executed by supporting with either: 1) a hinge barré upon arriving at IX position, or, even better, 2) a hanging barré from ④. The latter, by keeping 1 as a guide finger, allows for a smooth transition between the initial Interpositional adduction of the upper arm to the intrapositional forearm rotation towards supination that places the hanging barré. The return to 2nd position, likewise, seamlessly links the upper arm abduction/rotation with the forearm pronation. The arm's movements follow a curvilinear trajectory, devoid of any jolting angularity.

Although this third alternative provides the most organic solution to the passage, the subtle but important differences among the three approaches provide opportunities for deepening the kinesthetic awareness of the left limb, as well as various training protocols for improving left-hand mobility. Other possible fingerings, like one avoiding any slurs, are also possible and might prove useful for training purposes, though hardly so for performance.

An important consideration, disregarded in the previous discussion, is that of string noise when using guide fingers. This has become an important, valid, issue in modern guitar playing and pedagogy. In the passage in question, as well as in many other similar passages, the guide-finger principle should be applied, when studying the passage for the first time, with no consideration given to the problem of noise. As the technique becomes more fluent and effective, the player will discover that the trajectory of the well-aligned hand in its movements along the fret board allows for shifts during which the guide finger does not have to maintain contact with the string and still feel the connection between the departing and arrival positions as direct and unimpeded as if the finger had, indeed, slid throughout the shift. A premature preoccupation with the string noise question is a great obstacle to initial, more basic left-hand training.

For detailed discussions on this topic, see (Carlevaro 1984, 79); for a somewhat different approach, refer to (Romero 2012, 50).

Another important feature of the Villa-Lobos example and Estudo No. 2 in general is the role of the arm in helping the fingers reach their notes within a position: the minute intrapositional adjustments are continuous and should be executed flowingly and without staidness, lest they interfere with the interpositional *segue*.

Indeed, Matthay's description of the rotational processes taking place within the arm ("those *invisible* changes of state rotationally… which, although *unseen,* are needed for every note we play…" (Matthay, 50)) apply with particular appropriateness to this study.

The work is a landmark in the modern history of guitar technique from the standpoint of the requirements for agility and virtuosity in shifting imposed on the hand. It is symptomatic that the first commercial recording made of the work was in the late 1960's, by Brazilian guitarist Turibio Santos, some 40 years after its creation (Santos 1969). Players who, even today, cling to the orthodoxy of the perpendicular positional approach find it immensely challenging and at the outer limits of their technical know-how.

In this same study, the scalar passage studied in chapter 2 in reference to the right hand, shows an interesting instance of interpositional shifting,

Example 3-15. Heitor Villa-Lobos, Etude No. 2 (from *Douze Etudes*), bars 10-12

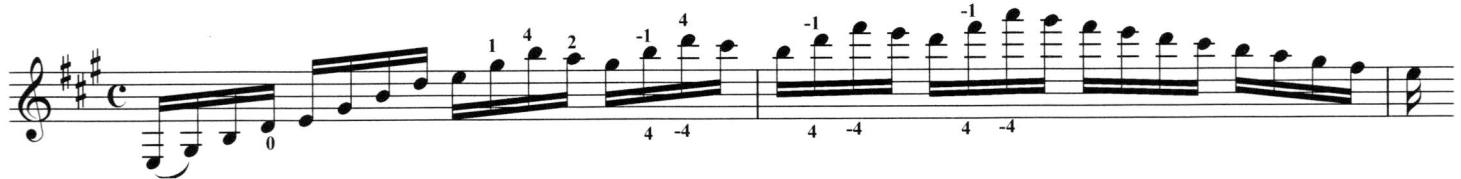

The two fingering options shown for the upward shifts (shifting on 1 or on 4, respectively) feel markedly different, given their distinct motivic configuration: Shifting on 1 works most closely with the end-accented cell natural to the melodic design of the passage, while shifting on 4 provides a slight stress to the culminating (highest) pitch of each motive. Physiomechanically, the shift on 1 will be quicker than on 4, because of the relationship between the weight of the hand and the finger sliding along the string (using 1 would be equivalent to moving a load downstairs while holding it from above, while shifting on 4 would equate to holding it from below).

However, the shifts on 1 feel somewhat more 'edgy,' tension-wise, than on 4: this is always the case when a shift occurs on a weaker rhythmic moment, that is to say, on the off-beat. In either case, the slightly diagonal (nested) presentation of the hand on the fingerboard, coupled with wrist flexibility, will provide the necessary 'aero-dynamic' swiftness to the movements, absent with a more perpendicular approach: the latter is the reason why some players avoid the one-string (interpositional) fingering of the scale and substitute other, 'safer' multi-string (intrapositional) fingerings (e.g. shifting to IX position when reaching the G# at the end of the arpeggio).

All of the examples above have been chosen to demonstrate a particular viewpoint: virtuosity, in regards to left-hand technique, is the consequence of the proper application of arm/hand/finger coordination of movements, not digital dexterity alone. The player's range of technical possibilities multiplies a hundredfold when this insight is assimilated and wisely applied.

Fingering: Player's Choice

Even though technical solutions that provide for a better distribution of the work-load throughout the limb are more ergonomic by diminishing the demands on fingerwork, individual differences among players should always be taken into consideration: bigger-limbed individuals, for instance, will probably find Koonce's positional fingering for the passage in Bach's Fugue from BWV 997 quoted above more secure than the more mobile interpositional alternatives, with their agile use of the arm. Smaller hands, on the contrary, might find the vertical extension between 3 and 2 and the subsequent horizontal stretch between 2 and 4, required in the former, onerous. It would be absurd for anyone not to consider these factors when deciding what to do in a given moment. Good technical solutions are always functional and contextual, never absolute.

This is one of the major issues facing anyone embarking on the study of an edited, fingered guitar score. By necessity, an editor's fingering decisions already show a high degree of personal interpretation. He or she is telling us, by the choices made, quite a bit about their individual techniques, information which might or might not be useful to the reader-player, who might or might not be similar, anthropometrically, to the editor (we are not considering, of course, the possibility of blatant incompetence on the part of the editor).

Aside from the musical consequences of fingering, any editorial fingering suggestion should be taken, particularly by teachers of younger players, as open for review and for adjustment according to the personal traits of the eventual performer of the fragment.

Furthermore, as our previous discussions imply, there is great merit in considering and studying multiple fingering options for the same passage. It is one of the better ways to enhance the player's knowledge of the instrument as well as liberating him/her from a narrow-minded sense of pseudo-security.

Some past masters considered their fingerings so sacrosanct that they would abuse, by word and deed, those unfortunate students who dared make changes without prior authorization. Nowadays, this risible attitude deserves nothing but derision. It is true that in the initial stages of learning a student is in no capacity to make informed decisions about fingering. This responsibility, however, properly belongs with the student's teacher, not the editor. Possible exceptions to this principle could be in those cases where the composer is, at the same time, the editor, or in those didactic materials where new technical procedures necessitating specific fingering approaches are introduced.

A Technical Analysis of Left-Hand Mobility in Fernando Sor's Study Op. 6, No. 8

Given its traditional role in the technical development of uncounted numbers of budding guitarists, it may be appropriate to finish this monograph with a detailed movement analysis of this beautiful didactic composition (Sor, Complete Works 1977, Sor, Twenty Studies for the Guitar 1945). As in many of Sor's three-voiced textures, the goal here is to achieve the homogeneity, balance and legato continuity of a string trio. When deemed necessary, notes explaining fingering changes from the standard Segovia edition have been added.

Example 3-16. Fernando Sor, Studio in C, op. 8 no 6, bars 1-6

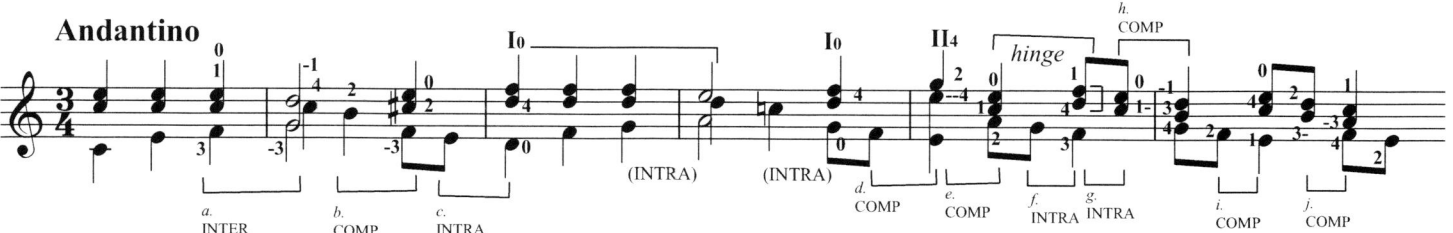

a. Seemingly a simple interpositional shift. In fact, despite the aforementioned 'stackability' of finger 4, the contraction requires an ever-so-slight forearm supination, i.e. an intrapositional shift component.

b. Compound shift, because of the change of string of finger 2, which is made easier by wrist flexion and forearm pronation, and by extension movements that also prepare the next move.

c. Intrapositional shift, to the hinge on fret 1, achieved through very slight wrist extension and upper-arm adduction/flexion. The hinge works much better than playing 1 on the F, which would necessitate a much more intricate intrapositional shift.

(Two very minor intrapositional shifts follow.)

d. Compound shift. The hinge brings finger 1 closer to the basses, thus making the move to the next E on ④ easier than if 1 were playing the F on its tip. The approach to the next chord needs a rather pronounced adduction, outer rotation and slight flexion of the upper arm, with some forearm supination and wrist flexion, slight radial deviation and finger abduction. A challenging move.

e. This compound shift should feel like a relief compared with the previous one. A freeing upper-arm abduction/extension will also free up the thumb retraction of the previous chord and will allow for forearm pronation, wrist extension and finger adduction.

f. Intrapositional. Slight upper-arm adduction and wrist extension will allow finger 1 to 'hinge' on its tip to end up in a partial barré covering the first two strings with minimal digital effort. The finger never lifts from the C on ②.

g. Intrapositional. The return movement from the previous position (slight wrist flexion, arm abduction).

h. Compound. Upper-arm adduction, pronounced forearm supination, wrist extension, finger adduction (with 2 slightly hyper-adducting in the cross-fingering over 3 to play the F on ④.

i. Compound. Upper-arm abduction, forearm pronation, wrist flexion (particularly marked in order to clear the open E string) and finger abduction.

j. Compound. Upper-arm abduction, wrist extension, finger adduction. A less movable approach would make the change almost intrapositional, by having the forearm supinate as the wrist extends and lightly deviates radially, with very minor upper-arm adduction. This process would require more effort in the wrist and fingers, as the final alignment of the elbow would still be with the 2nd position, rather than the first: indeed, the fingers would have stretched backwards to reach the frets of the F major chord.

Section 3. Compendium: Limits to the Possible

A series of examples, selected both from the didactic and concert literature, will serve as summary to this investigation.

Acknowledging the Limits I: Right-Hand Coordination Constraints

A curious instance of the influence of right-hand fingering on left-hand mobility occurs in passages like the one shown in Example 3-17:

Example 3-17

At first sight, the fingering seems to indicate simple interpositional shifts chromatically descending along ②, ③ and ④. In fact, the right-hand fingering (*m*, *p*, *i*) works better if 1 stretches backwards towards the next top note before the rest of the hand moves down a fret. If, on the other hand, the passage is played with *a*, *i*, *m*, instead of *m*, *p*, *i*, it would feel somewhat easier to shift the whole configuration, without the need for the extension of 1, thus making the shifting simple interpositional, instead of compound.

The difference lies on the particular kinesthesia associated with each grouping of right-hand finger movements: arpeggiated patterns involving *p* tend to group with the thumb stroke as the first note of the pattern. Likewise for patterns involving *i*, *m* and *a*, particularly when the accent falls on *a*, as would be the case here. Therefore, the latter fingering works better for the passage if the extension is to be avoided. The ties in the example below show the two interpretations made explicit by the two approaches:

Example 3-17a

In any case, the passage may be resolved with less strain by fingering it as follows,

Example 3-17b

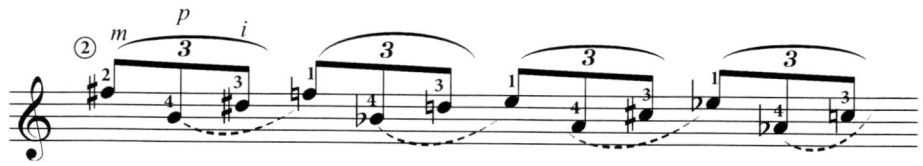

An even more interesting situation is presented in example 3-18a,

Example 3-18a

The indicated right-hand fingering tends to impose its strong tendency to create upbeat groups (starting with the note played by the thumb), risking left-hand anticipation of the next harmony. As before, the passage may be managed by substituting *a*, *i*, *m*, an alternative that will also prove to be less than ideal. The passage may be more easily resolved fingered thus,

Example 3-18b

These are exceptional instances where the principle of left-hand individualized finger placements of the chord-based arpeggio cannot be applied, given the speed of the passage and the particularities of the right-hand/left-hand coordination. Concrete instances of these situations can be found, for example, in the last of the Songs from the Chinese (Dance Song), op. 58 by Benjamin Britten, edited by Julian Bream (Britten1959). (Thanks to Jonathan Leathwood for important clarifications concerning these passages.)

Acknowledging the Limits II: Tempo Constraints
Certain textures exacerbate the situation described above and, in fact, may present unsolvable shifting demands to the left hand when a certain tempo limit is surpassed.

Example 3-19a

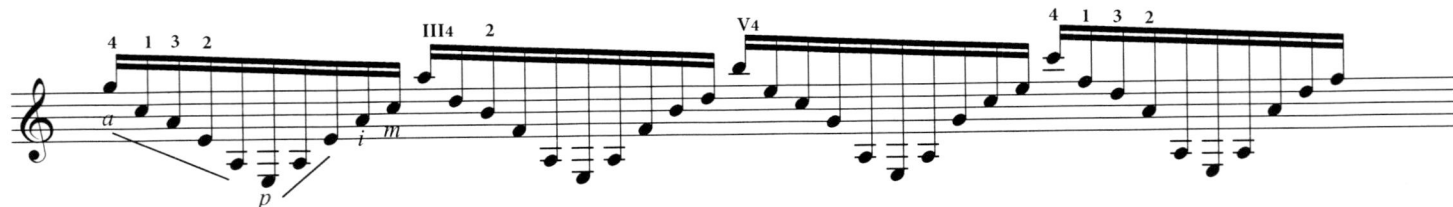

These arpeggios require a swift right-hand fingering approach, the quickest of which is having a slide from ① to ⑤, and p doing the same from ⑥ to ④ (i and m pluck ③ and ② normally). Using this fingering, as written and assuming a brisk tempo, the shifts are awkward, if not unplayable. The solution to achieve clear, smooth transitions between positions would be to anticipate the subsequent harmony in the second half of each group (the ascending arpeggio), thus using the 'dead time' afforded by the open bass strings. This permits a better coordination with the right hand for the reasons explained when discussing groupings of notes starting with the right-hand thumb stroke:

Example 3-19b

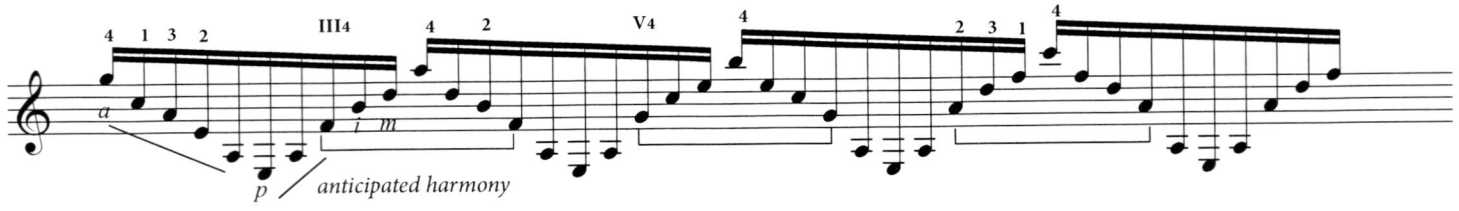

Other approaches, like crossing over i to execute the downward slide instead of a, slow down the pace somewhat and may be mastered so as to avoid the harmonic anticipation. Whether they achieve the same virtuosic *panache* and build-up in intensity as the former approach is open to debate.

Examples of these situations abound in the guitar music of Joaquín Rodrigo, the most famous instance being the passage in the Adagio, starting at bar 21, leading to the climax of the cadenza of the Concierto de Aranjuez (Rodrigo, Concierto de Aranjuez 1975).

Incidentally, Rodrigo's well-known *Invocación y Danza* shows a similar arpeggiated texture which, as revised and fingered by Alirio Díaz (Rodrigo, Invocation et Danse 1973, 49 ff.), is appropriately notated with the harmonic anticipations described above, the only practical and esthetically convincing way to solve the problem.

Pushing the Limits I: Maximum Speed Shifting

Modern guitar literature presents examples of extreme shifting situations where the speed of the movements falls well beyond the normal range expected in the major bulk of the literature. This is particularly true of some transcriptions, from the piano and orchestral repertoires, undertaken by a few virtuosos. Notable examples of these may be found in the path-breaking arrangements of Kazuhito Yamashita and Eliot Fisk. The exceptional left-hand capabilities of these two virtuosi allow them to use stretch fingerings more than would be possible, or even advisable, to less physically gifted individuals (Mussorgsky 1981, Paganini 1994).

The following example, drawn from the author's unpublished arrangement of Maurice Ravel's *Alborada del Gracioso,* is another case in point:

Example 3-20. Maurice Ravel: Alborada del Gracioso, transcribed by R. Iznaola, unpublished (Iznaola, Icarus 1995).

The key to this and similar passages is maintaining uninterrupted and smooth mobility of the arm, particularly as the hand comes to rest momentarily in a position (as it does, in the example, when arriving at V position). Any brusque end to the movements will accumulate a level of static tension that will immediately break the momentum necessary to keep the pace of shifting equal throughout the passage, as well as being an impediment to the appropriate handling of the changes in direction of the shifting movements. A good analogy would be to the way the ball is handled in a volleyball match, where players do not stop the ball's flight but rather control it by properly timed strokes that change the ball's vectorial trajectories. Of course, the best analogy is to the way dancers move on the floor, continuously changing direction, without stopping in place. In the example, an attempt has been made to pinpoint when specific arm shifting movements happen in the passage.

The left-hand task may be parsed as follows:
1.   All barrés are hanging.

2.   The intrapositional adjustment on position V is vital to the flowing departure of the arm towards position I. It consists of upper-arm adduction combined with forearm supination. The movement should feel as a release of the previous compound shifting effort (upper-arm abduction/lateral rotation), which it is.

3.   The upper-arm abduction/adduction movements in the compound shifts should seamlessly link with its outward/inward rotations. Otherwise, the ballistic impulse given to the arm may become too intense, in the rotation phase, to allow for accurate arrivals.

4.   As in all shifting passages involving chordal configurations, the finger presentation and distribution in the arrival chord, when taken in isolation, determines the proper movement form to get there. In other words, each chord should be studied individually at first, to properly feel and see what is the easiest, most effective way to play it. Only then can an appropriate shifting approach be determined.

Pushing the Limits II: Extreme Demands for Combined Finger Dexterity and Arm Agility

The fragments below present a more complex situation in which individualized fingerwork combines with rapid arm shifting in ever-changing ways. As before, movement indicators have been noted on the example.

Example 3-21. Frédéric Chopin, *Grande Valse Brillante*, op. 18, transcribed by Ricardo Iznaola, unpublished (Iznaola, Virtuoso 1995, Teicholz n/d)

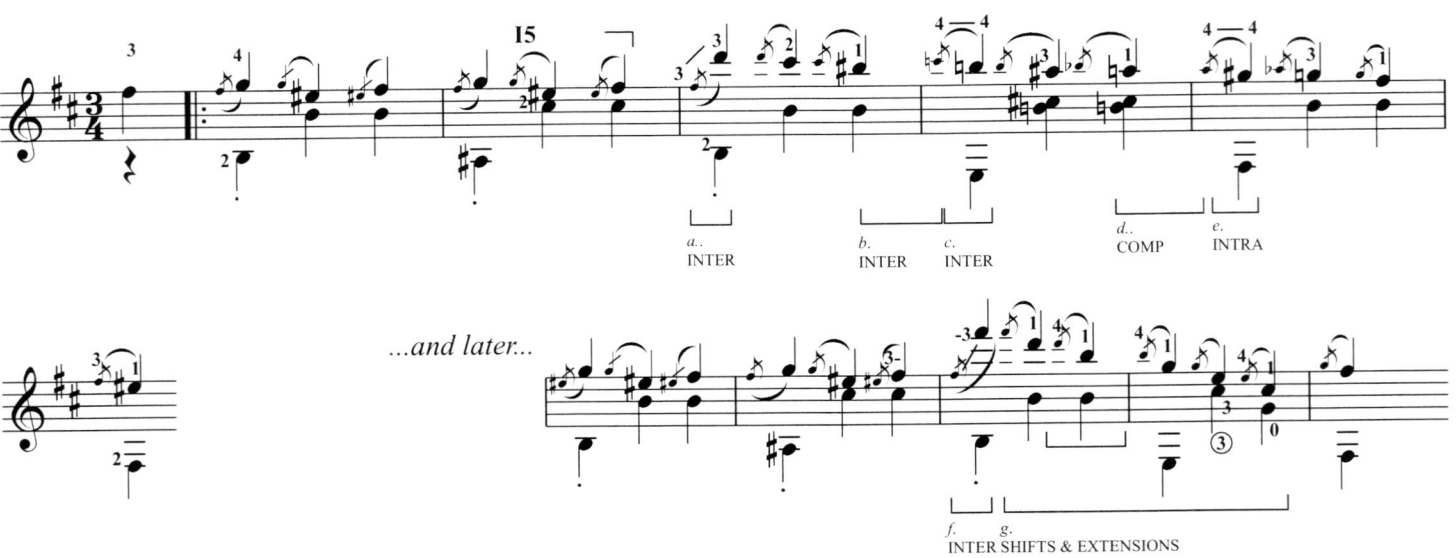

In general terms, the slurs should be supported by slight intrapositional adjustments of the arm, to lessen the amount of purely digital work required in each slur (as in bar 1 of the example, where the subtle upper-arm abduction/forearm supination executing the first slur resolve without hindrance into the opposing moves in the second, to then return, with additional wrist flexion, in the transition through the third beat to the barré in the second bar).

a. The slide is a simple interpositional shift that requires a supple wrist to ameliorate the potential risk of inaccurate arrival caused by the rather intense impulse provided to the hand by the upper-arm adduction/medial rotation. Care should be taken not to lose the nested attitude in this bar, as this would unavoidably affect, negatively, the two juxtaposed interpositional shifts in the next bar (at b and c).

b, c. These contiguous interpositional shifts in the same direction depend to a remarkable degree on the nimble poise achieved by the arm, hence, on the nested attitude of the hand. A perpendicular position, caused by letting the arm hang 'relaxed', would be disastrous to the execution of these two events. This would be so because of two factors: (1) the dead weight of the relaxed arm, and (2) the longer distance to be traversed, since the elbow would hang farther from the fingerboard.

d, e. A similar situation, made more complex by the fact that now the consecutive shifts are, respectively, compound (at **d**) and intrapositional (at **e**). Instance **d** is a form of what has been called previously a *bounce-back shift*, in which the upper arm's abduction links with a passive adduction movement, (in this case, accompanied by forearm supination and wrist flexion), thus 'cushioning' in position the new finger presentation.

f. In long, energetic interpositional shifts that arrive at position XI or higher, the player's fear of touching the body of the guitar is a common cause of faulty execution. The ballistic impulse of the shift should not be stopped by misguided concerns regarding this issue. In fact, realizing how convenient it is to have the body of the guitar as ultimate reference for the energy and length of a shift will make these movements some of the easiest and most effective.

g. A series of shifts and extensions. The risk here is to place 1 prematurely, thus starting a stretch effort before the shifting movement has been completed. A second risk is falling too perpendicularly in the changes of position: the stretches are more effective, and efficient, if the nested alignment is kept throughout, thus avoiding excessive finger abduction and relying, instead, on the natural 'spiraling' of the digits made possible by the different levels of extension among the fingers when the alignment is more diagonal to the fretboard.

Albeit daunting at first sight, there is nonetheless a certain feel of idiomatic appropriateness to passages like this that can be perceived only after the player's left-hand technique has become uninhibited, freed from all dogmatic formalism.

A perfectly managed functionality of movement is what the passage requires, which will seem to the onlooker as easy, nonchalant abandon.

And, though apparently far removed from the basic challenges offered by a modest study by Carcassi or Sor, this is precisely the same approach as the latter require: removing obstacles to the limb's motions through any piece is the way to overcome artificial limits to the possible and is, indeed, the key to discovering, and successfully traversing, the path to virtuosity.

> *...the one fact about the Future of which we can be certain is*
> *that it will be utterly fantastic.*
>
> Arthur C. Clarke
> (Clarke 1976, 17)

SOURCES

Adrian, M. J., and J. M. Cooper. *Biomechanics of Human Movement.* Madison, WI: Brown & Benchmark, 1995.

Aguado, Dionisio. *Método de Guitarra.* Edited by Regino Sainz de la Maza. Madrid: Unión Musical Española, 1943.

—. *Nuevo método para guitarra/New Guitar Method.* Edited by Brian Jeffery. London: Tecla Editions, 1981.

Alexander, F M., and Jean M. Fischer. *Man's Supreme Inheritance.* London: Mouritz, 1996.

Alexander, F. M. *The Use of the Self.* New York: E. P. Dutton, republished by Orion Publishing, 1932 (2001).

Andrews, Elizabeth. *Muscle Management for Musicians.* Lanham, MD: Scarecrow Press, Inc, 2005.

Artz, Alice. "The Ida Presti right hand technique for guitar." *YouTube.* 2009. http://www.youtube.com/watch?v=qW1pDXnSGxI (accessed July 31, 2013).

Bach, J. S. *Complete Works for Lute.* Edited by Frank Koonce. San Diego: Neil A. Kjos Music Corporation, 1989.

Beauchamp, Richard. 2000, rev 2012. http://www.musicandhealth.co.uk/default.html (accessed July 29, 2013).

—. *Anatomical Variations.* http://www.musicandhealth.co.uk/differences.html (accessed July 29, 2013).

Bendz, Per. "The Functional Significance of the Oblique Retinacular Ligament of Landsmeer. A Review and New Proposals." *Journal of Hand Surgery (British and European Volume)* 10-B, no. 1 (February 1985): 25-29.

Biberian, Gilbert. *Liber - The Book of Guitar.* Vol. 1. Cheltenham: Nouranexis Publications, 2012.

Britten, Benjamin. "Songs from the Chinese, op. 58." London: Boosey & Hawkes, 1959.

Caillet, Rene. *Hand Pain and Impairment.* Philadelphia: F. A. Davis Company, 1994.

Camus, Albert. *The Rebel - An Essay on Man in Revolt.* Translated by Anthony Bower. New York: Alfred A. Knopf Inc., 1956.

Carcassi, Matteo. *25 Melodious Studies, Op. 60.* Edited by Rey de la Torre. Columbus: Editions Orphée, 1996.

Carlevaro, Abel. *School of Guitar: Exposition of Instrumental Theory.* Translated by Jihad Azkhoul and Bartolomé Díaz. Dacisa S. A./Boosey & Hawkes, 1984.

Clarke, Arthur C. *Profiles of the Future - An Inquiry into the Limits of the Possible.* London: Pan Books Ltd., 1976.

Colditz, Judy C. *Anatomic Considerations for Splinting the Thumb.* Vol. 2, chap. 116 in *Hunter, Mackin and Callahan's Rehabilitation of the Hand and Upper Extremity,* edited by Evelyn J. Mackin, Anne D. Callahan, Terri M. Skirven, Lawrence H. Schneider, A. Lee Osterman and James M Hunter (emeritus), 1858-1875. Mosby, an affiliate of Elsevier , 2002.

Cole, Kenneth J., and James H. Abbs. "Coordination of Three-Joint Digit Movements for Rapid Finger-Thumb Grasp." *Journal of Neurophysiology* 55, no. 6 (June 1986): 1407-1423.

Conan Doyle, Arthur. "The Adventure of the Blanched Soldier." In *The Case Book of Sherlock Holmes (1927).* Infomotions, Inc. (infomotions.com), 2005.

Crosskey, Gordon. "The Under-Use Syndrome." *EGTA - UK.* 1990. http://www.egta.co.uk/content/underuse (accessed May 17, 2010).

Danner, Peter. "Rey de la Torre." *Soundboard* XXI, no. 2 (Fall 1994).

Duncan, Charles. *A Modern Approach to Classical Guitar.* 3 vols. Milwaukee, WI: Hal Leonard Publishing Company, 1996.

—. *The Art of Classical Guitar Playing.* Princeton: Summy-Birchard Music, 1980.

Eaton, Charles. *Normal Range of Motion Reference Value.* 2007. http://www.eatonhand.com/nor/nor002.htm (accessed July 27, 2013).

Einstein, Albert. In *Living Philosophies - A Series of Intimate Credos,* by Albert Einstein, Theodore Dreiser, James T. Adams, Bertrand Russell and others. New York: Simon and Schuster, 1931.

Feldenkreis, Moshé. *Awareness through Movement: Health Exercises for Personal Growth.* San Francisco: HarperSanFrancisco, 1990.

Fernández, Eduardo. *Technique, Mechanism, Learning: An Investigation into Becoming a Guitarist.* Pacific, MO: Mel Bay Publications, Inc., 2002.

Fiorini, Haroldo J., João B.G. Santos, Celso K. Hirakawa, Edson S Sato, Flavio Faloppa, and Walter M. Albertoni. "Anatomical Study of the A1 Pulley: Length and Location by Means of Cutaneous Landmarks on the Palmar Surface." *The Journal of Hand Surgery* 36, no. 3 (March 2011): 464-468.

Fishbein Adams, Deborah. *An Introduction to the Alexander Technique for Pianists and their Teacher.* 1995. http://www.ati-net.com/articles/debiadam.php (accessed July 31, 2013).

Fried, K., and G. Mundel. "Absence of distal interphalangeal creases of fingers with flexion limitation." *Journal of Medical Genetics,* no. 13 (1976): 127-130.

Galamian, I. *Principles of Violin: Playing and Teaching.* Englewood Cliffs, NJ: Prentice-Hall, 1962.

Glise, Anthony. *Classical Guitar Pedagogy - A Handbook for Teachers.* Pacific, MO: Mel Bay Publications, 1997.

Gonzalez, Mark H., Vivek Mohan, Bassem Elhassan, and Farid Amirouche. "Biomechanics of the Digit." *Journal of the American Society for Surgery of the Hand* 5, no. 1 (February 2005): 48-60.

Greene, David. "Performance-Related Medical Problems and the Guitarist: An Overview." *Soundboard* XX, no. 3 (Winter 1994): 31-35.

Grindea, C., ed. *Tensions in the Performance of Music.* London: Kahn & Averill, 1978.

Guyot, J. *Atlas of Human Limb Joints.* Berlin: Springer Verlag, 1981.

Haneke, E. "Surgical Anatomy of the Nail Apparatus." *Dermatologic Clinics* 24, no. 3 (July 2006): 291-296.

Hauger, Olivier, et al. "Pulley System in the Fingers: Normal Anatomy and Simulated Lesions in Cadavers at MR Imaging, CT, and US with and without Contrast Material Distention of the Tendon Sheath." *Radiology,* no. 212 (2000): 201-212.

Havas, Kató. *A New Approach to Violin Playing.* London: Bosworth, 1978.

Hay, J. G., and J. G. Reid. *The Anatomical and Mechanical Bases of Human Motion.* Englewood Cliffs, New Jersey: Prentice-Hall, 1982.

Holmquist, John. "Ricardo Iznaola's On Practicing." *Soundboard,* Winter 1994.

Isbin, Sharon. *Classical Guitar Answer Book.* San Anselmo, CA: String Letter Publishing, Inc., 1999.

Iznaola, Ricardo. "Alborada del Gracioso." *The Icarus Collection - The Dream of Icarus and Virtuoso Romantic Music.* Comp. Maurice Ravel. IGW 22874-5. 1995. CD.

—. "Grand Valse Brillante, op. 18." *The Icarus Collection - Virtuoso Romantic Music and the Dream of Icarus.* Comp. Frédéric Chopin. IGW 22874-5. 1995. CD.

—. *Kitharologus - The Path to Virtuosity.* Pacific: Mel Bay Publications, Inc., 1997.

—. "Left Hand Technique and the Limits of the Possible." Edited by Jonathan Leathwood. *EGTA Guitar Forum,* no. 1 (2001): 1-44.

—. *On Practicing.* Pacific, MO: Mel Bay Publications, Inc., 2000.

—. "Rest- and Free-Stroke Revisited." *EGTA Guitar Journal,* no. 1 (June 1990).

—. *The Physiology of Guitar Playing.* Reading: University of Reading, 2000.

—. "Two Circus Vignettes." In *Contemporary Anthology of Music for the Five Finger Technique,* edited by Charles Postlewate. Pacific, MO: Mel Bay Publications, Inc., 2009.

—. "Two Miniatures." *Modern Times.* Vol. IV. Edited by Robert Brightmore. Heidelberg: Chanterelle Verlag, 1993.

—. *Unleashing Talent: In Search of a Passionate Pedagogy.* 1994. http://www.egta.co.uk/content/unleashing_ talent (accessed July 29, 2013).

Juhan, D. *Job's Body: A Handbook for Bodywork.* Barrytown, NY: Station Hill Press, 1987.

Klickstein, Gerald. *The Musician's Way - A Guide to Practice, Performance and Wellness.* New York: Oxford University Press, Inc., 2009.

Koebke, J. *A Biomechanical and Morphological Analysis of Human Hand Joints.* Berlin: Springer-Verlag, 1983.

Koonce, Frank. "Left-Hand Movement: A Bag Full of Tricks." *EGTA Guitar Journal,* no. 3 (1992).

—. "Left-Hand Movement: A Bag Full of Tricks, part 1." *Soundboard* XVIII, no. 3 (Fall 1991).

—. "Left-Hand Movement: A Bag Full of Tricks, part 2." *Soundboard* XIX, no. 2 (Summer 1992).

—. "Left-Hand Movement: A Bag Full of Tricks, part 3." *Soundboard* XX, no. 1 (Summer 1993).

Kopfstein-Penk, A. "The Healthy Guitar: Finding a Guitar that Reduces Injury Risk and Improves your Playing." Bethesda, MD: Self-published, 1994.

Landsmeer, J. M. F. "Anatomical and Functional Investigations on the Articulation of the Human Finger." *Acta Anatomica* supl. 24, 2 ad vol. 25 (1955): 1-65.

—. "The Coordination of Finger-Joint Motions." *The Journal of Bone and Joint Surgery,* no. 45 (1963): 1654-1662.

Leinjse, J. N. A. L., J. E. Bonte, J. M. F. Landsmeer, J. J. Kalker, J. C. Van Der Muelen, and C. J. Snijders. "Biomechanics of the Finger with Anatomical Restrictions - The Significance for the Exercising Hand of the Musician." *Journal of Biomechanics* 25, no. 11 (1992): 1253-1264.

Leinjse, J. N. A., et al. "The Hand of the Musician: The Kinematics of the Bidigital Finger System with Anatomical Restrictions." *Journal of Biomechanics* 26, no. 10 (1993): 1169-1179.

Lessac, A. *Body Wisdom: The Use and Training of the Human Body.* New York: Drama Book Specialists, 1981.

Li, Zong-Min, and Jie Tang. "Coordination of Thumb Joints During Opposition." *Journal of Biomechanics* (Elsevier), no. 40 (2007): 502-510.

Littler, J. William. "On the Adaptability of Man's Hand (with reference to the equiangular curve)." *The Hand* V, no. 3 (1973).

Long, II, Charles. "Intrinsi-Extrinsic Muscle Control of the Fingers." *Journal of Bone and Joint Surgery,* no. 50 (1968): 973-984.

Mader, S. S. *Human Biology.* Dubuque: Wm. C. Brown Publishers, 1992.

Magee, David J. *Orthopedic Physical Assessment.* 5th. St. Louis, Missouri: Saunders (Elsevier, Inc), 2008.

Matthay, Tobias. *The Visible and Invisible in Pianoforte Technique (1947).* London: Oxford University Press, 1947 (rev 1997).

Mountcastle, V. B., ed. *Medical Physiology.* Vol. 1. St. Louis, MO: The C. V. Mosby Co., 1980.

Mussorgsky, M. P. "Pictures at an Exhibition, arranged for guitar by K. Yamashita." Tokyo: The Gendai Guitar Co., 1981.

Neumeister, Michael, Bradon J. Wilhelmi, and Reuben Bueno. "Flexor Tendon Lacerations." *eMedicine Orthopedic Surgery.* 2007. http://emedicine.medscape.com/article/1238823-overview (accessed July 29, 2013).

Nguyen Gillespie, Jessica, and Bradon J. Wilhellmi. *Intrinsic Plus Hand.* February 15, 2012. http://emedicine.medscape.com/article/1243815-overview (accessed July 27, 2013).

Nikanjan, Mina, Katarzyna Kursa, Steve Lehman, Lisa Lattanza, Edward Diao, and David Rempel. "Finger Flexor Control Patterns During Active Flexion: An In Vivo Tendon Force Study." *Human Movement Science,* no. 26 (2007): 1-10.

O'Rahilly, Ronan, Fabiola Müller, Stanley Carpenter, and Rand Swenson. *Basic Human Anatomy – A Regional Study of Human Structure.* 2008. http://www.dartmouth.edu/~humananatomy/index.html (accessed July 27, 2013).

Ortmann, Otto. *The Physiological Mechanics of Piano Technique.* London: Kegan Paul, Trench, Trubner and Co., 1929.

Paganini, N. "24 Caprices, op. 1, arranged for guitar by Eliot Fisk." Vol. 1 and 2. San Francisco: Guitar Solo Publications, 1994.

Palastanga, Nigel, and Roger Soames. *Anatomy and Human Movement - Structure and Function.* 6th. Edinburgh: Elsevier Ltd, 2012.

Phillips, Benjamin Z. *Nail Anatomy.* July 19, 2013. http://emedicine.medscape.com/article/1948841-overview#a30 (accessed August 4, 2013).

Pick, Richard. *School of Guitar: The Guitar in Pedagogy, Practice, Performance.* Columbus, OH: Editions Orphée, 1992.

Piscopo, J., and J. A. Baley. *Kinesiology: The Science of Movement.* New York: John Wiley and Sons, 1981.

Polnauer, F., and M. Marks. *Senso-Motor Study and its Application to Violin Playing.* Urbana, IL: American String Teachers Association, 1964.

Postlewate, Charles. *Homage to Villa-Lobos and Other Compositions.* Pacific: Mel Bay Publications, Inc., 2001.

—. *Right-Hand Studies for Five Fingers.* Pacific: Mel Bay Publications, Inc., 2001.

Puhaindran, M. E., S. J. Sebastin, Lim. A. Y. T., W. X. Xu, and Y. M. Chen. "Absence of Flexor Digitorum Superficialis Tendon in the Little Finger is not Associated with Decreased Grip Strength." *Journal of Hand Surgery* (European Volume) 33, no. 2 (2008): 205-207.

Pujol, Emilio. *Escuela Razonada de la Guitarra.* Vol. 1. 3 vols. Buenos Aires: Ricordi Americana, 1956.

Putz-Anderson, V., ed. *Cumulative Trauma Disorders: A Manual for Musculoskeletal Diseases of the Upper Limb.* London: Taylor and Francis, 1994.

Quine, Hector. *Guitar Technique - Intermediate to Advanced.* London: Oxford University Press, 1990.

Rodrigo, Joaquín. "Concierto de Aranjuez." Unión Musical Espanola, 1975.

—. «Invocation et Danse - Homage a Manuel de Falla.» Édité par Alirio Díaz. Paris: Editions Francaises de Musique, 1973.

Rolf, Ida P. *Rolfing: Reestablishing the Natural Alignment and Structural Integration of the Human Body for Vitality and Well-Being.* Rochester, VT: Healing Arts Press, 1989.

Romero, Pepe. *La Guitarra - A Comprehensive Study of Classical Guitar Technique and Guide to Performing.* Tampa, FL: Tuscany Publications, 2012.

Rybski, Melinda. *Kinesiology for Occupational Therapy.* Thorofare, NJ: Slack Inc., 2004.

Sagreras, Julio. *Las sextas lecciones de guitarra.* Buenos Aires: Editorial Ricordi Americana S.A.E.C., 1956.

Santos, Turibio. "Douze Etudes." *The Twelve Studies for Guitar.* Comp. Heitor Villa-Lobos. EMI ST-1007. 1969. LP.

Sataloff, R. T., A. G. Brandfonbrenner, and R. J. Lederman. *Textbook of Performing Arts Medicine.* New York: Raven Press Ltd, 1991.

Segovia, Andrés, and George Mendoza. *Guía para principiantes - mi libro de la guitarra.* Madrid: Ediciones Montena, S. A., 1980.

Selye, H. *The Stress of Life.* New York: McGraw-Hill Book Co., 1978.

Shearer, Aaron. *Learning the Classic Guitar.* Edited by Tom Poore. 3 vols. Pacific, Missouri: Mel Bay Publications, Inc, 1990.

Shearer, Aaron. "Left-hand Training." *Soundboard* XVIII, no. 1 (Spring 1991).

Shrewsbury, Marvin M., and K. Kuczynski. "Flexor Digitorum Superficialis Tendons in the Fingers of the Human Hand." *The Hand* 6, no. 2 (1974): 121-133.

Sor, Fernando. *Method for the Spanish Guitar.* Translated by A. Merrick. New York: Da Capo Press (re-print of ca. 1850 edition by R. Cocks, London), n/d.

Srinivasan, H. "Patterns of Movement in Totally Intrinsic-Minus Fingers Based on a Study of One Hundred and Forty-one Fingers." *Journal of Bone and Joint Surgery* American Volume, no. 58 (1976): 777-785.

Steinhausen, F. A. *Fisiologia della Condotta dell'Arco sugli Strumenti a Corda.* Translated by E. Polo. Padova: G. Zanibon, 1968.

Sullivan, Louis H. *The Autobiography of an Idea.* New York: Dover Publications, 1980.

Szende, O., and M. Nemessuri. *The Physiology of Violin Playing.* London: Collet's Publishers Ltd., 1971.

Taubman, Dorothy. "A Teacher's Perspective on Musicians' Injuries." *The Biology of Music Making Proceedings of the 1984 Denver Conference.* St. Louis: MMB Music, 1988. 144-153.

Teicholz, Marc. "Grande Valse Brillante, Op. 18, arranged by Ricardo Iznaola". *Valseana: 18 Classic Waltzes on 18 Vintage Guitars.* Comp. Frédéric Chopin. GSI 560. CD.

Tennant, Scott. *Pumping Nylon - The Classical Guitarist's Technical Handbook.* Edited by Nathaniel Gunod. Alfred Publishing Co., Inc., 1995.

Thomas, Donald H., Charles, III Long, and J. M. F. Landsmeer. "Biomechanical Considerations of Lumbricalis Behavior in the Human Finger." *Journal of Biomechanics* (Pergamon Press) 1 (1968): 107-115.

Thompson, C. W. *Manual of Structural Kinesiology.* St. Louis, Missouri: The C. V. Mosby Co., 1981.

Tubiana, Raoul. "Anatomy of the Hand and Upper Limbs." Chap. 2 in *Medical Problems of the Instrumentalist Musician*, edited by Raoul Tubiana and Peter C. Amadio. London: Martin Dunitz Ltd., 2000.

Villa-Lobos, Heitor. "Etude No. 2." *Douze Etudes pour Guitare.* Paris: Editions Max Eschig, 1953.

Watson, Alan H. D. *The Biology of Musical Performance and Performance-Related Injury.* Lanham, Maryland: Scarecrow Press, 2009.

—. "What Studying Musicians Tell Us about Motor Control of the Hand." 2006. http://musicianhealth.co.uk/anatomy.html (accessed July 29, 2013).

Wheeless, III, Clifford R. *Wheeless Textbook of Orthopedics.* 2008. http://www.wheelessonline.com/flexor_digitorum_superficialis (accessed July 27, 2013).

—. *Wheeless Textbook of Orthopedics.* 2008. http://www.wheelessonline.com/flexor_digitorum_profundus (accessed July 27, 2013).

Winspur, Ian, and Christopher B. Wynn Parry eds. *The Musician's Hand: A Clinical Guide.* London: Martin Dunitz, 1998.

Wright, Richard. "Articulation and the Myth of Difficulty." *EGTA Guitar Forum* (EGTA UK), no. 1 Autumn (2001).

Zatsiorsky, V. M., Z. M. Li, and M. L. Latash. "Enslaving Effects in Multi-Finger Force Production." *Experimental Brain Research* 131, no. 2 (March 2000): 187-95.

INDEX

ILLUSTRATION PAGE NUMBERS ARE SHOWN IN *ITALICS*

About the Author

For more than four decades **Ricardo Iznaola** has distinguished himself as an international performing and recording artist, composer, teacher and author.

Mr. Iznaola is Artist-in-Residence and Chair of the Guitar and Harp Department at the Lamont School of Music of the University of Denver, Colorado, USA, where he has been the professor of guitar since 1983, awarded the Distinguished Faculty Artist Award in 1990, and named the University Lecturer in 1994. In 2004, he received the John Evans Distinguished Professorship, a life-long distinction which is the highest bestowed by the university on its faculty.

An American citizen, he was born in Havana, Cuba, in 1949, and has resided since 1980 in the United States, after having lived in Venezuela and Spain, countries where he established deep roots and where he began and developed his international career as concert artist, composer and pedagogue.

Photo Wayne Armstrong, Denver

Winner of nine international prizes as performer and composer, he has published didactic texts and musical scores in Europe, the USA and Latin-America, as well as having produced numerous recordings, among which are the premières of the great Sonatas by Antonio Lauro and Antonio José, repertoire by the Spanish composers of the Generation of '27 and Venezuelan composers of the last hundred years, and his own compositions and transcriptions.

His pedagogical texts (*Kitharologus – The Path to Virtuosity, and On Practicing*, both published by Mel Bay,) have become standard required training materials for all serious guitarists. His exploration of the physiomechanical aspects of guitar playing, based on over three decades of deep study of the anatomy and functionality of the upper limb, culminates in this first volume of *Summa Kitharologica*, a comprehensive exposition of his thinking about these matters.

Mr. Iznaola lives in Denver, Colorado, with his wife, Victoria. He can be reached through his Websites at http://portfolio.du.edu, and http://www.iznaolaguitarworks.com.